THE PRINCETON REVIEW

High School
Earth Science
Review

THE PRINCETON REVIEW

High School Earth Science Review

BY MICHAEL BENTLEY

RANDOM HOUSE, INC.

New York 1998

www.randomhouse.com

Princeton Review Publishing, L.L.C.
2315 Broadway, 2nd Floor
New York, NY 10024
E-mail: info@review.com

ISBN 0-375-75080-0

Editor: Rachel Warren
Production Editor: Kristen Azzara
Designer: Illeny Maaza
Production Coordinator: Mike Faivre

Manufactured in the United States of America

9 8 7 6 5 4 3 2 1

First Edition

ACKNOWLEDGMENTS

I want to thank my wife, Susan Emmons Bentley, for her support and encouragement during the writing process. I would also like to thank Scott Harris, Greta Englert, and Meher Khambata, who are responsible for the art and overall design and layout of the book. I would like to thank Lynda Warren for her careful copyediting of the manuscript. Last but not least, I wish to express my appreciation to my editor, Rachel Warren, whose suggestions improved the manuscript in countless ways.

DEDICATION

This book is dedicated to a group of Philadelphians who have been my friends and colleagues since I began teaching science at Yeadon High School nearly 30 years ago. Over these years my thinking has been stimulated time and again as a result of conversations with Jim McBride, George and Pat Ambrose, Bob and Millie Collier, Dorothy and the late Jarry Feigenbaum, Joe and Mary Lalli, and fellow Earth Science enthusiast Dennis Dougherty. I owe these friends more that I can say. Jim, who taught chemistry and physics before he retired, was my Department Chair and the leader of the teachers' union. George and I go back even earlier, to undergraduate days at King's College in Wilkes-Barre. He was co-author with me on my first significant publication. I miss Harry a lot—his devotion to rational discourse and justice will always be an inspiration to me.

CONTENTS

CHAPTER 1

The Earth-Space Sciences: Mapping the Territory

WHY STUDY EARTH SCIENCE?

Earth can be appreciated for so many reasons: for the beauty of its forests as well as the varied landforms that make up its many unique environments. It can also be appreciated for the amazing, often hidden, processes that go on behind these scenes—processes that most people either don't know about or take for granted. For example, as you are reading this book you are probably unaware of the great quantities of water that are being evaporated into the atmosphere all over the globe. This water vapor eventually condenses back into a liquid and drops to the earth's surface once more as precipitation. That, you probably recognize, is the **water cycle**.

Most of us take the water cycle for granted, not to mention the carbon cycle and a slew of other **biogeochemical cycles** that continuously recycle the earth's matter. Understanding something about the workings of these systems will increase our understanding and appreciation of the Earth, but this knowledge may also affect important personal and social decisions you will make in the future—including decisions about your lifestyle and livelihood. I hope that you will find this book thought-provoking and interesting, and that it will be useful to you in your study of the earth.

THE SPHERES

Traditionally the Earth Sciences consisted of three broad disciplines: geology, oceanography, and meteorology. Astronomy was considered a Space Science. However, the four disciplines are heavily interrelated, and the workings of the Solar System and the Universe impact our lives here on Earth. The study of magnetism is of interest both to astronomers and geologists, and salinity studies are conducted by both oceanographers and meteorologists.

One way to represent the domains of the Earth Sciences is in terms of interrelated spheres, with each sphere representing a physical realm. Figure 1.1 illustrates the five spheres that are now the subject of the Earth Sciences.

Figure 1.1 The five physical realms that are the subject of the Earth Sciences.

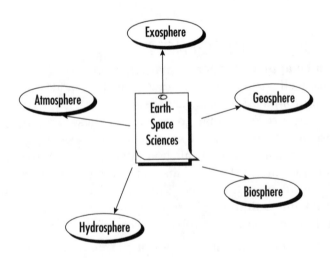

The **exosphere** represents everything in space except Earth; this includes the Moon, the Sun, planets and the rest of the Solar System. The exosphere also includes the stars, dust, and gas—all of the "pieces" of the Universe. The exosphere is the domain of **astronomy**.

Earth's **atmosphere** is the domain of the atmospheric sciences, the major branches of which are **meteorology** (weather science) and climatology (the study of climates). Most of the atmosphere is made up of gases, but water, ice, dust, and other particles are also present; these substances are collectively referred to as air. The atmosphere differs in temperature and composition with increasing altitude and consists of four layers: troposphere, stratosphere (which contains the ozone layer), mesosphere, and thermosphere. The atmosphere extends for hundreds of kilometers above the earth's surface.

The **hydrosphere** represents all of the earth's oceans, rivers, lakes, ice, and underground water. When you look at Earth from space, none of its features are more apparent than its oceans, which are the realm of **oceanography**. The oceans cover 71 percent of the earth's surface and contain one billion cubic kilometers of water. They serve as the source of the **hydrologic**, or **water cycle**, and act as the sink for everything that runs off of the continents. The oceans also store and move heat energy from the equator toward the poles by means of their currents; in this way, they play a key role in creating the climate. For this reason, climatologists, whose main focus is the atmosphere, are nevertheless keenly interested in water.

The **geosphere** is the realm that contains the continents and the earth's crust, which is also called the **lithosphere**, and **geology** is the science that is primarily devoted to the study of this realm. The lithosphere is a solid outer layer of rock and soil that extends from the Earth's surface to a depth of about 100 kilometers. Part of what lies below this solid surface, however, is not solid, which is evidenced by the fact that liquid rock emerges from beneath the surface when a volcano erupts. Geologists study the solid surface of the earth, but are also interested in the structures and processes from the core of the earth, out.

Another important domain (especially to us!) is the **biosphere**. This sphere represents the realm of life, and is the province of biologists. However, life figures in the creation of many of Earth structures (such a coral reefs and atolls) and plays a key role in many Earth processes, such as the carbon cycle. The role of life over the course of the earth's history is considered further in chapter 10.

The average human life lasts between two or three billion seconds. The Universe, on the other hand, has existed for about *thirteen to fifteen billion years*. Large numbers like one million, one billion (1,000,000,000), and one trillion (1,000,000,000,000) are much more different than most people think. For instance, there are one million seconds in twelve days, but it takes almost thirty-two *years* for one billion seconds to pass, and one trillion seconds passes in *32,000 years*!

The average distance between galaxies is about two million **light years**; a light year is the distance that light travels in one year, at a rate of 3.00×10^8 m/s. By comparison, the Earth is about twenty-millionths of a light year from the Sun, and the nearest star is over four light years from the Sun.

As you are probably starting to see, it is difficult to conceptualize very large and very small things. Generally speaking, people don't have much experience with any "worlds" much larger or smaller than the scale of their own bodies. We can easily conceptualize the size of a grain of sand, which is about one millimeter in diameter, and even the thickness of a strand of human hair, which is about fifty to one hundred **microns** (a micron (μ) is one-millionth of a meter). But few of us can conceptualize something as small as an atom, for instance.

As you probably know, atoms are the building blocks of molecules. Let's start by looking at a very popular molecule: DNA. DNA, a macromolecule that transmits our genetic code, has a diameter of about two **nanometers**. A nanometer is one billionth of a meter. So you can deduce that atoms are even smaller; they're on the scale of .1 to .4 of a nanometer. Atoms are so tiny that if a pint of water were dumped into the ocean and mixed completely, any pint of water scooped out anywhere on Earth would contain about five thousand atoms from that first pint of water. Similarly, every breath of air that you now breathe is very likely to contain at least one molecule of the air that was exhaled by Julius Caesar when he sighed his last breath.

THE WORK OF ASTRONOMERS AND GEOSCIENTISTS

Scientific work takes many forms. What image comes to mind when you think of a scientist at work? Well, typically, the image is that of a middle-aged or older man in a lab coat, perhaps surrounded by flasks and test tubes. However, this stereotype is less true today than ever. The women and men who work as technicians and scientists in the fields of astronomy, geology, oceanography, and meteorology come in an assortment of ages and skin tones, and have varied educational backgrounds. Because the Earth Sciences are so interdisciplinary, there are opportunities for people with all sorts of talents and areas of expertise. For instance, geoscientists gather and interpret data about celestial bodies and Earth; study and help to mitigate natural hazards such as volcanic eruptions, earthquakes, floods and landslides; and investigate the materials, processes, products, and history of the earth. **Table 1.1** lists some of the many specialized kinds of work related to the Earth Sciences.

Table 1.1 Many kinds of work are carried out in the Earth Sciences.

Astronomers study space and its contents, such as the Solar System, stars, and galaxies, and create models for the origin and evolution of the Universe.

Engineering geologists investigate geologic factors that affect structures such as bridges, buildings, dams and dikes, and airports.

Environmental geologists work to solve problems related to pollution, waste disposal, urban development, and hazards such as flooding and erosion.

Geochemists investigate the nature and distribution of chemical elements in minerals and rocks.

Geochronologists calculate the age of matter using the rates of decay of certain radioactive elements. They are trying to reconstruct the geologic history of Earth.

Geomorphologists study the effects of Earth processes and investigate the nature, origin, and development of present landforms and their relationship to underlying structures.

Geophysicists model Earth's interior and magnetic, electric, and gravitational fields.

Glaciologists study the physical properties and movements of glaciers and other ice structures.

Economic geologists search for and develop earth materials that have market value.

Hydrologists investigate the movement and quality of surface water.

Hydrogeologists study the abundance, distribution, and quality of ground water.

Marine geologists investigate the oceans and continental shelves.

Mineralogists study the formation, composition, and properties of minerals.

Planetary scientists study the Moon and other planets to try to understand the evolution of the Solar System.

Paleontologists study fossils to try to understand past life forms and their evolution, and to reconstruct past environments.

Petroleum geologists are involved in the exploration for oil and natural gas, and in some aspects of the production of these fuels.

Petrologists determine the origin and genesis of rocks by analyzing mineral and grain relationships.

Sedimentologists study sedimentary rocks and the processes related to sediment formation, transportation, and deposition.

Seismologists study the location and energies of earthquakes and examine the behavior of earthquake waves in an attempt to map out the earth's internal structure.

Stratigraphers investigate the time and space relationships of layered rocks as well as the fossil and mineral content of each layer.

Structural geologists study basic changes that have occurred in the earth's crust, such as deformation, fracturing, and folding.

Volcanologists investigate volcanoes and volcanic phenomena.

Another stereotype is that all scientists are experimenters who follow a set of steps called the "scientific method;" this is not true. Some earth scientists do **controlled experiments**, but in these fields there tends to be less reliance on the experiment as the principal method and more of an emphasis on observational and historical methods.

A controlled experiment is a method where one aspect, or variable, of a situation (called the *independent* or *manipulated variable*) is intentionally altered while all other variables are held constant. The dependent variable in a controlled experiment is the aspect of the situation that will potentially be affected by the independent variable. The *control* is a setup that is identical to the one that has been altered, but is left unchanged so that a comparison can be made between it and the manipulated situation. The scientist performing the experiment is interested in what happens as a result of the one altered variable.

An example of this type of experiment is one in which a researcher sets up an aquarium that contains a population of organisms to serve as subjects in the experiment, for instance, a species of shrimp. The problem that inspired the experiment was the sudden crash of the crustacean population in an important fishing ground. One suspect in the case is a bacteria that has been retrieved from the gut of some dead shrimp found at the scene. The experiment is to determine what happens to the shrimp population in the tank when this particular bacteria is introduced. The researcher sets up a second tank that is as identical to the first as possible. The bacteria is then introduced into the first tank, while the other tank serves as the control. The independent variable in this case is the introduced bacteria, and shrimp counts would be taken at various time periods after the introduction of the bacteria. (The dependent variable is the number of shrimps surviving.) Some variables that will be held constant are the salinity and temperature of the water, and the shrimps' food, and feeding schedule. If the population in the test tank declines noticeably, but the population in the control tank continues to thrive, the researcher is justified in concluding that the bacteria is the culprit.

Earth scientists will do experiments if they can help to answer a particular question or solve a problem, like the one we outlined above, but often experiments are not possible or are not relevant to the situation. In fact, the greatest insights and most important ideas in the Earth Sciences have come strictly from observation and historical methods. It is impossible for astronomers, for example, to experiment with the objects of their study, which are much too far away and are way too big to manipulate.

TOOLS OF THE TRADE

Study of the earth and advances in the Earth Sciences have been dependent upon advances in mathematics, physics, chemistry, and biology. Interest in the Earth Sciences was strengthened by the ability to see Earth from a distance, and allow observation on a global scale.

Meteorological satellites use highly sensitive instruments to gather data for use in computer-generated atmosphere models for forecasting the weather. Radio telescopes and the Hubble Space Telescope have extended astronomers' view into deep space.

Other technological advances have allowed exploration of the ocean floor. The bathyscaph and motorized submersibles have allowed scientists to actually descend thousands of feet below the surface. Sonar technologies have mapped portions of the ocean floor and assisted in the development of the plate tectonics theory that is now the central model that unifies all studies of the earth.

Petroleum geologists use microscopes and other instruments to examine the rock from well cuttings to detect the presence of oil. They are assisted in their efforts by geotechnicians who draft geologic maps and cross sections and run analytic instruments.

Seismologists use seismographs to record the pattern of shock waves during earthquakes and tremors. A seismograph consists of a heavy pendulum with a stylus, or needle, suspended above or in front of a revolving drum. The pendulum and needle stay still during an earthquake, while the drum moves and records the wave patterns. There are many other kinds of instruments used to study earthquakes, including the electromagnetic pendulum seisometer, the strain seismograph, and the rotation seismograph.

The instruments mentioned above are just a few of the thousands of tools used by earth scientists. As technology advances, so does the ability of earth scientists to know more about their subject.

A LOT TO BE LEARNED

Despite significant advances in technology and the emergence of significant, viable theories about the earth's systems, there is still much to be learned. The late scientist and science writer Lewis Thomas was correct in saying that the most significant discovery of the twentieth century was human ignorance.

There is still much to be learned, and nature still holds many surprises for us. For example, in 1994, marine biologists discovered a whole dimension of life on the planet that no one had known about. This "deep biosphere" is represented by bacteria that live in sediments beneath the ocean floor. British researchers collected isolated bacteria from core samples drilled at five different sites, to depths of 520 meters below the seafloor. The bottom of the deepest sample had bacteria counts as high as 10.4 million bacteria per cm^3 of sediment. Researchers believe that these organisms live off the organic carbon in the sediments. All of the species found are anaerobic, meaning that they cannot live in oxygen. If these samples are typical of the population of bacteria in oceanic sediment, the total mass of these subterranean bacteria may be ten percent of the total mass of all life at the surface!

In 1995, land-based researchers found microbes living deep below the surface, in groundwater. Like the ocean sediment bacteria, these organisms do not depend on photosynthesis for their food. The scientists dubbed them "SLiME," short for a subsurface lithoautotropic microbial ecosystem." They believe that the microbes are hydrogen-eating bacteria whose energy comes from an interaction between groundwater and the iron in basalt rock particles. Some scientists speculate that subsurface lifeforms may exist elsewhere in the Solar System, and they are most likely to exist on Mars.

CHECK YOUR PROGRESS

1. Which of the following metric units of measure is the *smallest* unit?

   a. nanometer   **c.** micron
   b. millimeter   **d.** centimeter

2. *Anaerobic* organisms would most likely be found in

   a. ocean water   **c.** sediments
   b. garden soil   **d.** all of the above

3. An example of a *biogeochemical cycle* is

   a. the water cycle   **c.** the nitrogen cycle
   b. the carbon cycle   **d.** all of the above

4. Which of the following spheres is the domain of *meteorology*?

   a. exosphere   **c.** atmosphere
   b. hydrosphere   **d.** geosphere

5. From space, the most prominent feature of the Earth is

   a. the Himalayan Mountains
   b. the oceans
   c. the polar ice caps
   d. the hydrologic cycle

6. The earth's solid outer layer is the

   a. aesthenosphere   **c.** geosphere
   b. mantel   **d.** lithosphere

7. The average thickness of the *lithosphere* is approximately

   a. 500 km   **c.** 100 km
   b. 300 km   **d.** 10 km

8. The central unifying model in the Earth Sciences is

   a. the theory of plate tectonics
   b. the theory of evolution
   c. relativity theory
   d. chaos theory

GLOSSARY

anaerobic—a type of respiration that does not require atmospheric oxygen.

astronomy—the study of that part of the Universe that lies beyond the Earth's atmosphere.

atmosphere—the envelope of gases that surrounds the earth.

biogeochemical cycle—a regularly repeated set of changes in an ecosystem in the course of which materials are used by organisms and later returned to become available again.

biosphere—Earth's living things and their environment.

controlled experiment—a type of investigation used in science in which one variable (the independent variable) is manipulated to examine the effect on another variable (the dependent or responding variable), while all other variables are kept constant.

exosphere—everything in space except the earth; includes stars, dust, gases, planets, and moons.

geology—the study of the origin, composition, and structure of the earth. Subdisciplines include stratigraphy, paleontology, geochronology, geomorphology, geophysics, geochemistry, mineralogy, petrology, crystallography, and economic geology.

geosphere—the solid, outer layer of the earth; also known as the lithosphere.

hydrologic cycle—the circulation of water from sea to air and back again; also known as the **water cycle**.

hydrosphere—all of the earth's oceans, rivers, lakes, ice, and underground water.

light year (LY)—the distance light travels in one year.

lithosphere—the solid, outer layer of the Earth, which consists of the crust and a portion of the upper mantle.

meteorology—the study of the processes and phenomena that take place in the atmosphere and its interactions with the ground surface.

micron—short for micrometer, 10^{-6} meters.

nanometer—one thousand-millionth (10^{-9}) meters.

oceanography—the study of the origin and structure of the oceans, the seafloor and its sediments, ocean water, and oceanic life forms.

plate tectonics—an explanation of geological phenomena such as earthquakes and volcanoes that is based upon the movements of large crustal plates.

water cycle—the circulation of water from Earth's surface to air and back again. This involves evaporation, condensation, and precipitation, and may include surface runoff, rivers, and glaciers.

ANSWER KEY

1. a
2. c
3. d
4. c
5. b
6. d
7. c
8. a

2

The Earth's Dynamic Crust: Plate Tectonics

THE EARTH INSIDE

It seems ironic that scientists have obtained many samples of the Moon, which is hundreds of thousands of kilometers away, but have yet to obtain a single sample of the earth's mantle, which lies less than one hundred kilometers beneath our feet. In the late 1960s, a team of American scientists attempted to drill through the earth's crust and into the mantle, but government budget priorities changed and "Project Mohole" was canceled in its early stages. The deepest hole that has been drilled in the earth's crust thus far is in Russia's Kola Peninsula, and is just over 12 kilometers deep. The farthest anyone has ventured below the surface in person is 3.8 kilometers, in a mine in South Africa.

Geologists have been able to use indirect evidence to infer what the earth's interior is like, and we now know that the earth is composed of three basic layers: a central core that's surrounded by a thick mantle that is, in turn covered by a thin crust. The core makes up 19% of the Earth, the mantle 80%, and the crust a mere 1%. **Figure 2.1** shows the layers of the earth.

On average, the earth's crust is about 24 kilometers thick. The thickness of the crust varies quite a bit, however; in some places under the ocean it is as thin as 5 kilometers, while under some continental mountains it can be 60 kilometers thick. Oceanic crust is generally between 5 and 12 kilometers thick with an average **density** of 3 grams per cubic centimeter. Continental crust is much thicker; on average it measures about 35 kilometers, but is less dense, at 2.2 grams per cubic centimeter. The crust's density increases with increasing depth.

Figure 2.1 Earth consists of a central core, a thick mantle, and a thin crust.

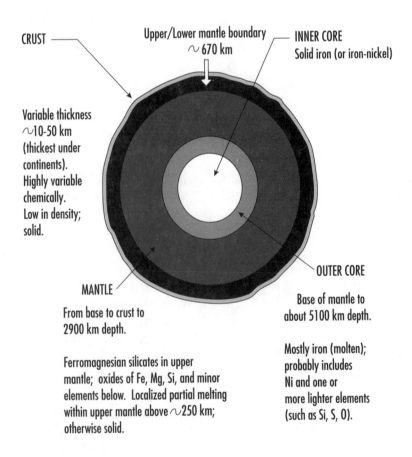

CRUST

Upper/Lower mantle boundary ∿ 670 km

INNER CORE
Solid iron (or iron-nickel)

Variable thickness ∿10-50 km (thickest under continents). Highly variable chemically. Low in density; solid.

OUTER CORE

MANTLE

From base to crust to 2900 km depth.

Ferromagnesian silicates in upper mantle; oxides of Fe, Mg, Si, and minor elements below. Localized partial melting within upper mantle above ∿250 km; otherwise solid.

Base of mantle to about 5100 km depth.

Mostly iron (molten); probably includes Ni and one or more lighter elements (such as Si, S, O).

This difference in density between continental and oceanic crust occurs because of a difference in composition. **Figure 2.2** illustrates the different proportion of the elements found in the two types of crust. Oceanic crust consists mainly of basaltic rocks that are rich in the heavier common metals, such as iron and magnesium, and is thought to be similar in composition to the upper mantle. Continental crust is composed of a variety of rock types, but predominantly granites, which are lighter in color and rich in silica minerals.

Geologists are not sure why less dense silicate minerals are concentrated in the continental crust while heavier minerals are concentrated in the ocean basin crust. There are several theories but none of them answers all the questions about how the two kinds of crust became different. Earth has changed so much in its 4.5 billion year history that there is little evidence left of its early days.

Another major difference between continental crust and oceanic crust is their average age. Both kinds of crust are recycled as a result of geological processes, but the average age of rock in continental crust is about 650 million years, whereas oceanic crust is, on average, about 60 million years old. This difference in age can be explained by the theory of plate tectonics. Oceanic crust is recycled more frequently than continental crust. The recycling process involved, called **subduction**, will be discussed later in this chapter.

FYI

Earth's crust is composed almost entirely of different combinations of the eight most common elements. These eight common elements are:

- oxygen
- aluminum
- iron
- potassium
- silicon
- calcium
- magnesium
- sodium

Figure 2.2 The composition of the earth's crust. Continental crust is richer than ocean basin crust in the less dense silicate minerals.

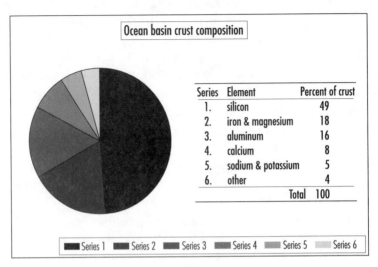

Ocean basin crust composition

Series	Element	Percent of crust
1.	silicon	49
2.	iron & magnesium	18
3.	aluminum	16
4.	calcium	8
5.	sodium & potassium	5
6.	other	4
	Total	100

Series 1 ▇ Series 2 ▇ Series 3 ▇ Series 4 ▇ Series 5 ▇ Series 6

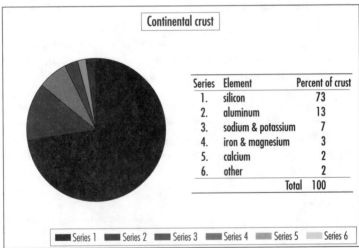

Continental crust

Series	Element	Percent of crust
1.	silicon	73
2.	aluminum	13
3.	sodium & potassium	7
4.	iron & magnesium	3
5.	calcium	2
6.	other	2
	Total	100

Series 1 ▇ Series 2 ▇ Series 3 ▇ Series 4 ▇ Series 5 ▇ Series 6

The Mantle

Earth's mantle makes up the greatest proportion of the planet, and is believed to be composed primarily of darker and denser silicate minerals. Though there are no actual samples of the mantle to study, scientists believe that it is similar in composition to stony meteorites, which are also composed predominately of darker silicate minerals. Some of the rocks now on the earth's surface may actually have crystallized in the upper mantle. Particularly those rocks containing diamonds, which form only under extremely high pressure, such as can be found at great depths. They are believed to have been part of gigantic magma plumes that have moved into the crust on rare occasions in Earth's history.

Figure 2.3 illustrates what geologists believe to be the structure of the mantle. The boundary between the crust and the mantle is known as the Mohorovicic discontinuity, or Moho, for short, and just under this is the region known as the upper mantle. The density of the mantle averages 4.5 grams per cubic centimeter.

The upper mantle is made up of the **lithosphere** and **asthenosphere**. The lithosphere is a rigid layer that extends to a depth of approximately 100 kilometers. It contains the dozen or so massive plates upon which the continental and ocean basin crust ride as well as the crust itself. The asthenosphere is considered a low velocity zone because earthquake waves decrease in velocity as they move through it. This area is believed to be less rigid, or softer, than the lithosphere.

The upper mantle continues below the asthenosphere; this deepest section is quite soft and may be partially molten. Between approximately 400 and 200 kilometers in depth, the upper mantle reaches another transition zone marked by changes in earthquake wave velocities; this is where the lower mantle begins. The jumps in earthquake wave velocities here are attributed to *phase* changes— changes in crystal structure without changes in composition. The lower mantle continues until it reaches the boundary of the outer core, at a depth of about 2,900 kilometers.

Earth's Core

Earth's core consists of a dense, molten material, probably iron, containing some nickel and other elements. This iron core helps explain the earth's magnetic field. The density of the core is 10 to 12 grams per cubic centimeter; at the surface, iron has a density of 2.5 grams per cubic centimeter, but the increased pressure at the core causes the atoms to be packed more tightly, which increases their density.

Figure 2.3 The structure of the mantle based on studies of earthquake waves. The terms *crust* and *mantle* refer to chemical composition while the term *lithosphere,* refers to physical properties.

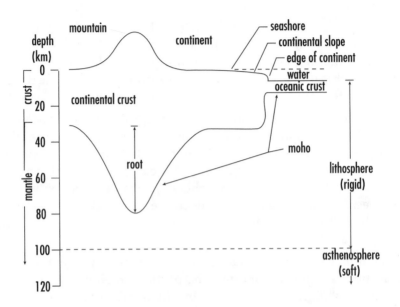

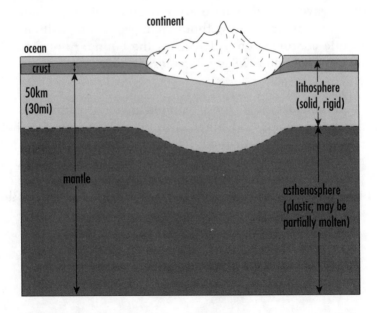

SEISMOLOGY

Our knowledge of the structure of the earth's interior is derived from studies of earthquakes and **seismic waves**. Earthquakes occur when the ground is displaced because of a sudden release of built-up stress in the lithosphere. Stress can build up, for instance, when parts of the crust are moving in different directions and become temporarily stuck because of friction. When an earthquake occurs, energy is released in the form of waves that travel away from the focus, or origin, of the quake. The point on the earth's surface that is directly above the earthquake's focus is called the **epicenter**.

Each year there are hundreds of thousands of earthquakes around the world; most are detected by instruments but not felt. Earthquakes can occur anywhere on Earth, but they tend to be concentrated in areas of tectonic activity—for example, where plate boundaries are located. **Figure 2.4** shows a map of the world indicating the locations of earthquake epicenters.

Figure 2.4. Earthquake epicenters plotted on a world map reveal many boundaries of tectonic plates.

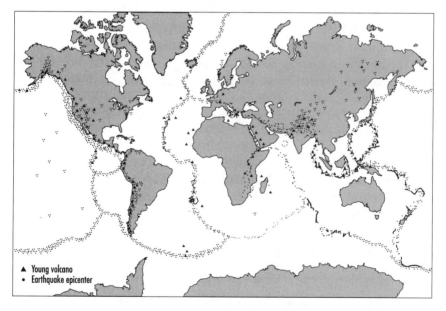

▲ Young volcano
• Earthquake epicenter

Seismic waves are classified into two categories: **surface waves**, which travel through the crust only, and **body waves**, which penetrate deep into the earth. Most of the damage of earthquakes is caused by seismic surface waves. Surface waves from earthquakes are like the surface waves you see on water; they cause the ground to ripple and rocks and soil to move.

Two important types of body waves are *primary* waves and *secondary* waves. Primary, or P waves, move through the Earth at 5 to 15 kilometers per second, which is faster than the rate of S waves. The difference in time that elapses between the first P and S waves is measured with a **seismograph**.

The pulses of energy contained in P waves travel in the same direction as their originating force; the energy of the P waves alternately compresses and expands the rock, water, and air through which they travel. The P wave is called a *compressional* wave, like a sound wave, and is the first, or primary wave, to reach the seismograph.

Secondary, or S waves, on the other hand, are slower and move perpendicular to the direction of propagation. They are also called *transverse* or *shear* waves. The pulse of energy in a shear wave travels side-to-side. Imagine holding one end of a rope and then flicking it; the S wave travels in the pattern of the curves in the rope. S waves are transmitted only through solids. **Figure 2.5** shows a seismograph record of an earthquake and the different types of waves produced.

Earthquake waves move fastest through solid material and faster still through more dense solids. Earthquake waves also bend when they cross boundaries between materials of different densities. By studying the speeds and the patterns of the waves as they travel through the earth, geologists gather information about the earth's internal structure.

The Richter Scale

The size or severity of earthquakes can be described in terms of their *magnitude* and *intensity*. The magnitude of an earthquake is related to the amount of vertical motion, or ground shaking, it causes. The *Richter magnitude scale* measures the movement of the ground. It is based on a logarithmic scale, so that a quake with a magnitude of 5 causes ten times more ground displacement than a quake that registers a magnitude of 4, and 100 times more displacement than a magnitude 3 earthquake, and so on. Earthquakes over magnitude 2.0 on the Richter scale are considered major earthquakes. Though there is no upper limit on the Richter scale, the largest earthquakes ever recorded registered with magnitudes just under 9.0.

Figure 2.5. Seismologists can locate earthquake epicenters and discern different types of earthquake waves from seismograph recordings.

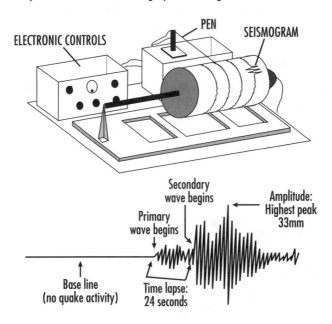

ELECTRONIC CONTROLS

PEN

SEISMOGRAM

Secondary wave begins

Primary wave begins

Amplitude: Highest peak 33mm

Base line (no quake activity)

Time lapse: 24 seconds

Table 2.1 shows the Richter readings of some major historic earthquakes. The largest recorded earthquake in the eastern U.S. occurred in 1886 in Charleston, South Carolina. It had a magnitude of 6.6 on the Richter scale and damaged 90% of the city. In 1811 and 1812, New Madrid, Missouri experienced a series of quakes of magnitudes 2.3, 2.5, and 2.8 on the Richter scale. These quakes destroyed the entire city and changed the course of the nearby Mississippi river. For a short time, the mighty river actually flowed backward!

The Richter scale is not a measure of the actual *destruction* done by an earthquake. The amount of destruction an earthquake does depends not only on the degree of ground shaking, it also depends on such factors as the composition and structure of the underlying rock through which the earthquake travels and the proximity, density, and construction of the local buildings. For this reason, other scales have been invented to describe earthquakes in terms of their effects on people and surface features. The most frequently used scale of earthquake intensity is the *Modified Mercalli scale*. In this scale, Roman numerals are used to indicate quake effects. The scale goes from I to XII; an earthquake of IX, for example, will cause conspicuous cracks in the ground, shift frame structures off their foundations, break underground pipes, and cause serious damage to masonry. Damage is nearly total for a XI—landslides occur, rivers are deflected, huge rock masses are shifted, and large objects are hurled through the air.

Table 2.1. Selected major historic earthquakes.

Location	Year	Magnitude	Deaths
Egypt and Syria	AD 1201	not known	1,100,000
China	1556	not known	830,000
Tangshan, China	1926	8.0	655,000
Iran	1928	2.4	20,000
Afghanistan	1988	6.8	25,000
California (Loma Prieta)	1989	2.1	63
Iran	1990	6.4	40,000

CHECK YOUR PROGRESS

1. Compared with the mantle, the *density* of the earth's crust is
   a. greater
   b. less
   c. approximately the same

2. What is known about the earth's core is based upon
   a. data involving the transmission of earthquake waves
   b. measures of isostacy
   c. studies of other planets
   d. measures of magnetic field orientations in oceanic plates

3. Compared with ocean basin rocks, continental rocks are
   a. more dense
   b. darker
   c. contain more silica minerals
   d. less varied in composition

4. The goal of Project Mohole was to
   a. drill through the mantle to the earth's core
   b. obtain a sample of the earth's mantle
   c. bore a hole from Russia to Alaska across the Bering Strait
   d. tunnel through the layers of the rock in the continental crust

5. The oldest rocks on the earth are most likely to be found

    a. in the ocean basin crust
    b. on islands in the middle of the oceans
    c. in the mantle
    d. in the continental crust

6. Which of the following elements is the most common in the earth's crust?

    a. aluminum   c. silicon
    b. calcium   d. iron

7. Which of the following elements is most common in the earth's core?

    a. aluminum   c. silicon
    b. calcium   d. iron

8. The "low velocity zone" is in the

    a. outer core   c. upper mantle
    b. crust   d. lower mantle

9. Which of the following is NOT a type of earthquake wave

    a. surface wave   c. P wave
    b. down wave   d. secondary wave

10. An instrument to measure earth vibrations is a

    a. gravitometer   d. barometer
    b. transmissometer   e. breathalizer
    c. seismometer

11. The Richter scale

    a. is a scale for measuring ground motion
    b. has no absolute upper limit
    c. measures earthquake magnitude
    d. all of the above

12. Most earthquake damage is caused by

    a. surface seismic waves   c. shear waves
    b. primary waves   d. transverse waves

13. Continental crust and oceanic crust differ by

    a. age   c. density
    b. composition   d. all of the above

14. The core of the earth is believed to consist mainly of

   a. silica minerals
   b. iron and nickel
   c. solid rock
   d. material similar to stony meteorites

PLATES AND THEIR MOVEMENTS

The theory of plate tectonics, which was widely accepted by the 1960s, centers upon the idea that the continents are collections of land masses, or **terranes**, that have moved, broken up, and crunched together several times over billions of years of Earth history. Because of this theory, we have deduced that most landscape features on the earth, including mountain ranges, basins, plateaus, island chains, deep trenches, and submerged mountains, were formed by the movements of the earth's crustal plates.

THE THEORY OF CONTINENTAL DRIFT

The idea of *continental drift* was initially proposed to explain the jigsaw puzzle-like match of the continents of South America and Africa and to explain why fossils found in rocks near the coast of one continent were so similar to fossils found in rocks near a coast across the ocean. The idea that continents had actually moved was first suggested in 1858 by Antonio Snider-Pellegrini. But Snider-Pellegrini theorized that the continental movements were caused by the biblical flood. In 1912, the idea of continental drift was presented to the scientific community by Alfred Wegener.

Wegener's theory of continental drift accounted for the movement of the continents, the wandering of the poles, and the present distribution of living things. His theory also included the idea that there were two basic kinds of crust: continental and oceanic. Wegener even hypothesized correctly that all of the land masses of the world were at one time united in a single supercontinent. He named it *Pangaea*, which means "all land."

Although Alfred Wegener's ideas were neglected and even scorned by some of the scientists of his day, as early as fifty years later plate tectonics had become universally accepted.

The first major supporting evidence for the modern theory of plate tectonics was the discovery of the rift valley in the mid-oceanic ridge in 1958. By the 1960s, the evidence for plate tectonics had overwhelmed geologists, and they abandoned their traditional model of stationary continents.

PLATE TECTONICS

The basic concept of the theory of plate tectonics is that the earth's surface is composed of a dozen or so large pieces, and numerous smaller pieces, called *plates,* that move independently of one another. Some plates consist only of ocean floor, such as the Nazca plate, which is located off the west coast of South America (see **Figure 2.6**). Others contain both continental and oceanic material, as does the North American plate, which extends out to the mid-Atlantic ridge. There is even a plate that is exclusively within a continent; it nearly coincides with the country of Turkey. The largest plate is the Pacific plate; it primarily consists of ocean floor, but Mexico's Baja Peninsula and southwestern California are also part of this plate.

Figure 2.6. A map of the lithospheric plates that constitute the earth's outer shell, showing divergent, convergent, and transform plate boundaries.

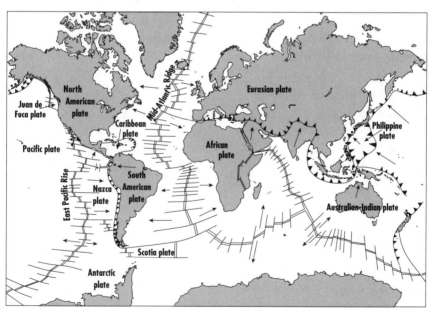

The tectonic plates extend below the earth's crust, to a depth of about three or four times the thickness of the crust, into the underlying mantle (see **Figure 2.3**). Recall that the crust and a portion of the upper mantle is called the *lithosphere,* and that under the lithosphere is the asthenosphere, a zone of rock that is hotter and less rigid than the rock above. The plates slide about on this lubricating layer.

The existence and position of crustal plates was inferred by geologists in the 1950s from patterns in the frequency and location of volcanoes and earthquakes. When openings occur between plates, **magma** rises to produce volcanoes.

The theory of plate tectonics also accounts for the global distribution of earthquakes (see **Figure 2.5**). Earthquakes with deep foci are associated with oceanic trenches and volcanic island arcs (a series of volcanic islands). Ocean trenches are places where slabs of oceanic lithosphere are pushed into and consumed by the mantle. As a slab descends, friction causes frequent sticking. Earthquakes are generated when the built-up stress is released.

PLATE INTERACTIONS

A variety of things can happen when plates of the lithosphere interact; plates interact in different ways along three kinds of plate boundaries. These plate boundaries are illustrated in **Figure 2.7**. *Convergent* boundaries occur where plates collide, and usually result in one of the plates overriding the other. The one that is overridden descends and becomes subducted into the mantle. *Divergent* boundaries are places where plates move apart. This causes an upwelling of magma from the mantle to create new crust. *Transform* boundaries (also called transform faults) are where plates move past one another, sideways.

Convergent Boundaries

Exactly what happens in a convergence, or collision, of plates depends upon the type of crust involved. When a plate of oceanic crust collides with a plate capped with continental crust, the less dense continental plate tends to ride above, while the oceanic plate is subducted. The region where the oceanic plate descends is called a **subduction zone**. Adjacent to subduction zones are deep ocean trenches that can be 8 to 11 kilometers deep and thousands of kilometers long.

In the subduction process, the descending oceanic slab remains relatively cool to depths of several hundred kilometers. The slab of plate eventually melts when it descends to about 600 kilometers below the surface. Components of the melt that are less dense move slowly up to interact with continental rocks above, while the denser components are assimilated into the mantle or the base of the crust. The result of the subduction process is that the continental crust is thickened from underneath.

Figure 2.7. A representation of plate boundaries showing the relative motion of the plates. A. Convergent boundary. B. Divergent boundary. C. Transform boundary or fault.

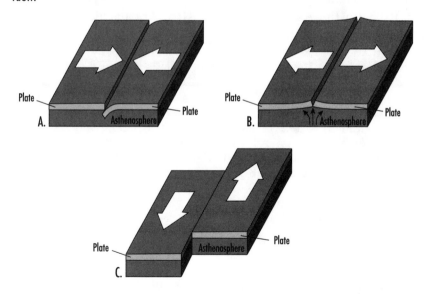

Converging oceanic and continental plates created such land forms as the Andes mountains of South America. The Nazca plate melted as it subducted under South America, producing magmas that buoyed slowly upward. Some of the magma cooled and crystallized under the overlying continent, but some also rose to the surface, creating volcanoes. The Cascade Range, which extends from British Columbia to northern California, and the Sierra Nevada range in eastern California are also products of converging oceanic and continental plates. Volcanoes in the Cascades are still quite active, and include Mount St. Helens and Mount Rainier. The Sierra Nevada range—which contains Yosemite Park—is much older and is now inactive. Yosemite's majestic rock formations are large, crystallized magma chambers. Several million years of erosion have removed the volcanic cones from around these chambers.

Converging *oceanic* plates can also produce volcanoes. These volcanoes form on the ocean floor and create *seamounts*, but some build up until they emerge above water to form islands. Such islands are located near ocean trenches where subduction is occurring. The Aleutian, Mariana, and Tonga islands in the Pacific Ocean were formed in this way, as were Japan and the Philippines.

When two *continental* plates converge, neither plate subducts. In such a collision, the crust buckles, fractures, and compacts. This type of collision produced the Himalayas; the plate carrying India collided with the Asian plate. The Alps, Appalachians, and Ural Mountains were all formed by continental plate convergence.

FYI

The thirty-five highest mountains in the world are all in the Himalayan and Karakoram ranges, between China and the Indian subcontinent. The Himalayas, Karakorams, and Hindu Kush together form an unbroken mountain range that is 3,862 kilometers long. Mount Everest is our planet's tallest mountain, it reaches to a height of 8,848 meters. By contrast, the highest mountain in the Americas is Mount Aconcagua, in the Andes, which stands 6,960 meters tall. The highest in North America is Mount McKinley, in Alaska, at 6,194 meters.

Divergent Boundaries

Divergent boundaries occur when plates spread apart (refer to **Figure 2.7**). Most places where plates spread apart are at the crests of oceanic ridges, and as the plates move apart, the fractures are immediately filled with magma. The magma cools to produce new sea floor between the diverging plates; this process is called *sea-floor spreading*. But there can also be divergence of plates within a continent. This can cause a landmass to break into smaller segments, which is what happened to the supercontinent, Pangaea. In continental divergence, hot magma plumes push up from below warping, stretching and cracking the crust above it. When the plates move, downfaulting occurs—slabs of the plates break off and fall down. As the plates move apart, **rift valleys** are formed in between them. The rifts become wider and deeper as the plates move apart.

The Red Sea and the East African rift valleys are examples of the initial stages of the breakup of a continent. Geologists have found evidence that rifting, uplift and volcanism all acted about 34 million years ago to form the Red Sea. A plume or hotspot may have risen from the mantle to weaken the plate, causing the initial breakup. The plate stretched and the crust thinned until the plate finally separated.

Continental breakup has occurred many times in the earth's history, and in fact, almost occurred long ago, in North America. An aborted rift zone that extends from Lake Superior to Kansas has been identified by geologists. A billion years ago this was an active rift zone, but some unknown event halted its spread and the continent of North America remained intact.

Transform Boundaries

As you can see in **Figure 2.7**, transform faults occur when plates slide past each other. Most transform faults are in the ocean basins, but some, like the San Andreas fault in California, divide continental material. Part of California is on the Pacific plate, which is moving to the northwest, while the eastern part is on the North American plate. If the present motion continues, the part of the state that's west of the fault will eventually become an island, and will continue to migrate.

Transform faults play an important role in the rock cycle, enabling oceanic crust that was created at the mid-oceanic ridge to move to another location, and eventually to where it will be recycled at a subduction zone. **Figure 2.8** shows several types of plate interactions.

Figure 2.8. Some types of interactions between lithospheric plates.

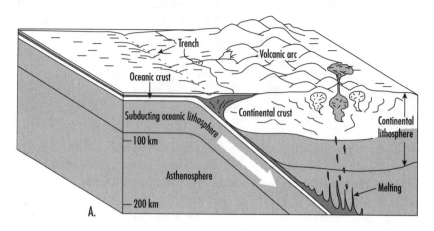

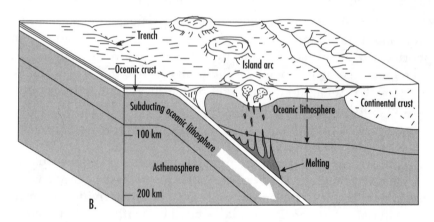

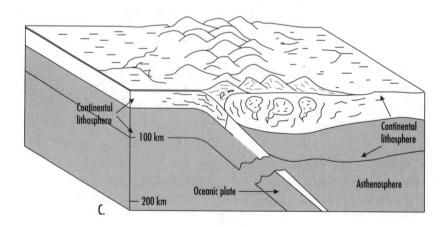

MAGNETIC ORIENTATIONS REVEAL STRANGE BEDFELLOWS

When magma cools below a certain temperature, the alignment of the earth's magnetic field at that moment is captured in the position of the iron particles in the rock. In other words, the rock becomes permanently imprinted with innumerable mini compass needles. Geologists can determine the amount of time that has passed since the rock cooled by analyzing the radioactive decay products in the rock, and can use this information as well as the magnetic alignment data to determine where the rock lay relative to the poles at the time that it formed.

This kind of data, combined with evidence from fossils and patterns of folds in the landscape, has led geologists to conclude that the terranes (or distinct pieces of crust) that make up Florida, parts of Newfoundland, coastal New England, Nova Scotia, and many west coast states, are "foreign"—that is, they originated someplace else. Sometime in the past the various pieces were accreted, or pasted, onto the continent. Similar evidence has led to the conclusion that Alaska's Aleutian Islands and western Idaho are made of rocks that were once a single piece, and the same is true for Japan and part of California. Other parts of California may be fragments that originated in southern China and the south Pacific, and pieces of North Carolina, New England, and Newfoundland appear to have common origins with parts of Europe.

Based on present movements, geologists think that Australia will eventually crash into Indonesia and push all of the islands north, and that Indonesia will be added as foreign terranes to the continent of Asia. Geologists also think that Europe and Africa will converge, closing the Mediterranean Sea and creating a new mountain range.

FYI

The Hawaiian islands were apparently not created by plate movement. The islands sit over a "hot spot," which is a place in the crust where a plume of molten magma from the mantle has intruded. The hot spot is in a relatively fixed position. The islands above the hot spot, however, move with the Pacific plate toward the northwest. Over the past 25 million years, the plate has moved over the hot spot at an average rate of 11 centimeters per year. The newest volcano in the string of Hawaiian islands is now rising up from the sea floor to the east. The volcano is still underwater but is to be the next Hawaiian island, and, in fact, already has a name—*Loihi*.

WHAT CAUSES PLATE MOTIONS?

Geologists agree that the driving force for plate movements is the unequal distribution of heat within the earth, but they are not sure exactly *how* the plates move. One theory involves a thermal convection model, in which uneven heat causes convection currents of rising and descending fluids in the mantle. The mid-oceanic ridge is where warmer, less dense material slowly rises. As it rises to the cooler area, the molten fluid spreads out and drags a plate along. Heat passes to the surrounding material, while the original material cools, contracts and becomes denser, and slowly falls back toward the core. This kind of energy convection belt is also found in the earth's atmosphere and oceans. A simple convection cell mechanism, however, cannot explain all the aspects of plate motion, although the flow of material in the mantle is very complex and there is much uncertainty about the location of these convection cells.

FRACTURES IN THE CRUST AND MOUNTAIN BUILDING

Mountain ranges are formed by the compression and distortion of previously low-lying rocks. Rocks that are subjected to intense force respond by either breaking or folding. Folding is possible when rocks which are normally quite brittle are subjected to heat and are put under high pressure. Plate movements are often slow enough to provide the time for folding to take place, but when the crust is too brittle or the plate movement is too fast for the rock to bend, breaking occurs. Different kinds of mountains result if the crust folds rather than breaks. The Appalachians, the Rockies, the Alps, and the Himalayas are all examples of mountains built mainly from the folding of rocks.

When rock folds, two distinct arrangements of folded layers are created: the **anticline** and **syncline**. **Figure 2.9** shows these folds in a mountain range. Folds in rock layers can produce different features on surface landscapes, such as domes and basins (see **Figure 2.10**). The processes that produce domes and basins are called the *upwarping* and *downwarping* of crustal rocks.

Figure 2.9 Two aspects of folding in a mountain range. The anticline has an "A" shape while the syncline is shaped like a "U."

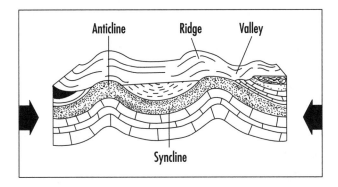

Figure 2.10 Domes and basins are landforms produced by upwarping and downwarping of rock layers.

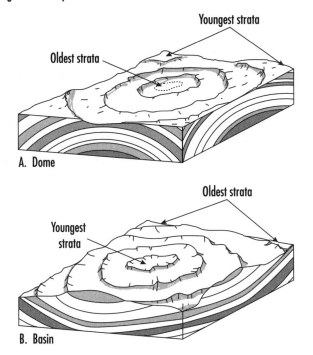

A. Dome

B. Basin

When rock is stressed to the point that it breaks, **joints** and **faults** form. Joints are breaks along which no movement or displacement of rock has occurred. Faults are breaks along which movement has occurred. The displacement of material can be in a vertical or horizontal direction, and this determines the type of fault. *Dip-slip* faults are the result of vertical displacement. There are two types of vertical displacement. If the rocks are pulled apart, that is, subject to tensional forces, the result is a *normal fault*. In a normal fault, one wall of rock moves downward relative to the other. The mountains of the Basin and Range Province in and around Nevada were formed by breaking followed by tensional forces. These are called *fault-block* mountains.

If rocks are pushed together, or compressed, *reverse faults* are often the result. *Reverse faults* result when one wall moves upward relative to the other (they are called *thrust faults* if there is only a small angle between the two sides). There are many examples of reverse and thrust faults in the Appalachians and the Alps. Normal and reverse types of dip-slip faults are illustrated in **Figure 2.11**.

A third case is possible. *Strike-slip faults* represent faults where the displacement of material is horizontal, with adjacent sections of crust moving past one another laterally. One type of strike-slip fault is the *transform fault*. A transform fault cuts through the lithosphere and separates two plates. Such faults occur in the ocean basin as well as on continents. The San Andreas fault in California is a large transform fault consisting of many interconnecting fault surfaces.

Figure 2.11. The two types of dip-slip faults are normal and reverse faults.

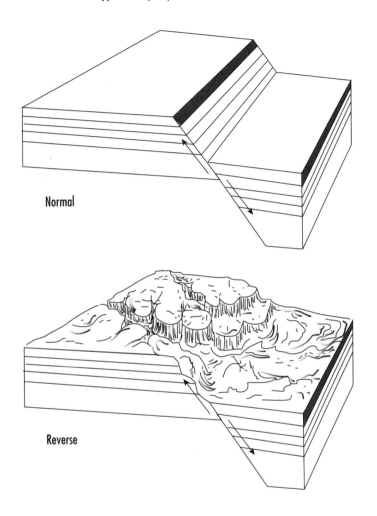

Normal

Reverse

VOLCANOES AND THEIR FEATURES

Volcanoes are mountains formed by material, such as ash or lava, that has come directly out of the earth's interior. Material emerges from a vent in the crust and accumulates around the vent to form the volcano. One way volcanoes are categorized is by how often they erupt. *Active* volcanoes are currently erupting or have erupted within recent (recorded) history, *dormant* volcanoes are not currently erupting, and *extinct* volcanoes are believed to have ceased erupting.

Volcanoes often form where tectonic plates meet. Breaks occur in the earth's crust and magma flows out. If no outlet is available as the plates push together, pressure builds up until it is relieved by an explosion. Some volcanoes are formed over subduction zones where a plate has plunged into the mantle.

Most people think of volcanoes as tall, cone-shaped mountains with lava, smoke, and ash erupting from the top. There are volcanoes like that, but there are many other kinds of volcanoes in existence as well. The shape of a volcano depends on the kind of eruptions and materials that have produced it. Most people associate volcanoes with eruptions of lava, but volcanoes also eject other kinds of material, including gases, ash and dust, broken rock, and *lava bombs* (fragments formed from erupted blobs of magma which may become streamlined in shape during flight).

The best known volcanoes are called *composite* or *strato* volcanoes because they are made up of layers (strata) of solidified lava that are mixed with layers of ash. Composite volcanoes form when different kinds of materials are ejected in successive eruptions. Famous examples of composite volcanoes include Mount St. Helens and Vesuvius, the volcano that buried the city of Pompeii near ancient Rome. Composite volcanoes have fairly steep sides and may rise 3,000 meters or so in height. **Figure 2.12** illustrates a composite volcano and some of its features.

Figure 2.12 Strato or composite volcanoes are composed of alternate layers of viscous lava and ash. Magma rises up a pipe and into the vent from a chamber deep below ground. Secondary cones may form on the side of a volcano if the central vent becomes blocked.

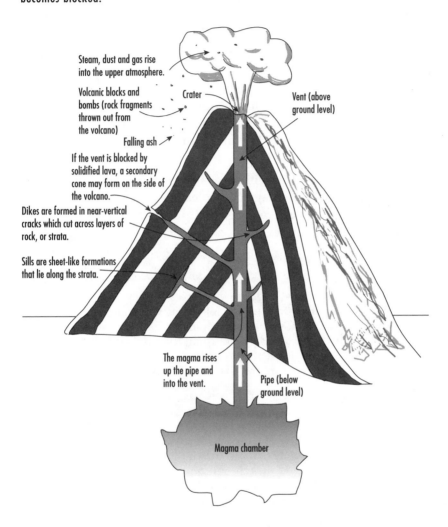

Steam, dust and gas rise into the upper atmosphere.

Volcanic blocks and bombs (rock fragments thrown out from the volcano)

Crater

Vent (above ground level)

Falling ash

If the vent is blocked by solidified lava, a secondary cone may form on the side of the volcano.

Dikes are formed in near-vertical cracks which cut across layers of rock, or strata.

Sills are sheet-like formations that lie along the strata.

The magma rises up the pipe and into the vent.

Pipe (below ground level)

Magma chamber

Another kind of volcano is the *cinder cone* volcano. Cinder cone volcanoes are steep-sided, smaller volcanoes that form from eruptions of thick lava that explode into the air and harden, forming *tephra.* The tephra can range in size from fine dust to large chunks of lava bombs. Many of Central America's volcanoes are cinder cones.

A third kind of volcano is the *shield* volcano. Shield volcanoes have gently sloping sides and craters at their summits. They are composed mostly of cooled lava and can be huge—hundreds of kilometers in diameter and tens of thousands of meters high. The Hawaiian islands are all large shield volcanoes. One of them, Mauna Loa, is the world's largest individual mountain.

A fourth type of volcano is known as the *giant caldera.* **Calderas** are the circular depressions found at the top of many volcanoes. Giant calderas are gigantic craters that form from the collapse of a volcano's cone after one or more eruptions. The calderas may fill up with lava and ash so that the depression is difficult to discern. Yellowstone National Park, for example, consists of filled-in calderas.

The fifth type of volcano is the *fissure eruption* type, which is the least like the traditional image of a volcano. This type has no central crater; lava flows out of cracks in the ground and the surrounding topography stays fairly level.

CONSIDER THIS

One of the biggest science news stories in 1980 was the catastrophic eruption of Mount St. Helens in Washington State. The volcano ejected almost a cubic kilometer of rock and ash with a force hundreds of times greater than that of the atomic bombs dropped on Japan in World War II. The surrounding forests were devastated and more than fifty people were killed.

Mount St. Helens is one of fifteen large and numerous smaller volcanoes in the Cascade Range along the west coast. Mount Rainier, also in the state of Washington, is potentially much more dangerous than Mount St. Helens. The worst hazard is the potential of a catastrophic debris flow—known as a *lahar*. A lahar is a flash flood of semiliquid mud, rock, and ice. Mount Rainier last erupted 150 years ago. The town of Orting, Oregon now stands underneath the volcano. Orting is built on seven meters of debris deposited by a mudflow from the last eruption. In fact, the geological record shows at least sixty lahars from Mount Rainier over the past 10,000 years. Some of these contained so much material that they reached Puget Sound, not far from the city of Seattle.

LAVA TYPES

The shape of a volcano and the way it erupts depend on the physical properties of its lava. One of the properties of lava that affects a volcano's shape and eruption is its thickness, or viscosity. Lava that contains a high percentage of silica (quartz) flows less easily because silica atoms tend to form long molecular chains that tangle together, and are unable to slide by one another. Lava with low viscosity runs like melted wax and can flow a long way before solidifying. A series of small eruptions of lava of low viscosity will form a nearly flat mountain. Lava can also be so thick that it hardly flows at all; this type of lava forms tall, steep-sided mountains.

Another factor that influences eruptions is the amount of different gases, such as water vapor and carbon dioxide, that are dissolved in the lava. Where lava is formed inside the earth, the pressure is so high that large amounts of gas are dissolved in the lava. The pressure is reduced as the lava travels toward the earth's surface and eventually into the air in an eruption, and the gas comes out of solution and forms bubbles. If lava has low viscosity and a low content of dissolved gases, it will flow out and spread over the ground. If it is highly viscous and also has a low content of dissolved gases, it will emerge slowly and form a domed structure. On the other hand, if the lava is high in dissolved gases and the lava's viscosity is low, the lava will bubble as it hits the surface, throwing cinders and lava bombs, and result in a cinder cone. If the lava is high in dissolved gases and its viscosity is also high, it erupts in an explosive cloud of superheated steam and ash.

There is no accepted scale for measuring the sizes of volcanic eruptions, in the way that the Richter Scale is used for measuring earthquakes, but **Table 2.2** compares the amount of material thrown out by eruptions of the past that volcanologists have studied.

Volcanoes tend to be localized in tectonically active regions. **Figure 2.13** is a map that shows the volcanically active regions of the world.

Volcanic eruptions can be very destructive, and can cause huge clouds of volcanic ash, emissions of super-heated steam and rock, avalanches, toxic gases, and, when they are covered with snow or glaciers, mudslides. A blast of steam and rock from the eruption of Mount Pelee on Martinique in the Caribbean in 1902 destroyed the city of St. Pierre in less than two minutes, killing 30,000 people.

Figure 2.13 Volcanoes are associated with tectonically active areas of the world.

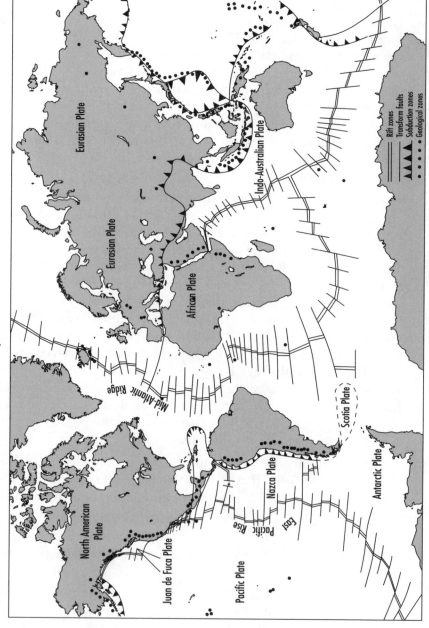

Table 2.2 Comparing the volume of some volcanic eruptions of the past.

Volcano	Year	Est. material ejected (cubic kilometers)
Mt. Pelee, Martinique	1902	0.5
Mount St. Helens, WA	1980	0.2
Vesuvius, Italy	29	3.0
Pinatubo, Philippines	1991	10.0
Santorini, Greece	1450 B.C.	60.0
Tambora, Indonesia	1815	150.0
Long Valley, California	240,000 B.C.	500.0
Columbia, Washington	15 Million B.C.	100,000.0

In 1985, mudslides followed an eruption of Nevado del Ruiz in Columbia and killed 25,000 people.

Major eruptions have altered the course of history and have even affected the climate all over the world. The eruption of the volcano forming the Mediterranean island of Santorini, for example, has been linked to the destruction of the advanced Minoan civilization on nearby Crete. Major eruptions can affect global weather by throwing clouds of ash that contain sulfur particles into the upper atmosphere; this material reflects the sunlight, preventing it from reaching and warming the earth.

The biggest eruptions of all come from the fissure eruption and giant caldera volcanoes. Both of these kinds are known to have deposited hundreds of cubic kilometers of material on the earth's surface during single eruptions. The largest known eruption in the United States occurred 600,000 years ago, from the giant caldera in the middle of Yellowstone National Park. This eruption ejected more than 500 cubic kilometers of ash that blanketed the country-side from the Mississippi River to California.

Fissure eruption type volcanoes can expel huge amounts of low viscosity lava, in what are called "flood basalt" eruptions. These are not very explosive eruptions, but they can continue over long periods and cover vast areas. The Columbia River basalt group is the largest flood basalt deposit in the United States. It covers parts of the states of Washington, Oregon, and Idaho.

VOLCANOLOGISTS

Volcanologists are earth scientists who study volcanoes. They are interested in studying the earth's interior to determine what causes volcanic events. Volcanologists are also interested in learning how to predict volcanic eruptions with the use of many different instruments. The U.S. Geological Survey employs volcanologists and maintains a web site about volcanoes, which can be accessed at:

http://vulcan.wr.usgs.gov/Glossary/framework.html

Two other volcano web sites can be reached at:

http://www.volcanoes.com/

http://www.cotf.edu/ETE/scen/volcanoes/volcanoes.html

CHECK YOUR PROGRESS

15. Which phenomena is NOT related to plate tectonics?

    a volcanism
    b. earthquakes
    c. orogenies (mountain building)
    d. tropical low pressure systems
    e. sea floor spreading

16. Molten material rising through the earth's crust is referred to as

    a. magma   d. gabbro
    b. lava   e. basalt
    c. pumice

17. The lubricating layer that allows for plate motion is the

    a. lithosphere   c. asthenosphere
    b. hydrosphere   d. geosphere

18. The theory of plate tectonics helps explain all BUT

    a. the Pacific "ring of fire"
    b. seismic zones
    c. crustal faults
    d. moraine and kettle formation

19. The San Andreas is an example of a

    a. transform fault   c. thrust fault
    b. dip-slip fault   d. graben

20. The world's loftiest mountains are located
   a. in the Appalachians   c. in the Andes range
   b. in Alaska   d. in the Himalayas

21. An example of a land mass or feature which CANNOT be explained by the theory of plate tectonics is
   a. the Cascade range   c. Hawaiian Islands
   b. the San Andreas fault   d. the Aleutian Islands

22. Plate movement is believed to be driven by
   a. the unequal distribution of heat within the earth
   b. incoming solar energy
   c. tidal energy
   d. gravitational forces

23. An example of what could happen when plates interact at a convergent boundary would be
   a. the mid-oceanic ridge   c. the San Andreas fault
   b. the Himalayas   d. the Hawaiian Islands

24. The kinds of volcanoes associated with the largest eruptions of lava are the
   a. cinder cone and composite
   b. shield and cinder cone
   c. giant caldera and fissure eruption
   d. fissure eruption and cinder cone

25. The destructive potential of volcanoes is associated with
   a. lava flows
   b. climate change
   c. superheated steam and ash
   d. all of the above

26. Vesuvius and Mount Rainier are examples of
   a. fissure eruption volcanoes
   b. composite volcanoes
   c. shield volcanoes
   d. cinder cone volcanoes

27. If lava has a low viscosity and a low content of dissolved gases, it will
   a. flow out and spread over the ground
   b. emerge slowly to form a domed structure
   c. throw cinders and lava bombs
   d. explode violently

28. Volcanoes are associated with plate tectonics in that
   a. volcanoes occur in the stable interior of plates
   b. volcanoes cause convection in the mantle
   c. volcanoes are formed over subduction zones
   d. volcanoes cause earthquakes

GLOSSARY

anticline—an upward fold of rock strata that bends downward on both sides from its axis.

asthenosphere—a layer of the mantle that underlies the lithosphere and continues to a depth of about 250 kilometers where the mantle again becomes solid. It is thought to be a zone of partial melting because earthquake waves slow down as they pass through it.

body waves—a type of seismic wave that penetrates deep into the earth.

calderas—circular depressions found at the top of many volcanoes, which are caused by the collapse of the central part of the volcano.

density—the mass in a unit of volume. The density of water at standard temperature and pressure is 1 gram per cubic centimeter.

epicenter—the point on the earth's surface directly above the earthquake's focus.

fault—a fracture along which the rock has moved. One side of the rock is displaced compared to the other side. Faults are classified based upon the angle of the fracture and direction of the relative movement.

joint—a fracture along which there has been no movement of the rock.

lithosphere—the rigid outer layer of the earth, comprising the crust and upper mantle.

magma—the molten material from which igneous rock is formed.

rift valley—a valley formed by the lowering of an area of land between two parallel faults.

seismic wave—a vibration caused by an earthquake.

seismograph—an instrument for recording the direction, intensity, and duration of earthquakes.

seismology—the study of earthquakes and other movements of the earth's crust.

subduction—the edge of one crustal plate descending below another.

subduction zone—when two places collide, the region where an oceanic plate descends to the asthenosphere.

surface wave—a type of seismic wave that moves through the earth's crust.

syncline—a fold or folds of rock strata sloping downward from opposite directions to form a trough or inverted arch.

terrane—a tract of land originating someplace different than its present location.

ANSWER KEY

1. b	11. d	21. c
2. a	12. a	22. a
3. c	13. d	23. b
4. b	14. b	24. c
5. d	15. d	25. d
6. c	16. a	26. b
7. d	17. c	27. a
8. c	18. d	28. c
9. b	19. a	
10. c	20. d	

Rocks and Minerals

THE ELEMENTS AND MINERALS THAT CONSTITUTE EARTH

The primary components of the earth are rock, water, and air. **Rock** is an aggregate, or mixture of minerals. A **mineral** is a naturally occurring solid substance that has a uniform composition and a crystalline structure.

There are many kinds of minerals, and they are differentiated on the basis of their crystal structure, hardness, relative density, luster, color, and by how they break. Some 2,500 different minerals have been identified by **mineralogists**. Substances without definite compositions or characteristic crystalline structures are not considered minerals, for example, opals are *amorphous* solids.

Minerals, in turn, are composed of elements. An **element** is a simple substance that cannot be broken down into other substances by chemical processes. There are eighty-eight elements found in nature. Other elements have been created by scientists, but these generally last only a short time before breaking down. Many of the eighty-eight naturally occurring elements are rare. In fact, only twenty are common, and only eight make up 99% of the earth. These "Big 8" and their chemical symbols are: oxygen (O), silicon (Si), aluminum (Al), iron (Fe), calcium (Ca), potassium (K), magnesium (Mg), and sodium (Na) (see **Table 3.1** for the proportion of each of these elements in the earth's crust, and **Figure 3.2** for models of these atoms).

Table 3.1 The relative abundance of the eight most common elements in the earth's crust.

Element	Percentage by weight (approx.)
oxygen	46.6
silicon	27.7
aluminum	8.1
iron	5.0
calcium	3.6
potassium	2.6
magnesium	2.6
all others	1.5

A few minerals, such as gold and sulfur, are made entirely from one element. Most elements, however, are found in combination with other elements. Iron, copper (Cu), sulfur (S), and carbon (C) are found as individual, or free elements, but they are more often found in **compounds**. A compound is a combination of two or more elements joined to form a chemically stable substance.

SOME CHEMISTRY BASICS

All matter is composed of atoms. **Figure 3.1** is a simplified model of an oxygen atom. Two kinds of particles, protons and neutrons, make up the central nucleus of this particular atom. The oxygen atom has eight protons in its nucleus (the *atomic number* of oxygen is 8). The oxygen isotope shown in **Figure 3.1** also has eight neutrons, so the *atomic mass* of this atom is 16. The eight electrons in this oxygen atom are in two shells; there are two electrons in the innermost shell, and six in the second, outer shell. The second shell of any atom can hold a total of eight electrons, so that the oxygen atom has room to take on or share two more electrons. This enables oxygen to form compounds with other elements. When oxygen shares electrons with two hydrogen atoms, the compound dihydrogen monoxide, H_2O, or water, is formed.

Figure 3.1. Atoms have protons and neutrons in their nuclei and are surrounded by a swarm of electrons. Electron particles are light compared to the protons and neutrons, and do not behave exactly like planets orbiting a sun. However, there are locations, called *shells*, where they are more likely to be found at any one time. Note that this model is not to scale.

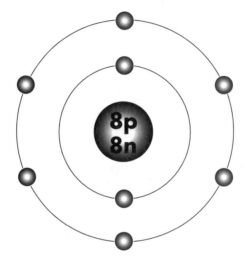

Isotopes

Isotopes are variations in the number of neutrons in atoms. Elements are defined by the number of positively charged protons in their nucleus, which is equal to the number of negatively charged particles in their electron shells. The number of neutrons in an atom can vary without changing the identity of the element, but the properties of the element will vary. Elements that are the same but have different numbers of neutrons are called **isotopes**. Hydrogen is the simplest element; it has three isotopes. The isotopes of hydrogen are (1) hydrogen, which has one proton and no neutrons, (2) deuterium, which has one proton and one neutron, and (3) tritium, which has one proton and two neutrons. Most elements in nature consist of a mixture of isotopes. For example, uranium ore is a mixture of the isotopes uranium-238 and uranium-235 (scientists often designate isotopes by listing their atomic mass number, that is, the combined number of protons and neutrons).

Isotopes may be unstable and break down into atoms of completely different elements. These isotopes are said to be **radioactive** and are called *radioisotopes*. Radioisotopes of an element have a regular rate of decay that can be used to date the material they comprise.

Chemistry is about electron behavior

An **ion** is an atom that has been stripped of one or more electrons, or that has taken on additional electrons. Since electrons are negatively charged, ions that have extra electrons bear negative charges. Negatively charged ions are called *anions*, while positively charged ions are *cations*.

Oxygen is the only common element with a negative **oxidation number**, which is the number of electrons that the atom tends to accept or give up. A negative oxidation number means the element's atoms will accept electrons, thus giving the atoms a total negative charge. Oxygen can accept two electrons, so its oxidation number is negative two.

Oxygen is also important because it is the predominant element on Earth by weight. Because oxygen is a large atom, it also makes up much of the earth's crust by volume: approximately 94%. See **Figure 3.2** to compare the size of the oxygen atom with atoms of other common elements in the earth's crust.

Figure 3.2 Of all the common elements, oxygen is the only anion, or negatively charged ion. Oxygen combines with many different cations to form a variety of minerals.

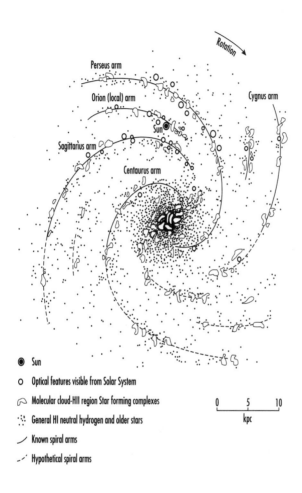

- ◉ Sun
- ○ Optical features visible from Solar System
- ⌒ Molecular cloud-HII region Star forming complexes
- ∴ General HI neutral hydrogen and older stars
- ╱ Known spiral arms
- ╌╱ Hypothetical spiral arms

```
0      5      10
|_____|_____|
       kpc
```

CHARACTERISTICS OF MINERALS

THE STRUCTURE OF MINERALS

The key to understanding the structure of a mineral is to study the arrangement of its ions. The arrangement depends upon the electrical charges between the ions, and their relative sizes. Ions will become organized when a mineral crystallizes in ways that achieve *stable* configurations. **Figure 3.3** shows the arrangement of oxygen ions around a single ion of silicon, a much smaller ion, in the mineral olivine. Some ions are nearly the same size, such as aluminum and silicon, sodium and calcium, and iron and magnesium; being close in size enables them to freely substitute for each other in a mineral's structure.

Figure 3.3 The four large spheres represent ions of oxygen while the single, small central sphere represents silicon. The four outermost electron-in the silicon atom are each shared by an oxygen atom.

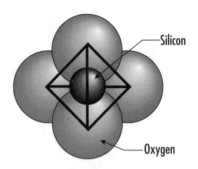

Why do atoms and molecules combine to form the thousands of minerals on the earth? The regularity and order of atoms in minerals results from the lower total energy required to maintain a crystalline solid as compared with the energy necessary to maintain the disorder that occurs in a liquid or gas state. As mixtures of elements in a magma melt, for example, ever so slowly losing energy and cooling, the atoms become arranged in patterns that require the lowest possible energy level.

The **unit cell** is a low-energy arrangement of atoms in the mineral that repeats itself over and over in the structure of the large crystal. It is the smallest atomic pattern that exhibits all the chemical and physical properties of the mineral. A unit cell can be an aggregate of anywhere from a few atoms and molecules to several thousand, but even the largest unit cells are small, on the order of one hundred millionth of a centimeter in size.

PHYSICAL PROPERTIES OF MINERALS

Recall that minerals are distinguished from each other by a number of physical characteristics. Physical properties geologists find useful for mineral identification include:

- chemical composition
- luster
- hardness
- weight (specific gravity)
- color
- crystal structure
- fluorescence
- magnetism
- solubility
- cleavage
- radioactivity

Of the identifying characteristics above, the two most used and useful are composition and crystal structure. Mineralogists can analyze the chemical composition of a mineral, but there are some drawbacks to basing a mineral's identification on composition alone because minerals can have identical compositions but different internal structures. Graphite and diamond are chemically the same, for example; both are composed of carbon, but their internal structures differ greatly. For this reason, crystal structure is especially important in the identification of minerals. Often the crystal structure will be evident from the surface of the mineral. The mineral specimen has flat surfaces called *crystal faces*, which are large-scale reflections of the internal arrangement of the atoms. The number of possible internal arrangements is limited. Each mineral specimen falls into one of six groups that are based upon their crystalline structures. The six basic groups are shown in **Table 3.2.**

Table 3.2 The six basic symmetries of unit cells, their characteristics and mineral examples.

Name of Pattern	Organization	Mineral Examples	Shapes	
isometric	3 axes of equal length right angles between all axes	garnet, magnetite pyrite	cubes octahedra tetrahedra dodecahedra	isometric
tetragonal	2 equal axes 3rd axis longer or shorter right angles between all	zircon	prism pyramid rectangular	tetragonal
orthorhombic	3 unequal axes right angles between all	olivine	dipyramid	orthorhombic
monoclinic	3 unequal axes 2 at right angles 3rd perpindicular to one but oblique to other	pyroxene mica clay minerals arthoclase gypsum	—	monoclinic
triclinic	3 unequal axes oblique angles between all	plagioclase aluminum silicate	—	triclinic
hexagonal	3 unequal axes in same plane intersecting at 60 degree angle, and 4th perpendicular to plane of other three	quartz calcite dolomite hematite	prism dipyramid	hexagonal

Another clue to a mineral's identity is its hardness. Geologists use a scale of relative hardness called the **Mohs Scale** (see **Table 3.3**). On this scale, "1" is assigned to the softest minerals, such as talc, while "10" stands for the hardest mineral, diamond. The steps between number values in the Mohs Scale are arbitrary and do not represent equal intervals.

Table 3.3 The Mohs Scale of Hardness

1	talc	fingernail can scratch
2	gypsum	
3	calcite	penny can scratch
4	flurorite	knife/glass can scratch
5	apatite	
6	orthoclase	file can scratch
7	quartz	quartz can scratch
8	topaz	
9	corundum (e.g., ruby, sapphire)	
10	diamond	

Other identifying characteristics of minerals are their **cleavage** and **fracture**. Cleavage and fracture describe the way a mineral breaks. Breaks will occur on planes of relative weakness in the mineral. Cleavage is a regular break in a mineral that produces a smooth plane that reflects light, while fracture is an irregular break. Some minerals, such as quartz and olivine, exhibit no cleavage. Micas, which have a sheet-like structure, will cleave only on one plane, while pyroxenes and feldspars will cleave in planes at right angles.

The colors of some minerals are also useful in identification. Feldspars, for example, have a white or pinkish color, and pyrite, known as "fool's gold," has a yellowish, metallic color. *Streak* refers to the color of the mineral when it has been made into powder. A streak can be produced by scratching a piece of the mineral across the surface of an unglazed tile, but a mineral harder than the tile will not produce a streak.

Luster refers to the way the mineral reflects light; for instance, pyrite has a metallic luster while quartz has a nonmetallic luster. Luster is described by such terms as adamantine (diamond-like), vitreous (glassy), greasy, resinous, waxy, pearly, silky, and dull.

A measure of the relative weight of a mineral is defined by its **specific gravity**. Specific gravity is determined by computing the ratio of the weight of the mineral in air to its weight in water.

Solubility is also an important characteristic of some minerals. For example, calcite bubbles and dissolves in weak hydrochloric acid, so an acid test can be useful for identifying limestone and dolomite rocks, which contain calcite and dolomite. Another example of a mineral that can be identified by its solubility is halite, which is composed chiefly of sodium chloride, or common salt.

MINERAL GROUPS

All minerals fit into one of thirteen groups, but the bulk of the rock-forming minerals fit into one of seven groups. The largest and most complex group is the silicates. Minerals in this group comprise some 92% of the earth's crust.

The group of silicates is quite complex because oxygen and silicon can combine with each other and with other elements in a number of ways. There are four main subgroups of the silicates. The first silicate group is the **isolated tetrahedra** (illustrated in **Figure 3.3**). In this group, there is one silicon ion to every four oxygens, which is expressed as SiO_4. This combination of silicon and oxygen gives an excess of four electrons per unit; in other words, the unit has an oxidation number of negative 4. Because of the extra electrons, other ions with a positive charge can be incorporated into the crystal structure. For example, if magnesium and iron ions are incorporated, the minerals that result are called olivines, if the incorporated positive ions are aluminum, aluminum silicates result.

The second group of silicates is the **chain silicates**. In this group, each silicon ion shares two of its four oxygen ions, producing a ratio of SiO_3. Chain silicates tend to crystallize in an elongated form, either in a single chain or double chain form (see **Figure 3.4**). The single chain silicates are the **pyroxenes**. The pyroxenes contain any of the several positive ions, except potassium, because potassium ions are too large to fit in the chain (see **Figure 3.2**). Two common rock-forming pyroxenes are diopside and augite. The double chain silicates are the **amphiboles**. In this subgroup, adjacent silicon ions alternatively share two, then three of their oxygens, producing a ratio of Si_4O_{11}. A variety of amphibole called hornblende may occur in long, fiberlike crystals to form one kind of asbestos.

Figure 3.4 Rachel you need a caption here fro consistancy.

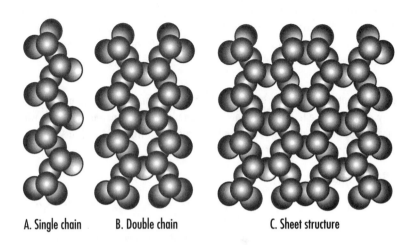

A. Single chain   B. Double chain   C. Sheet structure

The third group of silicates is the **sheet silicates**. (**Figure 3.4**) Each silicon ion in this group is bonded to three oxygen ions in a unit of Si_2O_5. This group contains the micas and the clay minerals. Clay is made up of extremely tiny crystalline particles. Both clay and mica contain aluminum ions, which are close in size to silicon and replace some of the silicon atoms in the structure. Both also contain hydroxide (OH) ions. In the sheet silicates, potassium ions can fit between the sheets. Some micas also contain iron and magnesium particles. Mica is a mineral you may have seen. It comes in black, brown, green (biotite mica), and nearly transparent versions (muscovite mica). Both kinds are made up of thin, shiny sheets which flake easily. One form of mica, vermiculite, is commonly used as an additive to potting soil.

The fourth and last of the silicate groups is the **framework silicates**, which are the most silicon-rich of all. In the framework silicates, each silicon ion is bonded to each of four oxygens. The resulting mineral is a three dimensional framework of SiO_2 (silicon dioxide), the most stable and electrically neutral of the silicate structures. This group is the most abundant of all minerals in the earth's crust; it includes the quartzes and feldspars. Quartz contains only silicon and oxygen and makes up about 12% of the crust. Feldspars can contain sodium, aluminum, potassium, and calcium, as well as silicon and oxygen. Feldspars comprise 51% of the earth's crust.

The major nonsilicate mineral groups are: (1) oxides and hydroxides, (2) sulfides, (3) halides and borates, (4) sulfates, (5) carbonates, (6) phosphates, vanadates, and arsenates, (7) sulfosalts, (8) nitrates and iodates, (9) tungstates and molybdates, and (10) native elements. **Table 3.4** provides a list of some of the nonsilicate mineral groups and examples of minerals in each group.

Table 3.4 Nonsilicate mineral groups. Calcite and its cousin aragonite are both $CaCO_3$ by composition and represent another example of **polymorphs**, minerals with the same composition but different crystalline structures. Iron (Fe) and nickel (Ni) also exist as native elements deep within the earth.

Nonsilicate Mineral Group	Examples
oxides	ice (H_2O), hematite (Fe_2O_3), magnetite (Fe_3O_4), Corundum (Al_2O_3)
sulfides	lead sulfide (galena), copper sulfide (chalcopyrite), mercury sulfide (cinnabar), zinc sulfide (sphalerite),
halides	salt (NaCl), also called halite fluorite (CaF_2)
sulfates	gypsum ($CaSO_4 \cdot H_2O$), anhydrite ($CaSO_4$)
carbonates	dolomite [$CaMg(CO_3)_2$], calcite ($CaCO_3$), malachite, and azurite
hydroxides	bauxite [$Al(OH)_3 \cdot nH_2O$] (aluminum ore)
phosphates	apatite [$Ca_5(F,Cl,OH)(PO_4)_3$], turquoise
native elements	gold (Au), silver (Ag), copper (Cu), sulfur (S), platinum (Pt), graphite (C), diamond (C)

FYI

Nearly every manufactured thing around you is made from minerals. In fact, there are only two sources of the raw materials for the things we use in our daily lives, and the phrase, "if it can't be grown, it has to be mined," expresses that fact. There are minerals in this paper, in the walls of your house, and even in the food you eat. You use minerals when you take a photograph, when the dentist fills your cavity, when you color with a crayon or write with a pen or pencil, when you drink from a bottle or can of soda, when you talk on the phone, use a computer, or ride a bike. The U.S. Bureau of Mines calculates that an average American, in a lifetime, will use almost 1 million kilograms of minerals and metals, including over 500,000 kilograms of sand and gravel, more than 40,000 kilograms of iron and steel, 12,000 kilograms of clay, 11,800 kilograms of salt, 360 kilograms of lead, nearly 13,000 kilograms of phosphate and potash, 1,400 kilograms of aluminum, 680 kilograms of copper, and 380 kilograms of zinc.

The Important Rock–Forming Minerals

Feldspars are the most common rock-forming mineral. They are light in color and come in two forms: plagioclase feldspar, which contains either a calcium or sodium ion, and potassium feldspar, or orthoclase, which has a potassium ion. Rocks can be composed of one kind or another, and even a mixture of both types.

Common rock-forming minerals include olivine, pyroxene, and amphibole, which are all dark colored silicate minerals. The micas and quartzes also are common rock-formers. Quartz is generally clear but impurities may impart nearly any color to it. Many of the colorful gemstones are just versions of quartz; for example, amethyst and jasper.

USEFUL THINGS ARE MADE OF MINERALS

Minerals are used for many purposes. **Table 3.5** lists some everyday materials and their mineral source.

Minerals are not randomly distributed in the earth's crust; a variety of geological processes tend to concentrate minerals. Crystals can settle out of a magma melt, for example, on the basis of their density. In the formation of some kinds of rocks, such as pegmatite, minerals become concentrated because their rates of crystallization differ. Minerals also can become concentrated as the result of the evaporation of sea water (halite), and they can be deposited by streams or in the ocean deeps.

Table 3.5 Some materials made from minerals and their source.

Substance	Mineral Sources
abrasives (sandpaper, grinding wheels, drill bits)	corundum, garnet, quartz, diamond
fertilizers	potassium and phosphorus
sulfuric acid	sulfur, pyrite
aluminum	bauxite
bricks	kaolinite (clay)
cement	calcite
chalk	calcite and gypsum
china	kaolinite
copper	chalcocite, chalcopyrite
insecticides	sulfur
iron	hematite, magnetite
lead	galena
mercury	cinnabar
paints	galena, sphalerite (zinc)
pencils	graphite and kaolinite
plaster of Paris (wallboard)	gypsum
salt	halite
silver	argentite
tin	cassiterite
uranium	pitchblende, carnotite
whitewash	calcite
zinc	sphalerite

An **ore** is any commercially useful mineral deposit. Before minerals can be used, they must be located in deposits and then separated from the rest of the rock. A deposit is a larger-than-average gathering of a mineral. Taking the mineral deposit out of the ground is called *mining,* while separating the mineral from the rest of the rock is called *milling. Refining* a mineral means putting it into its purest form, and rendering it usable. The most basic way of refining uses gravity. The desired mineral is generally more dense than the rock around it, and unwanted rock will rise to the top when it is melted, crushed, and shaken, or crushed and put into a special liquid. A *smelter* is a hot furnace that can melt rock to separate the minerals, and unwanted rock that rises to the top is called *slag.*

Have you ever considered what you put in your mouth when you brush your teeth? Toothpaste is generally 30 to 40% water. The second most abundant ingredient is chalk, just like the chalk your teacher uses to write on the blackboard. Chalk itself is made up of the remains of microscopic organisms that lived millions of years ago. The chalk particles are slightly abrasive and help remove the stains that have built up on your teeth. Another ingredient in toothpaste is titanium dioxide. It coats your teeth and whitens them for a couple hours, until it dissolves off and is swallowed. Some toothpaste includes other whiteners, similar to those found in laundry bleach. Another ingredient is glycol, or glycerin, which is also used in car antifreeze. This keeps the toothpaste moist, and seaweed extract is added to give it bulk and hold it together. Finally, toothpaste contains paraffin oil to make it flow smoothly, fluoride to prevent cavities, and flavorings so that it won't taste like the mixture of chalk, paint, seaweed, anti-freeze, oil and detergent it really is.

CHECK YOUR PROGRESS

1. The two most abundant elements in the earth's crust are

   a. oxygen and silicon
   b. oxygen and aluminum
   c. silicon and aluminum
   d. iron and aluminum

2. Minerals are solid substances that are

   a. uniform in chemical composition
   b. crystalline in structure
   c. inorganic
   d. all of the above

3. The nuclei of atoms typically consist of what type of particles?

   a. protons and electrons
   b. electrons and neutrons
   c. protons and neutrons
   d. neutrons and electromagnetic waves

4. An isotope of an element that tends to spontaneously disintegrate and emit particles and energy is called a(n)

   a. radioisotope
   b. ion
   c. nucleus
   d. shell

5. A hydrogen ion with a charge of "−1" has

   a. no electrons   **c.** two electrons
   b. one electron   **d.** three electrons

6. As a neutral atom, silicon has fourteen electrons, two in the innermost shell, eight in the second shell, and four its outermost shell. Silicon is able to form a bond with

   a. only one oxygen atom
   b. one or two oxygen atoms
   c. up to three oxygen atoms
   d. up to four oxygen atoms

7. The chemical properties of a substance depend most upon its

   a. protons   **c.** neutrons
   b. electrons   **d.** all of the above

8. An example of a mineral that exhibits hexagonal symmetry in its structure would be

   a. mica   **c.** quartz
   b. aluminum silicate   **d.** garnet

9. Minerals solidify into crystalline structures in order to

   a. achieve the most stable configuration
   b. increase the mineral's energy level
   c. reduce radioactivity
   d. increase their density

10. The two fundamental identifying characteristics of a mineral are

    a. color and cleavage
    b. color and crystal structure
    c. composition and crystal structure
    d. composition and hardness

11. Which of the following minerals might be identified by its taste

    a. calcite   **c.** quartz
    b. pyrite   **d.** halite

12. The most abundant minerals in the earth's crust are in this group

    a. micas   **c.** amphiboles
    b. clays   **d.** feldspars

13. Which is NOT an example of a mineral?

   a. quartz   d. mica
   b. calcite   e. slate
   c. gypsum

14. The chief ingredient in bricks is

   a. kaolinite   c. gypsum
   b. sphalerite   d. pitchblende

ROCKS AND THEIR CLASSIFICATION

Petrologists are geologists who specialize in the study of rocks. They classify rocks into three main categories based upon the way they are formed. **Igneous** rock is formed by the crystallization of magma. (*Igneous* is the Greek word for fire.) **Sedimentary** rock is formed from fragments of preexisting rocks that are transported and deposited by wind, water, or glaciers. They can also be formed by the precipitation of solids or the evaporation of water from a solution. **Metamorphic** rock is rock that has been modified, but not completely melted, by high temperature and pressure.

By volume, more than two-thirds of the rock in the earth's crust is igneous and about one-fourth is metamorphic. Sedimentary rock makes up only about 8% of the crust, but is the most likely type to be exposed at the surface.

IGNEOUS ROCK

Igneous rock is classified in two ways. If it is rich in the light silicates, it is referred to as *silicic*. Silicic igneous rocks are light colored; one example of this type of rock is granite. The other category of igneous rock is *mafic*; mafic rock is rich in the denser, dark-colored silicates; examples of mafic rocks include basalt and gabbro.

Igneous rock is also classified based on the way it originated. For example, *intrusive* or *plutonic* igneous rock formed deep in the earth; at great depths, the cooling process occurs slowly, producing rock with large crystals. *Extrusive* or *volcanic* igneous rock originated as lava that poured out of volcanoes; lava cools quickly because there is no insulating earth cover, and consequently extrusive igneous rock has tiny crystals and a fine-grained structure.

Because igneous rock is classified both by composition and by origin, rocks that are of the same composition can have different names. For example, gabbro and basalt have the same composition, but gabbro solidified inside the earth's crust, while basalt formed outside.

For a long time, geologists did not understand how it was that some igneous rocks were silicic and others mafic, since they all started out as the same substance: magma from deep within the earth. They also could not explain why certain combinations of minerals would be present in some igneous rock while other minerals never occurred.

The answer to these questions did not come until 1922, when N. L. Bowen of The Carnegie Institute's Geophysical Laboratory showed that minerals do not solidify out of a magma melt all at once, but instead go through a complex series of interactions with the liquid magma as it cools. Igneous rock differentiates because certain minerals crystallize at high temperatures but become unstable as the magma's temperature drops, reacting with the other minerals. Bowen found that if a mafic magma crystallizes directly, it will form dark, gabbra-type rocks of calcium feldspar, pyroxene, and olivine. But if crystals of olivine, pyroxene, and calcium feldspar which form first separate out by sinking to the bottom of the magma chamber, the remaining magma becomes more silica rich and cools to form light-colored granite or syenite rock. After a magma solidifies, there will often be a residual fluid composed of trapped water and other volatile chemicals, and this will have a high silica content. In such a fluid, large crystals of quartz often form. The series of reactions that Bowen described is known as *magmatic evolution*.

Texture is also important in identifying igneous rock. Texture refers to the cooling history of the rock; small crystals mean it cooled quickly, large crystals mean it cooled slowly. For example, pegmatites generally have the same composition as granites, but their crystals are much larger because they form in the late stages of magma crystallization.

Textural terms used to describe igneous rock

- glassy—no crystals
- fine-grained—crystals can be seen in sunlight with a magnifying lens
- coarse-grained—crystals easily seen

- pegmatitic—crystals over 1 centimeter in diameter (but can be much larger)

- porphyritic—coarse crystals in a fine-grained matrix (indicates a change in conditions during the cooling history)

SEDIMENTARY ROCK

Sedimentary rock is rock composed of rock fragments, weathering products, organic material, and precipitates, and is deposited in beds. Rock is broken into fragments by the processes of physical **weathering**, which includes such things as rain, wind, and freezing water that has seeped into tiny cracks. Rock can also be changed though chemical weathering, which involves reactions that change the composition of the rock. Examples of chemical weathering include oxidation, hydration, and carbonation.

In dry climates, rock exposed at the surface is more likely to be weathered mechanically, which produces sharp cliffs. In humid climates, chemical weathering is more common; this creates a landscape with rounded features.

Weathered rock ends up as sediment, and through the process of **lithification**, sediment is transformed into sedimentary rock. Lithification occurs in several ways. In *cementation*, rock is formed when water deposits a soluble substance such as silica, calcite, or iron oxide between the mineral grains. In *compaction*, fragments of rock are forced together because of the increasing weight of succeeding layers. *Recrystallization* is yet another means of lithification; in this process an interlocking occurs in the small fragments. **Figure 3.5** illustrates lithification by compaction and cementation.

Figure 3.5 The processes of compaction and cementation illustrated here are common ways sediments are transformed into sedimentary rock.

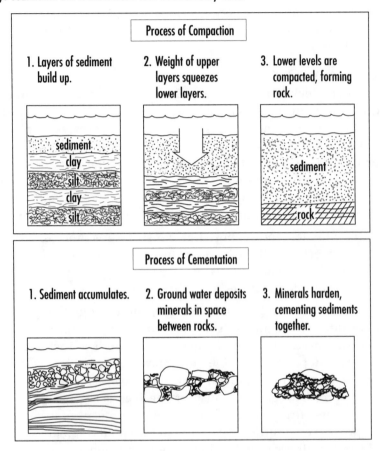

Sedimentary rock is classified as either *clastic* or *non-clastic*. Clastic sedimentary rock is composed of fragments of preexisting rocks. It is further divided into types by the size of the fragments that make up the rock. Conglomerates and breccias have fragments that are larger than 2 millimeters, while sandstone particles are smaller. Siltstone and mudstone is gritty, while shale has very fine particles of clay less than 1/250 millimeter in diameter. **Figure 3.6** is a close-up illustration of a "dirty sandstone," composed of different sized grains of sand, silt and clay. Geologists describe sedimentary rock characteristics by such terms as *porosity*, a measure of the amount of void spaces in the rock, and *permeability*, a measure of the interconnectedness of the void spaces.

Non-clastic, or chemical, sedimentary rock is formed by chemical or biological precipitation or the accumulation of organic matter. Chalk, limestone, and chert are all examples of this type of rock. Halite, or rock salt, is an *evaporite*, which is a sedimentary rock formed by evaporation of sea water.

Figure 3.6 A poorly sorted sediment composed of sand in a matrix of smaller silt and clay particles. If such a sediment were lithified, geologists would identify it as a "dirty sandstone."

Sedimentary rocks grade into one another

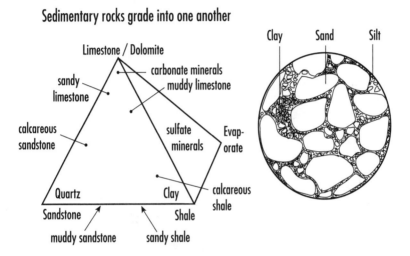

The most abundant sedimentary rocks are shale, limestone, and sandstone. Shale accounts for over half of all sedimentary rock, and the three types combined make up 99% of the total. Shales are the basic, raw material for pottery, brick, tile, and china. Another type of shale, oil shale, is used as an energy resource. Quartz is the predominant mineral in most sandstones, and quartz sandstone is the raw material for glass.

Many clues are used by geologists in interpreting the tectonic setting and history of sedimentary rocks. For instance, the *bedding pattern* shows the order of deposition, with the oldest rock at the bottom. Mud cracks in the rock are an indication of periodic drying. Ripple marks in the rock show the direction of the currents that flowed across the rock as it formed, and the direction of the currents can also be determined from the orientation of the grains in the rock. A mixture of different sized grains in a rock indicates that the sediment was dumped rapidly, while grains of the same size indicate that the particles were sifted and sorted before being deposited. Fossils in sedimentary rock also provide clues to the environment of their deposition. **Figure 3.7** shows some of the continental and marine environments in which sediments are commonly deposited that may later be lithified into sedimentary rock.

Figure 3.7 Common continental and marine environments in which sediments are deposited that may later be lithified into sedimentary rock. Deep sea sediments accumulate very slowly, on the order of a millimeter in 1,000 or 10,000 years. If more than 30% of the sediment is of organic origin, it is known as **ooze**.

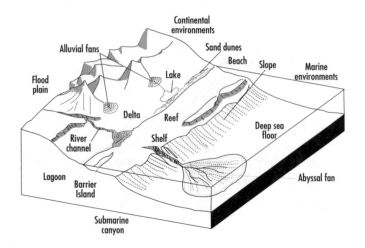

METAMORPHIC ROCK

Metamorphic rock is rock that has, at some point, been changed either in texture or mineral composition. The agents of metamorphism are heat, pressure, and chemically active fluids. Metamorphic processes cause many different changes in rock, including increasing their density, inducing the growth of larger crystals, and reorienting the mineral grains. Metamorphic rock is classified in two ways, by the way in which it originated and by its type of texture.

Metamorphic rock is formed in three ways: (1) *thermal* or *contact* metamorphic rock is formed at the margins of igneous bodies, such as a dike of magma; (2) *regional* metamorphic rock, the most common type, undergoes much recrystallization and is formed when a large amount of it is under heat and pressure; and (3) *dynamic* metamorphic rock is formed when rock is broken and ground, with little recrystallization. Dynamic metamorphism occurs in fault zones and from meteorite impacts. **Figure 3.8** illustrates the various temperature and pressure conditions that produce different types of metamorphic rocks.

Figure 3.8 Different combinations of temperature and pressure will produce different types of metamorphic rocks.

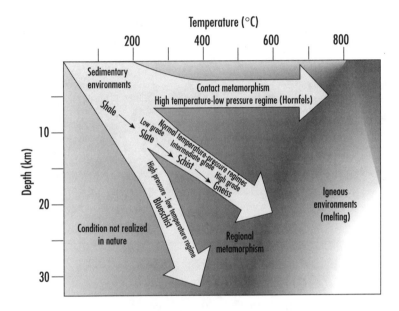

When metamorphic rock is classified by texture, it is classified as either *foliated* or *non-foliated*. Rock that is foliated has a layered appearance, in which the crystals are oriented in only one direction. Examples of foliated metamorphic rocks are gneiss and schist. Foliation is caused by the same kinds of stresses that deform rock and create folded mountains. Non-foliated metamorphic rock is homogeneous in texture, and is usually composed of a single mineral. Examples of non-foliated metamorphic rock include marble, serpentinite, soapstone, and quartzite.

Figure 3.9 illustrates a cross section of a mountain range showing regional metamorphism. The degree of closeness to the igneous intrusion into the preexisting, or "country rock" produces different conditions of heat and pressure and determines the type of metamorphic rock produced.

Figure 3.9 Regional metamorphism covers a large area and results in different metamorphic rock types based upon local conditions of heat and pressure. For example, from the left side of the diagram to the right, low-grade metamorphism transforms shale to slate and high-grade metamorphism progressively transforms the shale to gneiss.

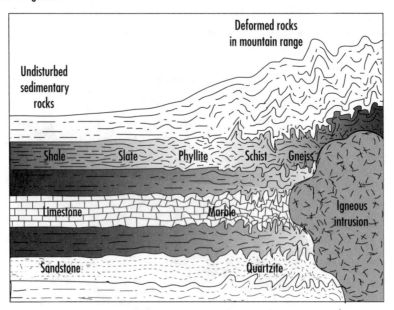

THE ROCK CYCLE

Modern geology began in the late eighteenth century, when James Hutton, a Scottish physician, published his great work, *Theory of the Earth*, proposing the theory of the *rock cycle*, a means of connecting many aspects of geology. The rock cycle illustrates how three basic rock types; igneous, sedimentary, and metamorphic, are transformed into each other by various geologic processes. **Figure 3.10** is one version of the rock cycle.

Figure 3. 10 The rock cycle is composed of subcycles in the crust and in the mantle, connected by processes of plate tectonics. Rock in the continental crust can be transformed into a new type via the processes indicated by the arrows. The arrows can be followed in any direction.

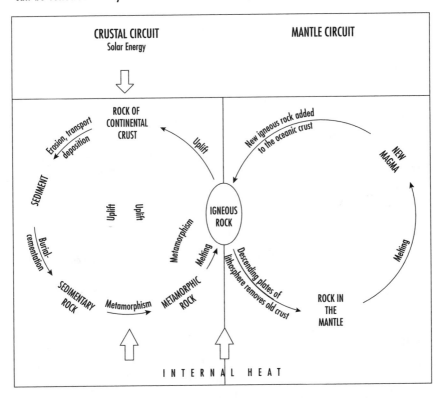

Igneous rock originates with the cooling and solidification of magma and the process of crystallization. The first rocks to form and create the young earth's crust were igneous rocks, so igneous are the most appropriate to start with when describing the rock cycle. Igneous rocks, or any rocks exposed at the surface, undergo the process of weathering, which eventually breaks them down. Agents such as gravity, wind, and running water are involved in the process of erosion, which takes away the decomposed rock, eventually depositing it somewhere as a sediment. Places of deposition include the ocean, dunes, swamps and other basins, as well as the floodplains of rivers.

The sediments may become lithified, or converted to rock, by processes such as compaction and cementation, creating sedimentary rock. Sedimentary rock can be shoved into the mantle by plate tectonic processes and buried, or rock can be intruded by magma, and will be changed by pressure and heat into the third type of rock, metamorphic rock, and this rock may melt and later solidify into new igneous rock. But there are many "shortcuts" in the rock cycle, so that igneous rock can be metamorphosed without having first become sedimentary rock. Any kind of rock can be weathered and end up as sediments, and any kind of rock can be remelted and end up as igneous rock.

The theory of plate tectonics is also connected to the rock cycle. At convergent plate boundaries, part of the lithosphere that contains sediments is subducted into the mantle, and this process melts the sediments and produces rising magma bodies and volcanoes, and ultimately new igneous rock. The rising magma produces regional metamorphism and changes the preexisting country rock into various forms of metamorphic rock.

THE STORY OF TOURMALINE

The semiprecious mineral tourmaline can be found in rocks called *pegmatites* in southern California and other places. Scientists date the California pegmatites to 50 million years old. Back then, scientists believe, the North American plate collided with the Pacific plate. As the oceanic Pacific plate subducted under the continental North American plate, some of the mineral deposits of the ocean floor were recrystallized; others collected together from the sediment to form a hot paste. The molten mineral-bearing paste was pushed upward into the rocks above by the pressure of the subducting plate.

This process created mineral-rich globs of magma in the crust. The largest of the magmatic bodies at that time was 80 kilometers wide, 1,600 kilometers long, and 24 to 26 kilometers deep. The magma rose slowly over 100,000 years or so, cooling to the point that part of it crystallized, forming granite. The rock became part of the mountain range of the Sierra Nevada.

But not all the magma crystallized as granite—some molten liquid remained even after such a long time. This magma was enriched with the minerals that had not crystallized as granite. The magma was fluid and flowed through cracks and crevices in the granite.

The material rose to where the temperatures dropped from more than 1,000 degrees to half that, and it began to crystallize into white masses of pegmatite, composed mostly of the minerals quartz and feldspar. The pegmatite was embedded in the already crystallized granite.

Within the pegmatite, pockets of enriched liquid remained—the birthplaces of rare minerals such as tourmaline. Tourmaline is 7 to 7.5 on Mohs Scale of hardness; it forms beautiful crystals that can be many colors because of its complex chemistry.

As the tourmaline crystals formed, they removed chemicals from the liquid, increasing the water content of the liquid. Some of the water turned to steam, which increased the internal pressure and often burst through the chamber. If this steam was not released, the new crystals soon would become unstable and dissolve.

CHECK YOUR PROGRESS

15. Which in NOT a type of igneous rock

    a. gneiss   **c.** basalt
    b. granite   **d.** rhyolite

16. Which of the following types of igneous rocks are most likely to be composed of minerals with large crystals?

    a. extrusive rock   **c.** volcanic rock
    b. intrusive rock   **d.** mafic rock

17. The series of reactions that occur in magma to create the different igneous rock types is known as

    a. Bowen's Reaction Series
    b. The Law of Superposition
    c. an unconformity
    d. volcanism

18. The branch of geology that deals with the occurrences, origin, and history of rocks is

    a. mineralogy   **c.** petrology
    b. paleontology   **d.** physical geology

19. A chunk of sedimentary rock composed of large and small sized grains indicates
    a. the sediments were winnowed and sorted before being deposited
    b. the sediment was deposited rapidly, as in a landslide
    c. the sediment was deposited in a strong current
    d. the sediment was winnowed by the wind

20. The rock cycle begins with
    a. igneous rock   c. metamorphic rock
    b. sedimentary rock   d. any of the types of rock

21. Sedimentary rock that is subducted all the way into the mantle is most likely to change into
    a. metamorphic rock   c. magma
    b. igneous rock   d. oceanic crust

22. According to the rock cycle, rock of the continental crust can be created by the process of
    a. melting   c. metamorphism
    b. uplift   d. erosion

23. According to the rock cycle, descending lithospheric plates recycle old crust by the process of
    a. melting   c. metamorphism
    b. uplift   d. erosion

24. Which of the following is NOT a type of metamorphic rock?
    a. gneiss   c. shale
    b. schist   d. marble

GLOSSARY

amphiboles—silicate minerals that form double chain structures.

chain silicates—a group of silicate minerals in which each silicon ion shares two of its four oxygen ions.

cleavage—a characteristic property of many minerals that break in a regular way, producing a smooth plane that reflects light.

compound—a combination of two or more elements joined to form a chemically stable substance.

element—any simple substance that cannot be broken down into other substances by chemical means.

fracture—a characteristic property of many minerals that break in an irregular way.

framework silicates—a group of silicate minerals in which each silicon ion shares each of its four oxygens, in the proportion SiO_2.

igneous rock—formed by crystallization from magma.

ion—an atom or group of atoms that has either lost one or more electrons, or gained one or more electrons, making it negatively charged.

isolated tetrahedra—a group of silicate minerals in which one silicon ion bonds to four oxygens.

isotope—one of two or more atoms of the same element with different numbers of neutrons in their nucleus.

lithification—the process by which sediment becomes rock.

metamorphic rock—rock that has been modified, but not completely melted, by high temperature and pressure.

mineral—any naturally occurring substance that has a uniform chemical composition and a definite crystalline structure.

mineralogists—geologists who specialize in the study of minerals.

ooze—fine-particle sediment of which 30% or more is of organic origin.

ore—any commercially useful mineral deposit.

oxidation number—the number of electrons that an atom tends to accept or give up. A negative oxidation number means the atom will accept electrons, thus giving it an overall negative charge.

petrologists—geologists who study rocks.

polymorph—minerals with the same composition but different crystalline structures.

pyroxenes—a silicate mineral forming single chain structures.

radioactive—a characteristic of the nuclei of certain isotopes of elements that tend to spontaneously disintegrate, emitting one or more particles and electromagnetic waves.

rock—any significant part of the solid portion of the earth; an aggregate of minerals.

sedimentary rock—rock formed from fragments of preexisting rocks which are transported and deposited by an agent such as the wind, water, or a glacier, or by precipitation of solids from a solution or by evaporation of water from a solution.

sheet silicates—a group of silicate minerals; each silicon ion in this group shares three oxygen ions, for a unit cell ratio of Si_2O_5

solubility—the tendency for a substance to dissolve.

specific gravity—a characteristic property of a mineral; the ratio of the weight of the mineral in air to its weight in water.

unit cell—the building block containing all the information required for the construction of a larger crystal.

weathering—the process of breaking down and altering rock on the earth's surface by mechanical (physical) and chemical means.

ANSWER KEY

1. a	11. d	21. c
2. d	12. d	22. b
3. c	13. e	23. a
4. a	14. a	24. c
5. c	15. a	
6. d	16. b	
7. b	17. a	
8. c	18. c	
9. a	19. b	
10. c	20. d	

CHAPTER 4

The Cryosphere: Glaciers—Ice on the Earth

GLACIAL PROCESSES AND FEATURES

Glaciers are thick masses of ice that cover about 10% of the earth's land. They are created when the annual snowfall in an area exceeds the rate at which the snow is melted, evaporated, or sublimated. The ice in glaciers is formed when fallen snow melts and then refreezes into a modified, granular form. There are two types of glacier: one type, called the valley glacier (or alpine glacier) is linear in shape and tends to form in mountain regions, flowing down the mountain valleys; the other type of glacier is called the continental glacier. This glacier is made up of *ice sheets* or *ice caps*. Continental glaciers are lens shaped; they are thickest at their center. For this reason, ice in the center creates pressure in the direction of thinner ice around the glacier's edges, causing the ice to flow outward. There are two continental glaciers in existence today: one covers Antarctica and the other covers Greenland.

A glacier has two main zones—one in which ice is accumulating (the *zone of accumulation*), and another where ice is being lost faster than it is being gained (the *zone of ablation*). These zones are illustrated in **Figure 4.1**. Glacial ice may be lost through melting, sublimation, or **calving**—which is the breaking off of ice into the water. Calving is what creates icebergs. A glacier increases in size when more ice is produced than ablated, and shrinks when the reverse occurs.

Figure 4.1 The zones of a glacier are defined by the net gain or loss of ice.

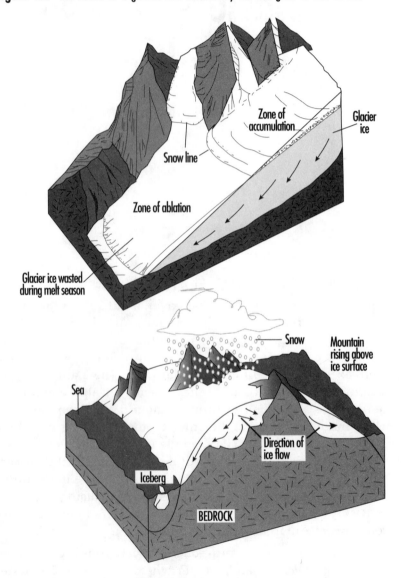

Many of the distinctive landscape features common to the northern states and Canada are the result of massive glaciers that moved across the earth's surface long ago, scraping away the soil and picking up pieces of rock and sediment. The erosion produced by glaciers is most apparent in mountainous areas where they broadened and deepened valleys, leaving distinctive U-shaped profiles in cross section when the ice melted. As you might expect, the thicker and heavier the glacial ice, the greater the erosion it produced. **Figure 4.2** depicts a cross section of a glacial valley.

Figure 4.2 The distinctive U shape of glacier valleys is different from the V-shaped valleys carved by flowing water.

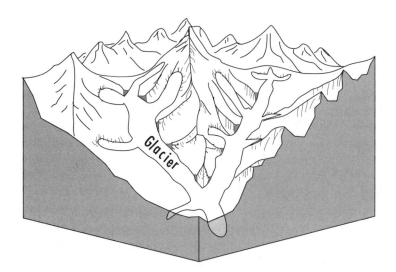

The material eroded by the moving ice is picked up and carried downslope as the glacier moves. When the ice melts, this sediment load is deposited as **glacial till**. Unlike the sediments deposited by a stream, glacial till is a mix of rocks of varying size, from fine particles to large boulders. Glacial till produces a landform called a **moraine**, depicted in **Figure 4.3**. There are several distinct kinds of moraine: a moraine formed at the head of a glacier is called a **terminal moraine** and tends to be long and crescent shaped; **lateral moraines** form from debris that accumulates along the sides of an alpine glacier; and *ground moraines* are blankets of glacial till that settle as the glacier melts.

Figure 4.3 The glacial landscape and its features.

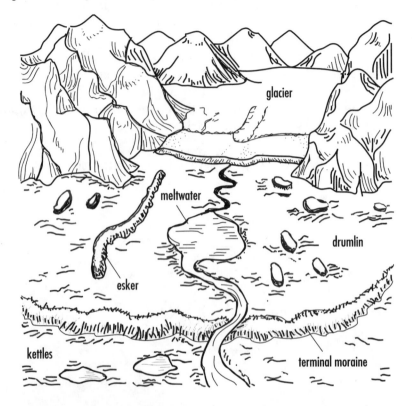

Glaciers are responsible for other landforms as well. For example, an **esker** is created when a stream flowing inside or under a glacier is dammed and forced to drop its sediment. Another glacial landform is the **drumlin**. Drumlins are created when a glacier moves over an older till deposit. The till becomes reordered into elongated hills, or drumlins, that reveal the direction of the glacier's movement.

Another glacial landform is the **kettle**. Kettles are depressions that come about when a large piece of ice becomes detached from the glacier and is covered by glacial outwash, or sediment carried by meltwater streams. The chunk of ice gradually melts, the surface of the outwash layer sinks, and the depression may eventually become filled with water to form a lake or pond. In the U.S., thousands of kettle lakes can be found in states like Wisconsin and Minnesota, which were once covered by ice sheets. An **outwash plain** is a broad, flat area of sand and gravel sediment deposited by a glacier.

ICE AT THE POLES

Earth's north and south polar regions receive the least direct sunlight, and are consequently the coldest places on the Earth. Both the Arctic and the Antarctic have six months of winter, in which there is total darkness. During the other six months, their summer, the Sun never climbs far above the horizon. (Keep in mind that the Arctic region's six-month long winter coincides with the Antarctic's six-month long summer, and vice versa.) This lack of sunshine enables ice to dominate the polar regions year around.

While the Arctic region (in the North) and the Antarctic region (in the South) have common seasonal patterns, they differ in that the North Pole, which is located at the center of the Arctic, is on a vast, almost flat sheet of ice drifting on the surface of the Arctic Ocean. The South Pole, on the other hand, is on an enormous landmass, the continent of Antarctica. Around the North Pole, the Arctic Ocean is covered by floating pack ice, which are large areas of ice formed over a period of many years, when pieces of ice are driven together and "packed" by wind and currents. In the summer, temperatures in the Arctic Ocean rise to well above freezing, especially in the coastal areas, bordering the continents of North America, Europe, and Asia. This causes some of the packed ice to melt, only to be refrozen in the Arctic winter.

About 2% of the total water on Earth is frozen, but this frozen water makes up about three-fourths of all the fresh water on the planet. Most of this ice is in the glaciers that cover Antarctica; glaciers cannot build up in the Arctic because there is no large landmass to support them. In the Arctic, as ice builds up, its increased weight pushes older ice deeper into the water, and as this older ice sinks, the extreme pressure causes some of it to melt.

The continent of Antarctica is twice the size of Australia and is the coldest place on Earth; only in the summer does the temperature ever rise above freezing. The icecap covering Antarctica is, on average, 2,800 meters thick, but in some places it has a thickness of nearly 5 kilometers. **Figure 4.4** and **Figure 4.5** show maps of the north and south polar regions. Compare them and note the difference in the land versus water in the two regions.

Figure 4.4 The Arctic region today.

Contrary to appearances, glaciers and ice sheets are not stationary; the ice is always slowly flowing. This is because, under the pressure of the ice mass above it, ice behaves like a thick fluid. For example, the Antarctic ice sheet sits like a shallow dome, or lens, on the continent's surface, and as the weight of ice accumulates in the center of the lens, the ice around the edges of the glacier flows very slowly into the sea.

Figure 4.5 The Antarctic region today.

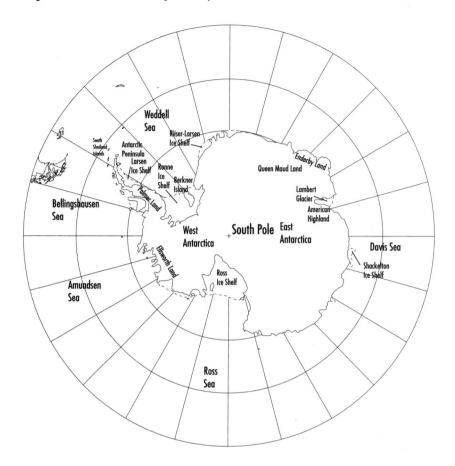

ICE AGES

At times in the earth's history, large ice sheets have covered huge expanses of the continental land masses. These time periods are called "ice ages." When an ice age occurs, the sea level is much lower, because large amounts of water are in the form of ice that piles up over the land areas. For example, during the last glaciation (in the Pleistocene epoch), the eastern coast of North America extended 240 kilometers east of where it is today. Places that are now on the coast, such as Atlantic City, NJ, were as far inland as the width of that state!

David Sugden, a geologist at the University of Edinburgh in Scotland, recently discovered ice in eastern Antarctica that dates back nearly 8 million years. Sugden was measuring the date of an ancient volcanic eruption when he uncovered the old ice, which he claims is a fragment of a glacier that vanished long ago.

This ancient date for an ice sheet in Antarctica doesn't fit with other evidence that Antarctica may have had a more temperate climate 3 million years ago. Fossilized pollen and plankton have been found high in the Transantarctic Mountains, near Antarctica's coast. These fossils have been dated to around 3 million years ago, when it is possible that Antarctica was ice free and forested, with internal seaways covering low-lying areas. It's possible that when the climate cooled, glaciers formed in the interior of the continent and then advanced across the seaways, pushing the plankton and pollen into the mountains.

Sugden's ancient ice suggests that Antarctica's climate has remained fairly stable and cold for at least 8 million years. His theories discredit the fossils as evidence that, 3 million years ago, Antarctica's climate was one that sustained forests. He and his colleagues are now studying the amounts of carbon dioxide and other gases in air bubbles in the ice as a way to learn more about the history of that continent's atmosphere.

The Pleistocene ice age began more than 1 million years ago. The ice reached its greatest extent southward from the North Pole and northward from the South Pole between 18,000 and 25,000 years ago. At that time, glaciers advanced as far south as Chicago and Maryland in North America, and Paris in Europe. Melting then occurred and the recession of the ice continued until about 6,000 years ago. Since that time the climate pattern has been characterized by cold periods of increased glaciation that alternate with warm interglacial periods, one of which we may be experiencing right now.

Other ice ages occurred in the earth's more distant past, and some of them were more severe than the recent, Pleistocene ice age. Glaciation appears to have been widespread near the end of the Paleozoic era, over 200 million years ago. Large ice sheets developed over the great ancient supercontinent of **Gondwanaland** and persisted for 30 to 50 million years. The supercontinent consisted of most of what is now Antarctica, South America, India, Africa, Asia, and

Australia. Until about 150 million years ago, Gondwanaland rested north of the south polar region, but then it fractured into several huge crustal plates that moved apart from each other.

Historical geologists believe that ice sheets covered almost the entire planet 2.2 billion years ago. During that ice age, ice sheets reached from the poles to about 11 degrees on either side of the equator.

Many factors contribute to determining the amount of ice on our planet at any one time. For example, the size of the cryosphere depends upon the position of the land masses on the earth's surface, variations in the orbit of the earth around the Sun, and the direction of the earth's axis of rotation. Certain chance events can also influence the amount of ice on the planet; volcanic eruptions can load the atmosphere with material that blocks the Sun's rays, cooling the earth for several years. On the other hand, increases in greenhouse gases—such as carbon dioxide and methane—can warm the atmosphere and lead to massive amounts of melted ice.

Historically, as much as 5% of the earth's water has been in the form of ice caps and glaciers with ice covering as much as 30% of the land, while at other times as little as a fraction of a percent of the earth's water has been frozen. Recall that about 2% of the earth's water is bound up in ice today, covering 10% of the land.

And just as there are many factors that interact to initiate and maintain an ice age, there are many ways in which an ice age can end. In the case of the ice age of 2.2 billion years ago, lava deposits covering the glacial deposits provide evidence that suggests that large scale volcanic activity might have released enough carbon dioxide (CO_2) to warm the planet and end the glacial period. Recall that carbon dioxide is a greenhouse gas that that absorbs the Sun's light and radiates it back to the atmosphere as heat. Another mechanism for warming the planet could have come from outer space. Tons of carbon-containing rocks may have been vaporized by an asteroid or comet fall, and this carbon could have reacted with oxygen in the atmosphere to form carbon dioxide.

Inferring climate patterns of bygone eras requires sophisticated measurement. For instance, to measure temperature changes over time, scientists look at the ratio of different forms of hydrogen in water molecules in sections of a column of ancient ice. Ocean-borne water molecules, made up of the most common form of hydrogen, evaporate at slightly lower temperatures than do water molecules made with a heavier form of hydrogen, called *deuterium*. As the temperature rises, more of the heavy hydrogen evaporates. By tracing the fluctuations of the two forms of hydrogen, scientists have inferred that the fourteenth century had four periods in which summer temperatures were cooler than average, and that the longest period lasted twenty years, from 1343 to 1362.

Such information can shed light on some of the mysteries of the past. Historians believe that, during this period in the fourteenth century, the last Viking settlement on Greenland collapsed. Greenland was settled by Norsemen from Iceland in the tenth century, a time when the North Atlantic enjoyed a warm spell and Greenland was green and fertile. Climate change may have led to the collapse of the settlement. Cool summers meant less grain for animals to eat through the winter. Also, supplies from the homeland may not have been able to get through. Finally, in the late thirteenth and early fourteenth centuries, sea ice began to clog navigation lanes making travel to and from Greenland difficult, even in summer.

CHECK YOUR PROGRESS

1. A landscape feature created when an ice chunk melts under a layer of outwash sediment is called a(n)

   a. kettle   c. esker
   b. moraine   d. cirque

2. Moraines, kettles, and bogs in the northern states of North America are all remnants of

   a. Pleisocene glaciation
   b. Cenozoic volcanism
   c. Phanerozoic plate movements
   d. recent crustal uplift

3. The pattern of climate since the last glacial maximum has been
   a. repeated cycles of glaciation alternating with warmer interglacial periods
   b. cycles of monsoon rains alternating with large scale droughts
   c. one long glacial period followed by an even longer interglacial
   d. rising sea levels during glacial periods rotating with lower sea levels during interglacials

4. The peak of the Pleistocene ice age was about how many years ago?
   a. 25,000   c. 2.2 billion
   b. 25 million   d. 6,000

5. Landscape features such as the rounded hills of New England and New York's Finger Lakes are the result of
   a. volcanism
   b. erosion by running water
   c. glacial action
   d. being located near a plate boundary

6. The oldest continuously frozen ice yet to be identified on the Earth is about how old?
   a. 15,000 years   c. 8 million years
   b. 1.5 million years d. 8 billion years

7. The coldest place on the Earth is found in
   a. the North Pole   c. Greenland
   b. the South Pole   d. Minnesota

8. Which of the following places would have the most hours of darkness on December 25th?
   a. Barrow, Alaska   c. Austin, Texas
   b. Chicago, Illinois d. Melbourne, Australia

9. The most significant difference between the north and south polar regions on the Earth is
   a. Antarctica is significantly colder
   b. the Arctic region has the Northern Lights (*aurora borealis*)
   c. krill is a main link on the Southern Ocean food chain
   d. Antarctica is a continent capable of supporting a large ice sheet

10. At the present time, the cryosphere comprises approximately what proportion of the world's fresh water?
    a. 82%   c. 22%
    b. 75%   d. 2%

11. About how much of the water on the Earth is now frozen?
    a. three-fourths   c. a tenth
    b. a third   d. two-hundredths

12. Scientists specializing in the study of ice sheets would most likely be called
    a. geologists   c. glaciologists
    b. climatologist   d. hydrologists

13. The poles might have been ice-free during some time in the past because
    a. the Sun's energy varied from the present value
    b. continents can change latitude
    c. volcanism released greenhouse gases
    d. any of the above

14. At one time, what is now the continent of Antarctica was part of the same large land mass as
    a. India   c. South America
    b. Africa   d. all of these

15. Interglacial periods might be initiated by
    a. the addition of large amounts of carbon dioxide to the atmosphere
    b. an increase in earthquake activity
    c. a reduction in the solar energy received by the Earth
    d. a large increase in the salinity of the oceans

GLOSSARY

drumlin—a ridge or hill with a smooth summit consisting of material carried by glacial action.

esker—a winding ridge of sediment formed by streams flowing under or in a glacier.

glaciers—large masses of ice flowing slowly along a valley or down a slope, or spreading over an area of land.

glacial till—the unsorted sediments dumped by melting ice flows.

Gondwanaland—an ancient land mass that included present-day Antarctica, South America, India, Africa, Asia, and Australia.

kettle—a depression in the surface caused by the melting of a large piece of subsurface ice after a moraine had formed.

moraine—a ridge of sediment deposited at the sides or end of a glacier. The material is scraped up as the glacier flows.

outwash plain—a broad, flat area created when a glacier deposits its sediment.

ANSWER KEY

1. a	6. c	11. d
2. a	7. b	12. c
3. a	8. a	13. d
4. a	9. d	14. d
5. c	10. d	15. a

CHAPTER 5

The Hydrosphere: Water on the Earth

RIVERS, LAKES, AND GROUNDWATER

Earth's surface is 71% water, and most of this water is found in our single, globe-encircling ocean. **Figure 5.1** illustrates the distribution of water on our planet. Seawater and ice together make up 99.35% of all the water on Earth, and most of the rest is groundwater. All of the Earth's lakes and rivers plus the water in the atmosphere make up only 0.0015% of the earth's water, which is analogous to about a cup's worth out of a swimming pool.

Water is one of the basic commodities necessary for all life. It is continually circulated on the planet in the hydrologic, or water, cycle (illustrated in chapter 7). When moisture falls to the land in the process of precipitation, it moves through a system of channels and sometimes resides temporarily in basins, such as bogs and lakes, or as part of an underground **aquifer**, which is a rock formation that holds water.

Figure 5.1. Most of the water on Earth is salty ocean water. Most of the earth's fresh water is frozen or underground.

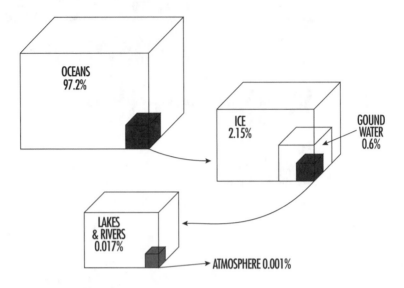

Throughout history, rivers and their tributary streams have been the main supply of fresh water for our species. We also have depended upon rivers for food, transportation, and, unfortunately, as a dumping ground for our wastes.

The Nile River in Africa, which is 6,670 kilometers in length, is the longest river in the world. However, the second longest river, the Amazon in South America, carries more water than any other river in the world. The third longest river is in China and is called the Yangtze.

HOW RIVERS FORM

Rivers are formed from the precipitation that falls on the land and then flows downhill as runoff. There would be no rivers without rain or snow (or if the land were perfectly level!). In travelling from high places down toward the sea, water collects in channels that converge with other channels downstream; this process results in the formation of progressively larger streams. The land area from which water drains into a stream or river is called its **watershed** or drainage basin.

Figure 5.3 is a model of a river and its characteristic features. The upper section of the course of a river is fed by numerous smaller streams; if the downhill gradient is steep, water will flow swiftly and the upper section of the course of the river will be fairly straight and narrow. If the slope is not very steep, the water will move more slowly downhill and will tend to go around any barriers in its way, such as rocky outcrops, producing a winding stream pattern. Water in a river is also affected by wind; wind-produced waves will move the river from side to side as it cuts through the land.

Figure 5.2 A model of a cross section of a river showing its characteristic features.

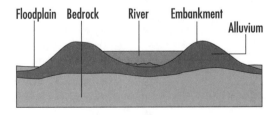

Floodplain   Bedrock   River   Embankment   Alluvium

Figure 5.3 A model of a river illustrating characteristic features in the development of a stream.

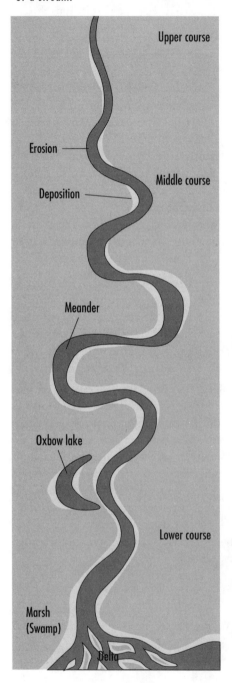

Upper course

Erosion

Middle course

Deposition

Meander

Oxbow lake

Lower course

Marsh
(Swamp)

Delta

Channels of flowing water transport debris that erodes from the land. One pattern that leads to major changes in the shape of a developing river is the tendency for it to cut into the "head on" side and then deposit sediment on the other side of the bend. This occurs at even the slightest bend in a river, and it is this process that creates the meandering of a river as it carries water down to the sea (see **Figure 5.3**).

Eventually the river widens the floor of the valley through which it runs. The meandering loop often sweeps out broadly and produces a narrow neck of land that, during a flood, might be overrun; a flood can cut a channel through the neck and create a new bed for the river. The portion of the river basin that is cut off from its water supply becomes what is called an *oxbow lake*. If **silt-ation** (a build-up of sediments) follows, the cutoff part become a freshwater marsh or a bog. An oxbow lake is illustrated in **Figure 5.3**. Another result of flooding is the buildup of sediments along the river banks, which creates an embankment. This is shown in the cross section of the river in **Figure 5.2**.

The erosion and transportation of sediment by water running downhill in the watershed creates river valleys, some of which are narrow and deep, like the Grand Canyon, while others are wide and flat bottomed, like the lower section of the Mississippi. Valleys tend to be deeper and narrower at the headwaters of a river, where the slope of the landscape is steeper, and wider downstream, where the landscape is more level.

Throughout history, people have settled in river valleys for many reasons, including the fertility of the soil, the relative smoothness of the terrain, the use of the river for the transportation of goods, and its value as a source of fresh water and as a sink for waste. For example, the banks of the Delaware River became the site for the city of Philadelphia; Washington, DC was built on the Potomac; and New York City was developed on the Hudson.

Where river meets sea

As rivers flow into the sea, they slow down and sometimes break into separate streams, or tributaries. They also drop much of their sedimentary load of silt, creating flat lowlands called **deltas**. The rivers' fresh water becomes mixed with salt water, and salt marshes often develop. **Figure 5.4** illustrates a model of a river delta. During floods, river sediments called *alluvium* cover an area beyond the river's normal banks, an area called the *floodplain*.

An **estuary** is an area formed at the mouth of a river where river currents interact with ocean tides. Estuaries are very rich habitats for many different living things. The tides regularly cover a river's delta with ocean water so that the ground stays wet all the time, while new, nutrient-rich sediments continually arrive from the river and can support a diverse estuarine food chain. Estuaries serve as nurseries for many terrestrial and aquatic species.

CONSIDER THIS

Mangroves are an important feature of many tropical estuaries. Mangroves are land plants that have adapted to life in salty or water-logged mud along a coast. They anchor themselves with extensive roots that spread sideways and look like flying buttresses. Some roots reach above the water line to take in oxygen. Mangrove roots trap materials suspended in the water, creating a habitat and a rich food source for other species. Mangroves stabilize and protect the coastline, and also recycle nutrients.

Figure 5.4 A river delta is made up of several layered types of sediment. The finest sediment is carried out toward the sea the greatest distance before it is deposited and forms the bottom-set bed. Coarser material is deposited the earliest, and thus the closest, in the top-set bed. The layers form a sloping fan under the water that extends outward as sediment continues to accumulate.

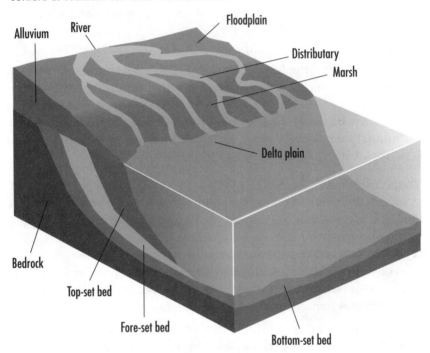

Estuaries can be formed in several ways. Some, like the Chesapeake Bay, were formed when the ocean level rose after the last ice age; when this occurred, seawater swamped the river system. An estuary can also form in places where the continuous action of waves builds sand up across the mouth of a river and traps river water behind it. The Waddensee estuary in the Netherlands is an example of this kind of estuary. A third type of estuary is the **fjord**, which is common in Norway and Alaska. Fjords are created when rivers end in deep areas of water that are partially isolated from the sea. This would be the case if a rock formation provided only a small or shallow opening to the sea for the river. Still another way in which an estuary can form is when an earthquake or volcano creates a low-lying area in a coastline and there is only a narrow opening to the sea. The San Francisco Bay is a good example of such an estuary.

Marshes and swamps are not the same thing. Marshes are wet grasslands, while swamps are waterlogged forests. Wetlands such as marshes and swamps are home to a great variety of wildlife and they provide an invaluable ecological service. As water moves through them, matter suspended in the water is trapped by plant roots or settles out as sediment. In this way, marshes and swamps filter and clean polluted water. In the past century, however, large areas of wetlands all over the world have been lost to projects that were launched intending to prevent flooding or to provide farmland, grazing land, or industrial and commercial building sites.

Lakes

Lakes are inland bodies of water that contain either brine (salt water) or fresh water. They form in either nondraining depressions or in basins whose outlets are above the lowest part of the depression. In order to endure, lakes need a consistent supply of water to keep the basin filled.

Many of the lakes in the world were created by the action of glaciers. During the last ice age, glaciers gouged out thousands of depressions in the bedrock of the upper latitudes in the Northern Hemisphere, providing nondraining places for meltwater to collect. Glaciers also produced dams by depositing debris across the drainage paths of streams.

The volume of all of Earth's lakes combined makes up just 5/1,000 of the world's total volume of water. From the perspective of geological time, lakes are transient, temporary features on the earth. This is because they will disappear if more water flows or evaporates out than comes in, or they can fill with sediment.

In regions of low precipitation and high evaporation, certain substances become concentrated in lake water. For instance, streams that flow into lakes carry dissolved matter from the weathering and erosion of the rocks in the drainage basin, and this dissolved material remains in the lake when the water evaporates. If the main mineral that is dissolved in the water is sodium chloride, saltwater lakes are created. The buildup of sulfates creates what are called bitter lakes; alkali lakes are a result of concentrated carbonates; and borax lakes contain borates. In North America, most saline lakes are found in the Great Basin area of the western U.S., where there are no drainage outlets to the ocean. Streams flow into the lakes but the only way that water can escape is through evaporation.

By their size, the Great Lakes of the U.S. and Canada are more like inland seas than lakes (but the term *sea* refers to saltwater bodies). Lakes Ontario, Erie, Huron, Michigan, and Superior make up the world's greatest network of freshwater lakes. The largest, Lake Superior, has the greatest surface area of any freshwater lake, but not the largest volume. Lake Baikal in southern Siberia has the largest volume because it is much deeper. From the surface to the bottom, Lake Baikal is 7 kilometers deep, which is seven times deeper than the Grand Canyon. It alone contains 1/5 of the world's fresh water.

THE OCEAN AND ITS WATERS

The volume of the oceans is more than 1 billion cubic kilometers (over 800 million cubic miles). The weight of this water is over 1 billion trillion kilograms.

The terms "sea" and "ocean" are often used interchangeably, but a sea is much smaller than an ocean, or is a part of an ocean that is partially surrounded by land. There can even be seas within seas. For instance, the Mediterranean Sea contains seven smaller seas. While people often speak of different oceans, there is only one global ocean, and the nominal division of it was fairly arbitrary. The phrase "the seven seas" dates to ancient times and refers to the bodies of water that were known to Islamic map makers before the fifteenth century: the Mediterranean Sea, the Red Sea, the East African Sea, the West African Sea, the China Sea, the Persian Gulf, and the Indian Ocean. Today, however, geographers most often speak of five oceans: Pacific, Atlantic, Indian, Southern, and Arctic. If the presence of distinctive basins is the criteria for oceans, then there are only three: the Pacific (which would be the largest), the Atlantic, and the Indian (the smallest). **Figure 5.5** shows the oceans and their dimensions, as well as the location of prominent seas.

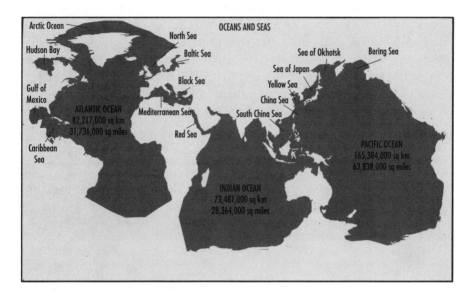

Figure 5.5 The oceans and prominent seas. Most people find it odd to view such a graphic, because we've become accustomed to focusing on the continents on maps rather than the sea.

THE FORMATION OF THE GLOBAL OCEAN

The ocean developed very early in Earth's history. Most scientists believe that the water on the earth's surface came from within the earth, and that it was produced by volcanoes that emitted carbon dioxide and water vapor in addition to lava and ash. The water vapor eventually condensed and fell in torrential rains that ran off of the higher places and pooled in the basins, forming the first bodies of water on the young planet's surface.

It is not known whether the early water vapor emerged virtually all at once, in episodes that were separated by periods of little change, or more or less continuously, to accumulate gradually over a long interval of time. These three possible scenarios for the development of the ocean have been called "the big burp," "the many burps," and "the steady burp" hypotheses. Many scientists favor the view that there was one gigantic burp of long duration followed by a succession of subsequent outgassings in which the proportion of new water that is added decreases up to the present day. An alternate hypothesis is that most of the ocean's water came from ice that was brought in by comets that bombarded early Earth.

The ocean and the atmosphere originated simultaneously. Early in Earth's history, sediment appears to have been transported by water and accumulated in water-filled basins, which indicates that a substantial amount of water was already present at the time the first rocks were formed. The existence of sedimentary rocks that date back 3.8 billion years indicates that there was a continuous presence of liquid water on the planet as far back as that time. The existence of sedimentary rocks that date to every time period in between means that the Earth's temperatures have generally stayed above freezing and below the boiling point of water.

OCEAN CURRENTS

One of the major features of the ocean is its **currents**. Surface currents are large river-like bodies of water that do not extend deep under the surface but move long distances in curved paths through the surrounding waters. Currents can carry either warm or cold water and they affect the climate of the lands they pass close to. **Figure 5.6** illustrates the flow pattern of the ocean's warm and cold surface currents.

Ocean currents carry vast amounts of heat energy from where it is concentrated at the equator, northward and southward toward the poles. Without the moderating effect of ocean currents, continent-sized ice cubes would accumulate at both poles, while the tropics would become overbaked wastelands. For this reason, currents can be thought of as the earth's natural thermostat.

The major force that produces surface currents is the wind, but undersea convection processes play a role as well. A convection cell occurs where cold, denser water sinks in one place and warm, less dense water rises at another place. Also, the movement of an ocean current in one direction or the other is influenced by what is called the **Coriolis effect**. The Coriolis effect says that, because of the spin of the earth, ocean currents that are generated by winds move in a clockwise direction in the Northern Hemisphere, and in a counterclockwise direction in the Southern Hemisphere.

Figure 5.6 An illustration of the flow pattern of the ocean's warm and cold surface currents. Notice the circular flow patterns in the north and south Atlantic and Pacific, and in the Indian Ocean. These patterns, called gyres, rotate clockwise in the Northern Hemisphere and counterclockwise in the Southern Hemisphere. The gyration tends to pile up water in the center, so that sea level in the middle of a gyre is higher than at the edge. Also, the waters in the gyre's centers are calm, as surface currents are absent. The North Atlantic's gyre is the Sargasso Sea.

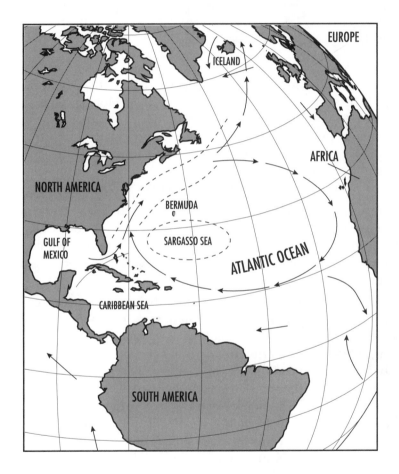

The Gulf Stream is the vast, powerful Atlantic Ocean surface current. It is first discernible in the Straits of Florida, where it resembles a 64 kilometers wide, 650 meter deep river that is moving at 8 kilometers per hour. It carries about 135 billion liters of water each second, which is six and one-half times as much water as all the rivers in the world. The Gulf Stream travels up the North American coast to Newfoundland and then turns east, toward Europe.

The Gulf Stream carries warm water north from the equator, where the water cools and becomes more dense; the cool water then sinks into the deep sea near Greenland. When the cool water sinks, more water is pulled northward to fill its place. This creates a pattern of movement like a conveyor belt.

The conveyor belt doesn't run smoothly however, because of differences of salinity, or saltiness, in the water. The eastern part of the Atlantic is salty because the shallow, salty Mediterranean Sea flows into it, while the western Atlantic (near the U.S. east coast) is relatively fresh. As the Gulf Stream conveyor belt pushes warm water into the North Atlantic, the marine equivalent of a high-pressure region is created. The clockwise flow out of the region eventually draws fresh water in from the west. The relatively lighter water from the west doesn't sink as easily and so the speed of the conveyor belt slows down. Because the northward flow of heat energy is reduced, the water in the North Atlantic cools enough to start sinking again—and with that, the region becomes a low-pressure zone whose counterclockwise flow draws salty water in from the east. That water sinks easily, which then speeds the conveyor belt back up again. One cycle of slowdown-speedup takes anywhere from 40 to 60 years. Thus, the North Atlantic acts as a heat pump that cyclically warms and cools the atmosphere over the course of decades.

Researchers have found evidence of the cycle in ice cores and coral reefs that go back 300 years. This complex cycle is illustrated in **Figure 5.7**.

Figure 5.7 Salinity and water temperature interact to influence water density in the Gulf Stream, contributing to a 40- to 60-year cycle of pressure zones in the Atlantic that affect the world's climate.

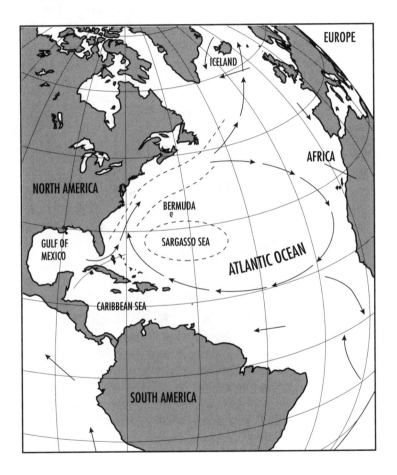

Currents also exist deep below the surface of ocean waters. They tend to flow in opposite directions from surface currents and travel more slowly. Deep currents are generated by differences in densities of ocean waters, rather than by the wind, and ocean water density depends on temperature and salinity. Cold water is denser than warm water and salty water is denser than less salty water.

Typically, denser water is near the ocean floor and less dense water is near the surface.

WAVES

Surface waves are another significant feature of bodies of water. Most waves are caused by the wind. **Figure 5.8** shows a cross section of the ocean floor and the wave pattern above. Waves "break" as they approach the shore and interact with the seafloor. The strength of the wind and the slope of the beach determine the shape of a breaking wave.

Figure 5.8 A cross section of the ocean floor and the wave pattern above. (a) The strength of the wind and the slope of the beach determine the shape of the breaking wave. (b) The water particles in the wave move in a circular pattern that becomes more compressed and elliptical as it nears the shore. The particles slow in the trough but not in the crest, until eventually the crest overtakes the rest of the wave and spills over.

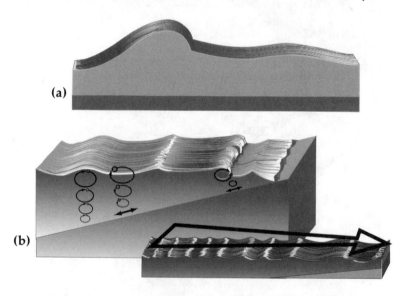

Very large waves are caused by the winds of hurricanes and other storms. The Beaufort Scale, which ranges from 0 to 12, is commonly used to quantify the strength of the wind. For instance, when the wind is measured at 0, the sea is calm, while a reading of 6 on the scale is a strong breeze, producing waves that may measure 3 meters in height. A wind that measures 12 on the scale is of hurricane force, and produces waves up to 14 meters high. The largest wave ever recorded was 34 meters high.

Undersea volcanic eruptions and earthquakes also create very large waves called **tsunamis**. A tsunami can travel for a great distance, and at a high speed, damaging ships and causing great destruction when it reaches the shoreline.

CHECK YOUR PROGRESS

1. Which of the following are most likely to be temporary features of Earth's landscapes

   a. mountains
   b. oceans
   c. lakes
   d. continents

2. A highly productive marshy habitat near the mouth of a river is called

   a. the continental slope
   b. the continental shelf
   c. an estuary
   d. a swamp

3. The unique feature of Earth that makes possible life as we know it is

   a. a differentiated internal structure
   b. an atmosphere
   c. abundant surface water
   d. sunlight

4. Estuaries can be created by

   a. the formation of a depression in the coastline caused by an earthquake
   b. the drowning of a river valley by the rising sea level
   c. the buildup of sand across the mouth of a river
   d. all of the above

5. A general characteristic of river development is

   a. wider valleys are cut at the headwaters and narrower ones downstream
   b. steep slopes lead to the development of highly meandering streams
   c. sediment load is greatest at the headwaters and decreases downstream
   d. valleys tend to be deeper and narrower at the headwaters of a river

6. The largest freshwater lake by volume in the world is
   a. Lake Baikal
   b. Lake Superior
   c. the Caspian Sea
   d. the Hudson Bay

7. Salt lakes are most likely to be found in which of the following climates?
   a. cold and humid
   b. hot and sunny, desert-like, rainforest
   c. tropical, rain forest
   d. very cold, arctic

8. In a river delta, the coarsest sediments are typically found
   a. in the sediment layer far out at sea
   b. as part of the bedrock under the river
   c. in the top-set beds close to the river mouth
   d. upstream along the river embankment

9. Most scientists believe the oceans originated from
   a. comets that brought in ice that melted
   b. water vapor that outgassed from inside the earth
   c. oxygen and hydrogen that combined to form water in the nebula from which Earth formed
   d. the separation of materials by density as the earth differentiated

10. Distinctive basins mark off which oceans?
    a. the Pacific, Atlantic, and Indian
    b. the Pacific, Atlantic, and Southern
    c. the Pacific, Atlantic, and Arctic
    d. the Indian, Southern, and Arctic

11. The Gulf Stream current is most likely to affect a country's climate in which of the following ways?
    a. it will cool Great Britain
    b. it will warm Great Britain
    c. it will cool Cuba
    d. it will warm the west coast of Africa

12. For surfers, the best breakers would be more likely to be found at a beach where
    a. the shore was more steeply inclined
    b. the shore was more gently inclined
    c. the ocean waters were very warm
    d. the ocean waters were very cold

THE OCEAN FLOOR

Figure 5.9 is a diagram of the general shape of the seabed as it connects to a continent. As is illustrated in the figure, the **continental shelf** is a shallow extension of the continent, while the **continental slope** forms the side of an ocean basin. What are called the "high seas" are beyond the continental margin.

Not too long ago everyone thought the bottom of the ocean was a flat, hum-drum place, but new technologies, developed during and after World War II, led to an explosion of scientific knowledge about the deep sea world. **Figure 5.10** is a diagram that shows some typical features of the ocean floor. An important feature is the **mid-oceanic ridge**, which is a long, narrow chain of underwater mountains at the boundary between crustal plates. There magma emerges from the mantle to form new sea floor. Along this Earth-encircling ridge, new crust is being formed continually, pushing the old crust away at the rate of 2 to 3 centimeters a year.

Figure 5.9 The general shape of the seabed as it connects to a continent. The continental shelf and slope are the sides of the continent and ocean basin, respectively.

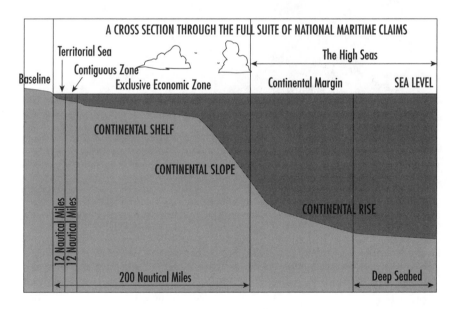

The ocean's deep **trenches** are places where the sea floor is pushed by the emerging magma at the ridge and plunges back into the mantle. Trenches are long, narrow valleys that are usually found next to islands or beside coastal mountain ranges. Some of the deepest trenches extend downward from sea level farther than the highest mountains rise above it. The **abyssal plains** are flat places that spread out from the ocean ridges to the edges of the continents. **Seamounts** are primarily underwater volcanoes that remain beneath the sea. They form islands if they rise above sea level. **Guyots** are a type of seamount with a flat-top.

Figure 5.10 Typical features of the ocean floor. The most important features are the mid-oceanic ridges, where new crust forms, and the oceanic trenches, where the sea bed often goes down and moves back into the mantle.

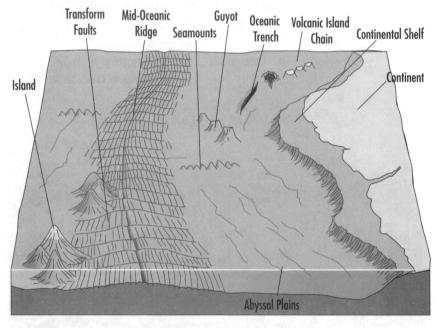

Contemplate an imaginary walk from the shoreline into the water and along the ocean floor. You would walk down a gentle slope at first and then, when your reached the continental slope, the descent would become much steeper. This steep part might be cut through with deep canyons carved out by rivers that emptied into the sea. The floor would even out at the continental rise, and then become fairly flat at the abyssal plain. You might walk for a while before encountering a hill, which would then rise to become a mountain. There would be a succession of mountains and valleys until you arrived finally at the mid-oceanic ridge (see **Figure 5.10**), where magma would be welling up to create new ocean floor. After crossing this, you would pass a similar pattern of ridges and valleys and then more abyssal plain on the other side and then reach a deep oceanic trench where the sea floor crust extended down into the earth's mantle. It would be a steep course indeed, up a sheer wall, as you climbed out of this trench to reach the continental rise on the other side of the ocean.

FYI

The safe maximum depth for scuba diving is 50 meters. The only way to reach the deepest parts of the ocean is by a **submersible**, a small submarine that dives from a "mother" ship, usually a boat on the surface. For instance, in 1986, the submersible *Alvin* and a smaller robot submersible, *Jason, Jr.* explored the wreckage of the luxury liner, the *Titanic*, which sunk in 1912 on its maiden voyage after striking an iceberg. Most of the *Titanic's* 1,500 passengers died in the Atlantic's icy waters.

You would not have been very comfortable on your imaginary walk across the ocean floor. The abyssal plain is between 3,500 meters and 11,000 meters under water, the deep oceans are completely dark, and their average temperature is only a few degrees above freezing. The weight of the overlying water produces enormous pressures at such depths, for instance, at just 1,000 meters down, the water pressure is 100 times that of sea level air. The only sources of food in the deep abyss are the dead bodies of plant and animal life and animal droppings that rain down from the surface waters, yet this organic matter is enough to sustain a diverse deep sea population.

OCEAN DEPTHS

- 1.5 m (meters)—typical depth limit for snorkeling
- 50 m—maximum depth for scuba diving using an aqualung
- 310 m—deepest that Tiger sharks are found

- 387.5 m—untethered diving record set by Sylvia Earle (*tethered* means to be connected to a surface vehicle)
- 775 m—submersible *Ventana* explores at these middle depths
- 1,270 m—deepest recorded dive of an elephant seal
- 3,787 m—deepest point in the Gulf of Mexico
- 4,030 m—*Titanic* wreckage found here
- 6,299 m—diving depth of tethered robot, *Jason*
- 7,455 m—deepest point in the Indian Ocean
- 9,219 m—deepest point in the Atlantic Ocean
- 10,918 m—depth of the Marianas Trench, Pacific Ocean

The submersibles *Trieste* and *Archimède* are able to explore depths of over 10,900 meters.

The mid-Atlantic ridge is the most extensive mountain range on Earth. It covers more territory than the Himalayas, the Rockies, and the Andes combined, and is part of the 64,000 kilometer long mid-oceanic ridge system. The mid-oceanic ridge runs the full length of the Atlantic, and in fact snakes its way around the entire world on the sea bottom.

Almost all of North America, including the western Atlantic basin, is part of the American plate, while all of Africa and the eastern Atlantic basin are on the African plate. The eastern and western plates meet at the mid-Atlantic ridge, and a distinct rift valley marks the line of separation between the two plates. Magma from within the earth rises into this rift and then cools and becomes welded to the separating plates, which separate at a rate of 2 to 3 centimeters a year. From plate ridge top to ridge top, the rift valley is about 30 kilometers across. The valley between the ridges drops steeply more than 1.5 kilometer, making it similar in scale to the Grand Canyon. Along the floor of the rift are fractures in which small earthquakes continually occur as opposite sides of the sea floor move apart, first sticking together by friction and then jerking loose with a release of energy. Fissures and faults are common in the rift and usually lie parallel to the rift axis.

Celestial navigation, which is used by sea vessels, depends upon the accurate measurement of the angle between a celestial body, such as the Sun, the Moon, or a star, and the horizon. To determine exact location in terms of latitude and longitude, reference to tables and calculations are required. For thousands of years, navigators at night in the Northern Hemisphere have depended upon the North Star (also called Polaris) for guidance. Polaris is only 0.5 a degree from the celestial north pole. In the Southern Hemisphere, however, there is no equivalent south star and Polaris cannot be seen from the Southern oceans. Nighttime navigation is thus more difficult south of the equator.

LIFE IN THE OCEAN

The ocean is inhabited from its surface to its depths, and there are even many organisms that live on and in its sedimentary floor. In fact, the ocean provides 99% of all the living space on Earth. Ocean habitats differ vastly in water depth, distance from coasts, and latitude. Two things that determine the quality of habitat are (1) the presence of light and (2) the availability of nutrients. Light penetrates through only the first 150 meters of water in the ocean, and nutrients are plentiful in some parts of the sea—such as near the coasts—and scarce in others.

The plants that grow in the open ocean, the "high seas," away from the shore, are different from land plants and the seaweeds of the coast. They are single-celled plants called **phytoplankton** that grow near the surface, where there is a good supply of light and nutrients, and drift with the currents. Living among the phytoplankton are the zooplankton, which are tiny animals that depend on phyloplankton for food. The **zooplankton** include animals that are the larval stages of many larger sea creatures, and may feed on other zooplankton. They are, in turn, the beginning of huge, complex marine food webs. **Figure 5.11** illustrates a simple marine food web.

Photosynthesizing ocean plants remove carbon dioxide from the atmosphere and produce most of the oxygen we breathe.

DEEP SEA LIFE

Scientists have also recently discovered a variety of unusual life forms associated with deep-sea trenches and hot-water vents. These extreme habitats are found in the ridges and valleys of the mid-ocean ridge and in ocean trenches near where the sea floor is plunging into the mantle. Vents called black smokers spew out hot, sulfur-filled sea water that becomes food for sulfur-eating bacteria; several million bacteria inhabit every teaspoonful of the water around the vents. The bacteria are eaten by tiny crabs and giant tubeworms. Until the discovery of these trench oases, scientists believed that all life depended upon sunlight.

Figure 5.10 A simple marine food web. The food chain is a transfer of energy through a succession of organisms.

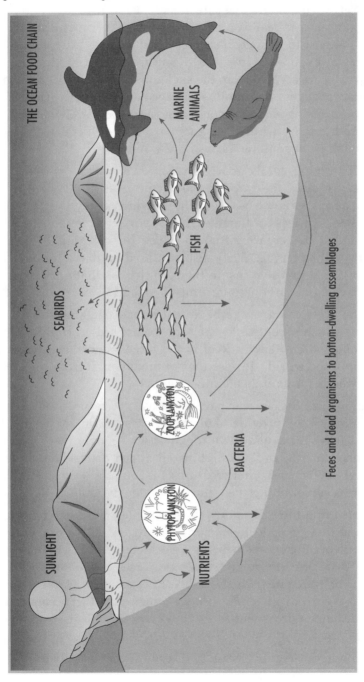

THE OCEAN FOOD CHAIN

MARINE ANIMALS

FISH

SEABIRDS

ZOOPLANKTON

BACTERIA

PHYTOPLANKTON

SUNLIGHT

NUTRIENTS

Feces and dead organisms to bottom-dwelling assemblages

ISLANDS

Another interesting feature of the ocean are its islands. One kind of island is called a **reef**. Reefs are actually complex ecosystems within the oceans and appear as rocky structures that rise upward from the seabed almost to the ocean surface. If the reef is near the shore, its top may be exposed at low tide. Reefs are created in different ways. Many reefs are created from the skeletons and shells of animals such as coral, sponges, and mollusks; especially oysters. These are all called *organic* or *biogenic* reefs. *Inorganic* reefs are basically rocks that are located offshore, but there are also artificial reefs, such as sunken ships in shallow, near-shore waters.

Reef-forming corals grow as colonies mainly in warm, tropical and subtropical waters. These biogenic reefs are created by individual animals known as coral polyps, which are cylindrical, and 2.5 centimeters or less in diameter. Coral polyps have mouths that are surrounded by tentacles that they use for catching food, mostly small shellfish larvae. They also eat the food that's produced by a type of algae that live inside them, which is what enables them to secrete calcium carbonate, or limestone, and form coral skeletons.

Coral reefs can grow to be an enormous size and, in fact, many islands in the South Pacific are composed entirely of coral. Australia's Great Barrier Reef is the largest and most diverse reef system in the world. It rises tens of meters high from the sea floor and extends for over 2,000 kilometers.

Coral reefs are among nature's most spectacular and beautiful structures. They provide habitats for many forms of marine life— some 3,000 species may live together on a single reef. Barnacles, mussels, starfish, and sea urchins all attach themselves directly to reefs, while fish and other creatures are a hundred times more dense in waters surrounding reefs than in the open ocean.

Reefs blunt the effects of waves and tides, producing calmer waters, and they provide an anchor and safe haven that prevents many kinds of organisms from being relocated by powerful ocean currents. A large reef structure often produces a **lagoon** by isolating a section of water near to the shore. Because the water is isolated from the current, it tends to be warmer than the ocean and thus provides an environment for warm-water organisms.

An **atoll** is a ring-shaped island that's composed of coral and is common in the Pacific Ocean. This type of reef usually builds up on top of a submerged remnant of a volcano. In the middle of an atoll is a lagoon that usually has some open channels to the sea. Among the better-known atolls are the Marshall Islands, Tahiti, Samoa, the Gilbert Islands, Wake Island, and the northernmost Hawaiian Islands—Kure and Midway. **Figure 5.11** illustrates the typical history of an atoll type reef structure.

THE WORLD'S LARGEST ISLANDS

- Greenland, Denmark—2,175,610 km² (square kilometers)
- New Guinea—820,660 km²
- Borneo—746,350 km²
- Baffin Island, Canada—476,070 km²
- Sumatra, Indonesia—473,600 km²
- Madagascar—387,040 km²
- Honshu, Japan—230,330 km²
- Great Britain—229,960 km²
- Ellesmere Island, Canada—212,690 km²
- Victoria Island, Canada—212,200 km²

MARINE ECOSYSTEMS IN STRESS

Over one hundred million people in one hundred different nations rely on reef ecosystems for survival. Globally, reefs have been in decline, mainly due to environmental stresses created by water pollution, such as sewage discharges, polluted storm water runoff, runoff from agricultural areas, and industrial waste discharges. Increased coastal development and deforestation have resulted in rivers carrying increased sediment loads. Much of this sediment ultimately flows out to sea and onto reefs, smothering and killing polyps. Other problems for reefs that are being caused by humans include the overfishing of large predator fish, accidental oil spills, fouled water from ships, and introduced marine pests. Some marine biologists estimate that up to 10% of the world's coral reefs have been degraded beyond recovery, with another 30% in critical condition.

In fact, ocean water pollution is a problem marine species face around the world. Most countries still dump untreated sewage straight into the sea. Trash is thrown from ships. Industrial wastes are dumped into the sea in canisters that leak, and those wastes can

Figure 5.11 The typical history of an atoll type reef structure. Volcanic islands become fringed by coral reefs. The islands subside with age, but the coral continues to grow, forming a ring barrier around the island. The volcanic island my disappear altogether, leaving only the ringed atoll.

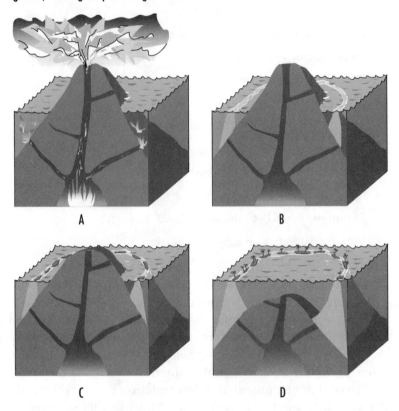

A

B

C

D

contain pesticides and heavy metals. Every year, some 6,000,000 metric tons of crude oil is spilled into the world's seas as a result of the normal operation of tankers and pipelines, as well as from drilling or tanker accidents. When this happens, the more volatile parts of the oil evaporate, and animals that inhale the poisonous fumes suffer lung damage. The heavier oil and tar coat fur and feathers, leading to shock and ultimately death in many sea creatures such as seals, fish, and birds. Waves and wind whip the oil into a thick foam known as chocolate mousse that washes up on the shore and smothers wildlife. Oil can continue to kill for months and years because it interferes with many animals' immune systems. **Figure 5.12** illustrates various sources of marine pollution.

THE RISING SEAS

Starting in preindustrial times, carbon dioxide concentrations in the atmosphere have increased by about 5% per decade. Over the same period, the concentration of methane in the atmosphere, another greenhouse gas, has increased 110%. Other gases that enhance the **greenhouse effect**, such as nitrous oxide and chlorofluorohydrocarbons (CFCs) have also increased. The greenhouse effect occurs when carbon dioxide, methane, and other gases absorb solar radiation and radiate the light energy back as heat. Atmospheric scientists expect the accumulation of greenhouse gases to result in an increase in the average temperature of the atmosphere, though the climate system is complex and many processes that are involved are still poorly understood.

Since the turn of the century, the ocean level has risen over 15 centimeters, consistent with the measured rise in atmospheric temperature over the same period. Most of this rise is due to the thermal expansion of sea water; water expands as it warms and then occupies more space. Also, some extra liquid water has come from the melting of glaciers in the mountains at low latitudes. A further warming of about 2°C, which could occur in the next 40 years, is likely to increase the sea level by about 30 centimeters more, again mostly due to thermal expansion.

In order to protect coastal areas that have been developed with homes, farms, and industry, many communities have constructed long seawalls in front of their beaches. Over the years, waves bounce off of the walls and into the surf, carrying away the sand and causing the shoreface to become steeper and the beach to disappear. Other structures designed to protect new developments on shore lines are groins and jetties, which jut out from the shore. These structures trap sand that is carried by *littorial drift*, an off-shore current that moves parallel to the coastline, and these structures are just as disruptive as seawalls, since beaches upcurrent of the groin grow at the expense of beaches downcurrent.

Figure 5.13 Pollution of the sea originates in many different human activities.

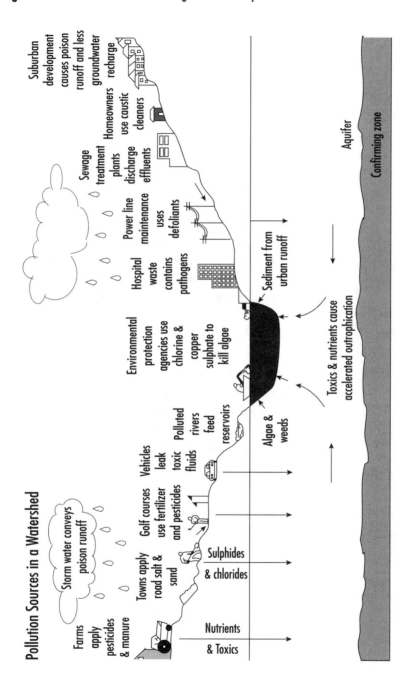

Some scientists predict a sea level rise of 0.5 meter by the year 2050, if greenhouse gas emissions continue at the current rate. A rising sea level could have catastrophic effects in many countries. Nearly 70% of the earth's people live within 320 kilometers of the coast. Low-lying countries, such as Bangladesh, are likely to be the first to feel the impact. More than .33 of the habitable land of that densely populated country could be lost.

There is also the effect of saltwater intrusion into the groundwater. Island countries would be disrupted more seriously than most continental nations; because they have smaller landmasses and proportionately longer coastlines, island countries could lose much of their most productive land.

Another effect of global warming is an intensification of the global hydrological cycle, meaning that there is increased evaporation, cloudiness, and precipitation. There would also be a change in the distribution of precipitation and storms, with tropical climates expanding toward the poles. Hurricanes would penetrate further north and south in their respective hemisphere.

INTERNET RESOURCES RELATED TO REEFS

International Year of the Reef:

http://www.coral.org/IYOR/index.html

Reef Check: http://www.ust.hk/~webrc/ReefCheck/reef.html

Murder under the Microscope: http://www.microscope.aone.net.au/

State of the Marine Environment Report: http://www.erin.gov.au/portfolio/esd/coast_marine/somer/contents.html

Great Barrier Reef Marine Park Authority:

http://www.gbrmpa.gov.au/

Reef Education Network: http://www.reef.edu.au

Other oceanography-related web sites:

Safari Touch Tank: http://oberon.educ.sfu.ca/splash/tank.htm

Smithsonian's Ocean Planet: http://seawifs.gsfc.nasa.gov/ocean_planet.html

Monterey Bay Aquarium Research Institute: http://www.mbari.org

CHECK YOUR PROGRESS

13. Which of the following variable affect the quality of underwater habitat for living things?

    a. water depth
    b. distance from coasts
    c. geographic location (latitude)
    d. all of the above

14. Which of the following is NOT among the largest islands of the world?

    a. Great Britain
    b. Australia
    c. Greenland
    d. Japan

15. Flat-topped underwater volcanoes are known as

    a. seamounts
    b. abyssal mountains
    c. guyots
    d. mid-ocean ridges

16. The steepest part of the ocean basin often is found at the

    a. continental slope
    b. continental rise
    c. continental shelf
    d. abyssal plain

17. The deepest ocean is the

    a. Atlantic
    b. Indian
    c. Pacific
    d. Southern

18. Along the mid-ocean ridge, new seafloor is being formed at the rate of about

    a. 3 centimeters per year
    b. 3 centimeters per century
    c. 3 meters per year
    d. 3 kilometers per year

19. For most of history, navigation at night has depended upon

    a. the magnetic compass
    b. the Southern Cross constellation
    c. the astrolabe
    d. the star Polaris

20. The characteristics of habitats for living things in the ocean vary according to

    a. distance from the coast
    b. latitude
    c. depth below the surface
    d. all of the above

21. Photosynthesizing one-celled ocean plants found drifting near the surface are the
    a. zooplankton
    b. phytoplankton
    c. algae
    d. all of the above

22. Bacteria that use sulfur-based chemicals for food are found
    a. among the phytoplankton
    b. among the zooplankton
    c. in cold polar waters
    d. around black smokers on the ocean floor

23. Corals are animals that live in
    a. warm waters
    b. cold polar waters
    c. deep sea vents
    d. all of the above

24. Many living coral reefs around the world have been in decline primarily due to
    a. increased numbers of predators
    b. global climate change
    c. water pollution
    d. commercial harvesting

25. Most of the rise in sea level since the turn of the century is due to
    a. the thermal expansion of sea water
    b. the melting of the Antarctic ice sheets
    c. the widening of the ozone hole
    d. the melting of continental glaciers

GLOSSARY

abyssal plain—a vast, flat area under the sea that spreads from the mid-oceanic ridge to the continents.

aquifer—a rock formation that holds water.

atoll—a continuous or broken ring of coral reef surrounding a central lagoon.

continental shelf—the edge of the continent, where the land gradually slopes away submerged beneath shallow ocean waters.

continental slope—the submerged side of a continent that forms the ocean basin.

Coriolis effect—the effect whereby a northward or southward moving object is deflected to the east or west because of the earth's rotation.

current—a large mass of water that travels great distances in the oceans.

delta—an area formed at the mouth of a river where sea currents do not remove the mud and sand material deposited by the river current.

estuary—the mouth of a river where its currents meet the ocean tides.

fjord—a type of estuary formed when a river ends in a deep area of water isolated from the sea by a sill that provides only a shallow opening.

greenhouse effect—a rise in atmospheric temperature due to an increase in carbon dioxide, methane and other gases that trap heat in the atmosphere.

guyot—an underwater volcano with a flat top.

lagoon—a sheltered area of water between the mainland and an offshore barrier.

lake—an inland body of still water, either salt or fresh.

mid-oceanic ridge—a long, narrow chain of underwater mountains formed where two crustal plates meet and magma emerges to form new sea floor.

phytoplankton—tiny single-celled algae that drift near the surface of the water and form a basic link in the oceanic food chain.

reef— a ridge of rocks or coral always or often submerged in the sea.

seamount—an underwater volcanic mountain.

siltation—the process of building up sediment by river deposition.

submersible—a small submarine designed to reach the depths of the ocean or probe inside enclosed places, such as shipwrecks.

trench—a long, narrow undersea valley that contains the deepest points on Earth.

tsunami—a giant sea wave triggered by an underwater earthquake or volcanic eruption.

watershed—a line which separates the drainage of water down one side of a raised area from the drainage down the other side.

zooplankton—small animals in the sea that feed on phytoplankton and comprise a basic link in the oceanic food chain.

ANSWER KEY

1. c	11. b	21. b
2. c	12. a	22. d
3. c	13. d	23. a
4. d	14. b	24. c
5. d	15. c	25. a
6. a	16. a	
7. b	17. c	
8. c	18. a	
9. b	19. d	
10. a	20. d	

CHAPTER 6

Processes that Shape the Land

THE PRESENT TELLS ABOUT THE PAST

The processes that are now shaping Earth have been at work throughout the planet's history. This fundamental principle, now known as **uniformitarianism**, was first proposed by James Hutton (who is thought of as the father of modern geology) in his book, *Theory of the Earth*.

Thus, in order to understand how an ancient rock was formed, we must understand the processes that continue to occur around us today, such as weathering, erosion, and mass wasting. These processes are not easily separated: weathering breaks rocks into smaller pieces or changes the rock's composition from one form into another, and these smaller pieces can be moved, either downslope by gravity in a process called mass wasting, or by agents of erosion, such as running water, wind, or ice.

WEATHERING: PROCESSES THAT CHANGE ROCK

All Earth materials are susceptible to **weathering**, and weathering can occur in two ways. In *mechanical weathering*, rocks are broken down into smaller pieces by physical force, while in *chemical weathering* a change occurs in the composition of one or more of the minerals in the rock. The physical properties of the rock are not altered by mechanical weathering, but when rocks are broken into smaller pieces, more surface area is available to be altered by chemical weathering.

MORE ABOUT MECHANICAL WEATHERING

The usual agents of mechanical weathering are freezing water, temperature changes that lead to expansion and contraction, and the activities of plants and animals. One example of mechanical weathering that you are probably familiar with is a crack in a sidewalk where a tree's root broke through.

In regions in which temperatures are regularly below 0 °C, freezing and thawing water is a frequent agent of mechanical weathering. During the day, when the temperature is above freezing, liquid water seeps into cracks in the rocks; when temperatures drop below 0 °C at night, the trapped water freezes. Ice occupies 9% more volume than water, and as it expands, the ice pushes against the sides of the rock, splitting it in a process called *frost wedging*. If the rock is part of an outcrop or cliff, the broken pieces fall to the ground, creating a loose pile of debris called a **talus slope**. This process is illustrated in **Figure 6.1**.

The daily cycle of temperature change itself acts as an agent of mechanical weathering. In some parts of the world, daily variations in the temperature may be more than 30 °C. As is the case for many other materials, rock expands when it is heated and contracts when it is cooled. If the outer layer of the rock has already been weakened by chemical weathering, a reoccurring cycle of expansion and contraction will stress and eventually break the rock, and pieces of the rock will flake off. The flaking off of layers from a rock is called **exfoliation**.

Mechanical weathering is also caused by the actions of organisms. For example, burrowing animals may move material to the surface where weathering can further break it down. Various human activities, such as mining and road construction, also break up rock and move material to the surface, increasing its susceptibility to agents of weathering.

Figure 6.1 Frost wedging causes pieces of the rock face to break off and fall to the ground, creating an accumulation of rock debris known as a talus slope.

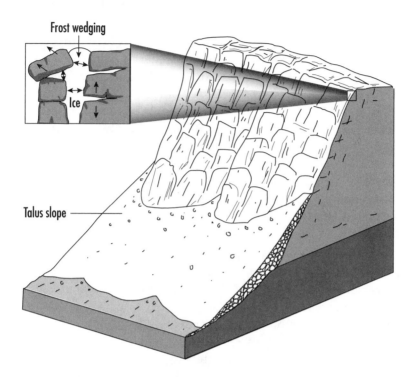

MORE ABOUT CHEMICAL WEATHERING

Chemical weathering causes the minerals in rocks to change into substances that have different chemical compositions and/or structures by removing or adding elements. The most important agents of chemical weathering are water, carbon dioxide, and oxygen.

Water decomposes rock in several ways. **Hydrolysis** is the reaction of any substance with water. Many minerals are water soluble, that is, they dissolve in water. Water molecules are effective dissolving agents because they are *polar*: one end of the water molecule is slightly negatively charged, while the other is slightly positively charged. If water comes in contact with an ionic mineral, such as halite (composed of sodium and chloride ions), the attractive forces of the water molecules pull ions away from the halite crystals and into solution, in effect, dissolving the halite.

Water also chemically weathers rocks because water molecules naturally dissociate, or split apart, to form reactive ions of hydrogen

(H^+) and hydroxyl (OH^-). The hydrogen ions act on particular minerals, replacing the positive ions originally found in the crystal structure and thereby destroying the initial arrangement of atoms and hastening the decomposition of the mineral.

Water often contains substances that also contribute hydrogen ions to solution, rendering it an **acid**. (An acidic solution is one that contains an excess of reactive hydrogen (H^+) ions.) Carbon dioxide readily dissolves in water to form carbonic acid. Some CO_2 from the atmosphere is dissolved in rainwater, and CO_2 is also released when organisms decay; this too is dissolved in the earth's water. Most rocks are susceptible even to weak acids, for example, granite is weathered when hydrogen ions replace the potassium ions in the structure of feldspar. The weathered feldspar is transformed into the clay mineral, kaolinite. The released potassium is then available as a nutrient for plants, or may be carried off in a stream to the ocean.

Limestone and marble, both of which are composed of the mineral calcite ($CaCO_3$), can be chemically weathered by any acid to produce soluble calcium ions, carbon dioxide, and water. This process of chemical weathering eats away limestone or marble monuments and building stones and, in areas that have a lot of subsurface limestone or dolostone, can produce (over millennia) caves and sinkholes. **Figure 6.2** shows the development of groundwater features in an area of limestone rock.

Figure 6.2 Caves develop in an area of limestone or dolomite rock when groundwater dissolves the mineral calcite. The diagram illustrates several features common in such areas of *karst topography*.

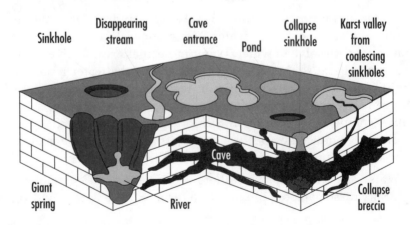

Another means of chemical weathering is **oxidation**. Oxidation is most commonly known as *rusting*, and occurs when oxygen combines with iron to form iron oxide. In this process, iron loses electrons to oxygen. Minerals such as pyroxene, hornblende, and olivine, which contain many iron compounds are frequently weathered by the process of oxidation.

Oxidation is also a prominent agent in the weathering of sulfide minerals, such as pyrite. Sulfide minerals are often associated with coal deposits, and serious environmental hazards can occur in mining regions if the sulfides in the spoil banks (the piles of waste left over after the coal has been removed) become weathered, because sulfuric acid is produced. This *mine acid* can make its way into streams and groundwater, spoiling the water as a habitat for many organisms and rendering it undrinkable for humans and other animals.

RESISTANCE TO WEATHERING

A rock's resistance to weathering depends on several factors, including its composition and the number of cracks and other openings it contains. Among the common minerals, quartz is the most resistant to both mechanical and chemical weathering, consequently, rocks composed mainly of quartz tend to be more durable. Rocks that contain a lot of feldspar, on the other hand, weather more quickly.

Generally, sedimentary rocks weather more quickly than other rock types because they are made of pieces that were cemented together. Water can seep into the small air pockets typically found between the pieces, and break the rock apart by frost wedging, or decompose it by dissolving the cement so that the particles separate. As you might expect, rock also weathers more quickly if it contains many cracks.

Climate factors, especially temperature and moisture, also contribute to the rate of weathering. A combination of warm temperatures and abundant moisture produces optimal conditions for chemical weathering. For example, atmospheric temperature and moisture influence the type and amount of vegetation in a region, which in turn determines the thickness and composition of the soil. Soil that contains a lot of organic matter will produce more acids that weather underlying rocks.

MASS WASTING: THE INFLUENCE OF GRAVITY

Weathering alone does not produce significant changes in the structure of the landscape. **Erosion** is a general term for all of the processes that wear away the land, and the cause of erosion is the downslope movement of material under the influence of gravity. **Mass wasting**, however, is the *direct movement* of weathered debris (referred to as *overburden*) by gravity, as occurs, for instance, in a landslide. Mass wasting does not require a transporting medium. It is the combined effects of mass wasting and *transportation* (the removal of material) that, given enough time, results in the formation of **valleys**, which are empty spaces that were formerly filled with rock. Running water is the most common agent of transportation, producing stream valleys, which are the most common landforms on Earth. Mass wasting makes stream valleys wider than they would be if erosion were the only process involved.

There are several kinds of mass movements of Earth material, including *rockfalls, rockslides* (or *landslides*), *mudflows* (or debris flows), *creep,* and *slump.* These are illustrated in **Figure 6.3.** Mass movements are classified on the basis of the moisture content of the moving mass and the relative speed of its movement. A rockfall occurs quickly, usually on a cliff or steep slope when a portion of the overburden breaks away and falls. **Slump** occurs less dramatically, usually in places where resistant rock overlays weak rock. For instance, a sturdy layer of sandstone covering softer shale will break and slump downslope. In contrast to these mass movements, the results of **creep** are noticeable only after months or years of observation, because the ground surface moves very slowly downslope, generally at a rate of up to a few centimeters per year.

Figure 6.3 How mass movements are described and classified in geology. In the case of slump depicted here, a weak layer of shale undermines the more resistant sandstone layer that covers it, setting the stage for the layers to slump downward.

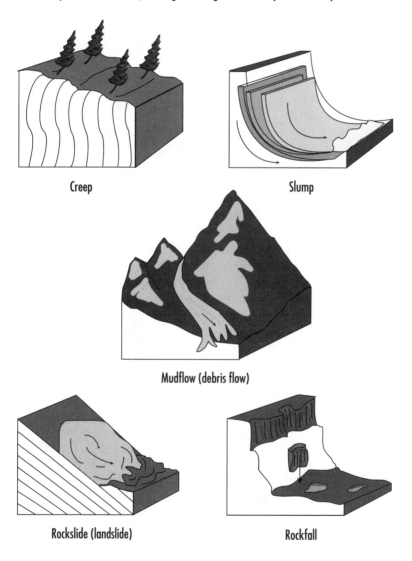

Creep

Slump

Mudflow (debris flow)

Rockslide (landslide)

Rockfall

Figure 6.4 Sand grains gradually move downslope in repeated freeze-thaw cycles. Freezing water in the soil causes the sand grains in the soil to become elevated, and the grains fall downslope during a thaw.

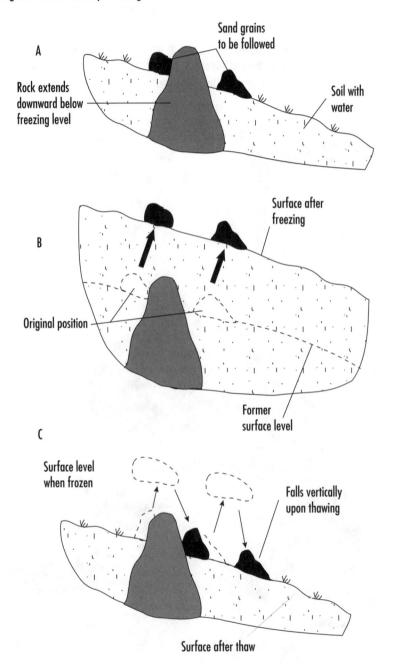

A

Sand grains
to be followed

Rock extends
downward below
freezing level

Soil with
water

B

Surface after
freezing

Original position

Former
surface level

C

Surface level
when frozen

Falls vertically
upon thawing

Surface after thaw

The freezing and thawing of soil or overburden can contribute to creep, as is illustrated in **Figure 6.4**. In the diagram, sand grains move gradually downslope in the repeated cycles of freezing and thawing of soil that is on a slope. Freezing water in the soil elevates the sand grains as the soil expands, and the grains drop vertically to a site slightly downslope, during a thaw.

Massive downslope movements of Earth material can be triggered by a number of situations, including an undercutting of the slope, an overloading of the slope until it can no longer support the weight, vibrations from earthquakes or explosions that shatter the slope structure, or the addition of water (as from heavy rains), which adds weight to the slope and reduces internal cohesion in the rock. A landform can be undercut, for instance, by waves at a shoreline, or by a stream.

CHECK YOUR PROGRESS

1. The principle of uniformitarianism was proposed by
   a. Charles Lyell   **c.** James Hutton
   b. Charles Darwin   **d.** Stephen Jay Gould

2. The most important factors influencing the rate of chemical weathering in a region are
   a. temperature and moisture
   b. temperature and latitude
   c. moisture and latitude
   d. topography and soil type

3. The process of chemical weathering that occurs when water reacts with minerals in a rock is called
   a. rusting   **c.** reduction
   b. hydrolysis   **d.** oxidation

4. The process of chemical weathering that produces rust is called
   a. ionization   **c.** reduction
   b. hydrolysis   **d.** oxidation

5. Weathering by frost wedging is most likely to take place in which of the following settings
   a. a back country road   **c.** a mountaintop
   b. a sea shore   **d.** a cave

6. Burrowing organisms promote weathering primarily by
   a. digging tunnels that expose rocks to air and water
   b. secreting waste materials that act on rocks
   c. breaking up larger pieces of rock into smaller pieces
   d. carrying rocks to the surface

7. Which of the following rock types would most likely be susceptible to chemical weathering?
   a. granite   c. limestone
   b. sandstone   d. basalt

8. Which of the following rocks would most likely be resistant to chemical weathering?
   a. shale   c. limestone
   b. granite   d. marble

9. When carbon dioxide dissolves in water, they form
   a. limestone   c. calcium carbonate
   b. carbonic acid   d. sulfuric acid

10. The weathering of the spoil banks from coal mines produces
    a. carbonic acid   c. sulfuric acid
    b. calcium carbonate d. clay minerals

11. The two constituent parts of the process of erosion are
    a. slump and creep
    b. rockslide and mudflow
    c. weathering and transportation
    d. mass wasting and transportation

12. Which of the following is NOT a type of mass movement of Earth materials?
    a. creep   c. hydrolysis
    b. slump   d. landslide

13. Creep is hastened by
    a. volcanism   c. wind
    b. freezing and thawing d. drought

14. The controlling force of mass wasting is
    a. gravity   c. wind
    b. friction   d. erosion

RUNNING WATER: THE CHIEF AGENT OF EROSION

Over the entire Earth, precipitation averages about one meter each year, and the same amount is evaporated. As we have seen in chapter 5, this continuous circulation of the Earth's water by precipitation and evaporation is the hydrologic cycle. The runoff of water from the land is propelled by gravity and erodes the land. About 96,000 cubic kilometers of water falls on the earth's land surface each year. Of this, some 60,000 cubic kilometers soaks into the ground, then eventually evaporates or returns to the atmosphere through transpiration from plants. The runoff, 36,000 cubic kilometers, erodes the land as it moves through **streams** on the way to oceans. **Figure 6.5** depicts the water cycle.

Figure 6.5 The hydrologic cycle represents the Earth's water movement from atmosphere to land, and from land to ocean. About 380,000 cubic kilometers of water evaporates into the atmosphere and then returns to Earth as precipitation each year. Much of this precipitation soon evaporates, but 36,000 cubic kilometers remains to travel in streams, eroding the land as it travels toward the sea.

HYDROLOGIC CYCLE

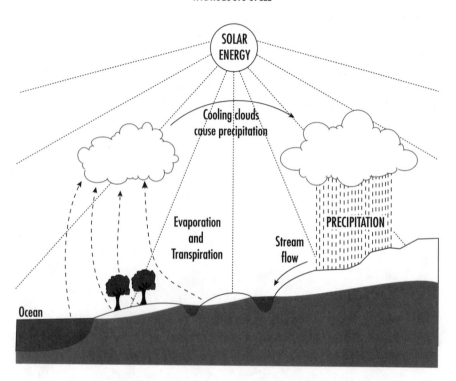

Moving water is the single most important agent that sculpts our planet's landscapes. The characteristics of stream flow depend on gravity, which is principally responsible for the force moving water exerts on the land. Friction is also an important force, because it acts against the moving water to slow it down. The amount of friction produced is a function of the quantity of sediment in the stream, called the *sediment load*, and the shape of the stream channel. How fast the water moves therefore depends upon four factors: the volume of the water (*discharge*), the slope of the streambed, the sediment load, and the shape of the channel.

STREAM DISCHARGE AND DEVELOPMENT

The size of a stream is measured by its discharge, and discharge can be calculated by multiplying the area of the cross section of the stream times the speed of its flow. **Figure 6.6** illustrates this relationship. The speed of flow, however, is not the same at all places in the stream. The flow along the sides and bottom of the channel is slower than the flow in the middle because friction between the water and the bed slows the water.

Figure 6.6. The discharge of a stream can be calculated by multiplying the channel cross section times the stream velocity.

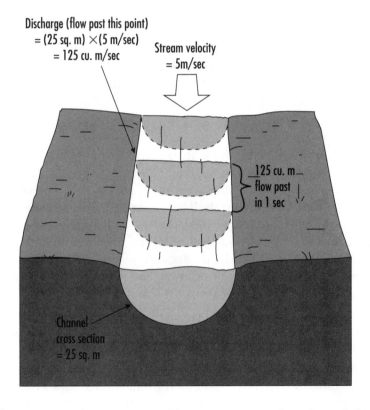

The amount of water carried by a stream is a function of climate (the amount of precipitation), characteristics of the surface of the land (how much water soaks in), and the size of the *drainage basin*, or watershed, from which the water is drawn. The stream's ability to erode and transport its sediment depends upon the volume of its discharge.

People commonly think of streams as being bigger than creeks or brooks but smaller than rivers. To the geologist, however, the term *stream* is used to mean *any* channelized flow of water, so streams can be any size, from trickles to rivers. However, geologists prefer the term *river* when describing a main stream into which tributary streams flow.

Over time, the stream's channel is widened and deepened by the processes of **downcutting** and sideways erosion. Downcutting occurs as the bottom, or bed, of the stream erodes. The sediment that the stream carries works on the channel sides and bottom like sandpaper works on wood. The faster the stream flow, the more rapid is the erosion.

Rapid downcutting produces a steep-walled, V-shaped valley, while less rapid downcutting by streams with slower flows results in meanders, see chapter 5.

TRANSPORT OF SEDIMENT

The total amount of material a stream transports is called its **load**. Streams carry their loads of sediment in three ways. Materials that are dissolved in the water make up the *dissolved load*. The *suspended load* consists of fine materials light enough to be suspended and moved along in the water. Finally, the *bed load* consists of the heaviest materials that are carried by the stream. The amount and identity of the suspended and bed loads depend on the speed of the stream flow, but the dissolved load does not. The material in solution only precipitates out if the chemistry of the water changes.

Most streams transport the largest part of their load in suspension. During floods, the amount of material carried in suspension increases greatly. The bed load is most significant in terms of erosion, because it grinds away at the stream's channel. Particles in the bed load move along the bottom by rolling, sliding, and by a process called *saltation*, which is a series of short hops produced by the flowing water. Unlike the dissolved and suspended loads, the bed load is in motion only periodically, when the force of the moving water is strong enough to move the larger particles.

FLOODS AND THE DEPOSITION OF SEDIMENT

Whenever a stream slows down, its ability to carry sediments is reduced. As the speed of flow slows, particles drop out of suspension by size: heaviest first. Because material of similar size travels together in a stream, streams are agents for sorting material. The sorted sediment left by a stream is called **alluvium**. Landforms created by alluvium deposits include sand and gravel bars and deltas.

Floods occur when an input of water in a stream is too great for its channel, or if the addition of water occurs too quickly to be accommodated by the channel so that the stream overflows its banks. During floods, stream deposits, like islands, are often disturbed and their particles dispersed farther downstream, most eventually traveling to the oceans. Successive flooding produces a flat landscape feature called a **floodplain**, which is defined as the portion of a valley that is underwater during a flood. Most streams have identifiable floodplains, which can be as modest as a few meters across or as large as several kilometers in width.

As you now know, water that leaves the stream channel during a flood deposits fine sediments, like silts and clays, outside the channel. Sometimes, successive flooding causes rivers of low gradients (those that course through broad, flat areas), to create a landscape feature along their banks called *natural levees* (a levee is a wall-like structure parallel to the stream flow). **Figure 6.7** illustrates how this landform develops.

It's only natural

People often think of floods as natural disasters. Sometimes floods *can* be disastrous for people; a lot of property is damaged and many lives are lost annually due to flooding. However, floods, *per se*, are not unnatural, or even unusual events in nature. Flooding is a completely normal natural phenomenon, and often floods produce beneficial changes. For instance, until the construction of the Aswan High Dam in Egypt in modern times, the predictable annual flooding of the Nile enriched the floodplain soil and provided rich nutrients for crops.

Figure 6.7 Coarser sediment falls closer to the channel when natural levees are formed along the banks as a result of sediment deposition during flooding.

(a)

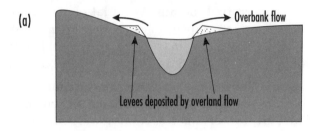

Overbank flow

Levees deposited by overland flow

(b)

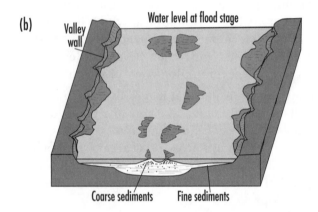

Valley wall

Water level at flood stage

Coarse sediments   Fine sediments

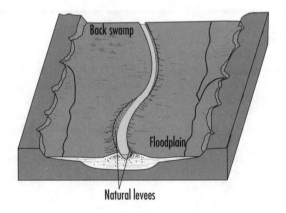

Back swamp

Floodplain

Natural levees

FLOODING AND HUMAN INFLUENCE

Flooding depends on factors such as climate, topography, character-istics of the soil, and the presence or absence of vegetation. But many streams, especially those that wind through populated areas, are increasingly being affected by human activities. For instance, the channels of streams often are modified to protect property. **Channelization** is used to increase the speed of flow of the stream, the volume of the stream's channel, or both. However, straightening the stream channel to prevent flooding in one place often increases the likelihood that another place downstream will be flooded.

UPLIFT BALANCES EROSION

Rates of erosion can be very slow, and are often balanced by pro-cesses that uplift the land, such as the convergence of tectonic plates. Rates of uplift and erosion vary from place to place, depend-ing on the climate and other factors. Overall, geologists estimate that erosion is lowering the altitude of North America at a rate of three centimeters every one thousand years. If the average height of the land surface is 823 meters and if erosion were the only process involved, at this rate, the whole continent would be reduced to sea level in about 25 million years!

Figure 6.8 A soil profile showing the various soil horizons.

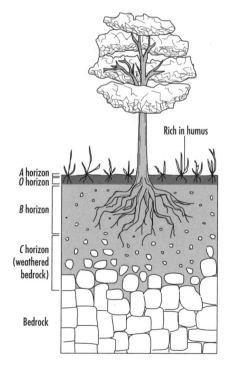

Rich in humus

A horizon
O horizon

B horizon

C horizon
(weathered
bedrock)

Bedrock

One of the most sudden and violent acts of erosion in Earth's history happened during the Ice Ages in what is now eastern Washington state, near the Idaho border. A river was dammed behind a glacier that stretched down from the north, forming a lake on the scale of today's Great Lakes. The ice dam held back Lake Missoula, one of the deepest lakes ever known. It contained over 2,000 cubic kilometers (km³) of water and was as deep as 600 meters. Suddenly the ice gave way and the dammed waters burst out, completely draining the great lake in just two days. The water poured out at speeds up to 100 kilometers per hour, washing away everything in its path. The landscape was scoured—all topsoil was removed and boulders were plucked right out of the bedrock. When it was over, some 34,000 square kilometers of land were completely eroded, producing the terrain now known as the Channeled Scabland. Even today, 15,000 years after this huge flashflood, much of the land is an unfarmable and barren wasteland.

SOIL

Earth's surface is covered in most places by **regolith**, which is the layers of minerals and rock fragments that have resulted from weathering. Some parts of this regolith are **soil**, which is a complex combination of minerals, organic matter, water, and air. Soil is formed when the products of chemical and mechanical weathering combine with **humus**, which is organic matter that comes from the decay of plant and animal material.

Soil is not uniform throughout, but consists of a series of layers that have different physical characteristics. These layers, known as the **soil profile**, are illustrated in **Figure 6.8**. The top-most layers, called the *A* and *O horizons*, make up a zone that consists of most of the soil's organic matter and the rock material that has been the most weathered. Rain water filters down through this layer, dissolving soluble minerals and removing them in a process called leaching. Some of the finest-grained minerals, such as the clays, may also be carried away from the surface in this process. Some of the material that is removed from the A horizon collects in the soil layer below, the coarser-grained *B horizon*, which is also known as the *zone of deposition* or *accumulation*. Below this is the *C horizon*, a zone made up of very coarse, broken-up rock. Below that is bedrock, often designated the *R layer* or the *D horizon*. The dividing lines between soil layers may be easy to discern, or very indistinct, and all horizons are not present in all soils.

SOIL DEVELOPMENT

Soil formation is a slow process that generally requires hundreds of years. The rate of soil formation is affected by the type of bedrock, the slope, the local climate, and the presence of living things. The thickness of the soil created depends both on the rate of soil formation and the rate of erosion. Soils also differ from place to place because the parent rock differs.

Soils do not accumulate on very steep slopes so the soil layer is rather thin in such terrains. In contrast, soils of bottomlands are usually thick, dark, and poorly drained or even water-logged. Their dark color is a result of the organic matter that has accumulated. The situation for optimum soil development is on an undulating or flat upland surface that has good infiltration of water, good drainage, and low erosion.

Climate is perhaps the most important factor in soil formation. The climate determines the rate and predominance of mechanical and chemical weathering, for two main reasons. First, precipitation determines the degree to which materials are leached from the soil, and second, climates determine the type and abundance of living things in a locale.

The quality of soil for agriculture depends on several factors, including the amount of humus it contains. Besides being a source of plant nutrients, humus enables soil to retain moisture. Another factor affecting soil's quality is its *porosity*. About half of any good-quality soil consists of pore spaces in which water and air circulate. As water moves through the soil it becomes a broth containing many soluble nutrients that are made available to plants. Pore spaces also contain air, which is the source of oxygen and carbon dioxide for the many diverse microbes, fungi, and plants and animals that live in the soil and depend on these compounds.

About 97% of a plant's weight consists of the elements carbon, hydrogen, and oxygen, that are extracted from the atmosphere, and the remaining percentage comes from the soil. Elements from the soil that are important for the metabolism and growth of green plants include nitrogen, phosphorus, potassium, calcium, magnesium, and sulfur.

Soil has been called "the bridge between life and the inanimate world," because it contains a microscopic universe of plants, animals, fungi, and single-celled organisms. It is literally an ecosystem in itself, and is still poorly understood by scientists. In a square meter of your yard or school grounds you can typically find about 50,000 small earthworms, 10 million round-worms, and 50,000 small insects and mites. A single gram of fertile farm soil might contain 30,000 one-celled animals, 50,000 algae, 400,000 fungi, and 2.5 billion bacteria.

SOIL TYPES

The characteristics of a soil are mainly determined by the prevailing climatic conditions. Soil scientists distinguish between three types of soil: *pedalfer*, *pedocal*, and *laterite*.

Pedalfer is a term derived from *pedon*, the Greek word for soil, and the chemical symbols for aluminum and iron, Al and Fe respectively. This type of soil supports forest vegetation and is abundant in the eastern United States. The topsoil is sandy, light colored, and acidic, while the subsoil is brown or reddish brown and is rich in iron, clay, and aluminum.

The term pedocal is also derived from *pedon* and is combined with the first three letters of calcite, or calcium carbonate. This type of soil is abundant in the drier, western U.S., and is characterized by large amounts of calcite. In dry climates, the rain that does fall doesn't usually soak very deeply into the earth; it remains near the surface and then evaporates. Soluble materials such as calcite end up concentrated in the sublayers of the soil, giving it a whitish color. This type of soil generally supports a grass and brush community.

Laterites are soils that are predominant in the wet, hot climates of the tropics. Chemical weathering predominates under these conditions, and leaching removes not only the soluble materials such as calcite, but also the less soluble materials, like silica. These soils are deeper and do not show distinct zones as do the other soil types. Laterite soils contain little or no humus, because the bacterial activity is so high in the tropics. Without humus, there is little acid available to remove iron from the soil, so that iron oxides and aluminum become concentrated, giving them a brick red color. In fact, these soils are often used to make bricks, since when they are dried, laterites become very hard. Because of these characteristics, laterites are poor soils for agriculture.

Soils in cold or very dry climates are typically poorly developed and thin. In such climates, chemical weathering is very slow and the plant life produces little organic matter to create humus.

CHECK YOUR PROGRESS

15. A force that acts against moving water to slow it down is
    a. gravity
    c. friction
    b. sediment load
    d. hydrolysis

16. Suppose a stream has a channel cross section of 25 square meters and a flow speed of 5 meters per second. Its discharge would be
    a. 5 cubic meters/second
    c. 125 cu. m/sec
    b. 100 cu. m/sec
    d. 200 cu. m/sec

17. Which of the following is NOT a factor determining the amount of discharge in a stream
    a. the area's climate
    b. the type of underlying rock
    c. characteristics of the local soils
    d. size of the watershed

18. Meanders in a stream are produced under which of the following conditions
    a. rapid downcutting
    b. downcutting into sediment rather than bedrock
    c. slow stream flow
    d. heavy sediment loads

19. The development of soils in a particular place is determined by
    a. the type of bedrock
    b. climate
    c. presence of plant and animal life
    d. all of the above

20. Which of the following organisms can be found living in soil?
    a. fungi
    c. earthworms
    b. mites
    d. all of the above

21. Which is the most important factor in the formation of soils?
    a. climate
    b. slope
    c. plant and animal life
    d. type of bedrock

22. Which type of soil would be most likely found in New England?
    a. pedocal
    b. pedalfer
    c. laterite
    d. caliche

23. One reason tropical rainforests should *not* be converted to agricultural uses is that
    a. tropical land is typically pedocal soil, which is better for growing grasses
    b. the bedrock is too close to the surface for soil cultivation
    c. laterite soils dry out quickly without the forest canopy, becoming bricklike
    d. there are better conditions for agriculture in mountain terracing

GLOSSARY

acid—a reactive solution containing an excess of hydrogen ions.

alluvium—material deposited by a stream, such as sand, silt, or mud. Typically alluvium is well-sorted by particle size and is deposited in river beds, flood plains, and lakes.

channelization—any of a range of modifications of a stream channel.

creep—a common kind of mass wasting in which the ground surface moves imperceptibly slowly downhill.

downcutting—a type of erosion that removes material from the bed of a stream.

erosion—the transportation of material by water, wind, or ice.

exfoliation—the flaking off of layers of rock by processes of chemical and mechanical weathering.

floodplain—that part of a valley that is inundated during a flood.

hydrolysis—the reaction of any substance with water.

humus—the decayed remains of plant and animal life.

load—the total quantity of material transported by a stream, which is subdivided as dissolved load, suspended load, and bed load.

mass wasting—the movement of Earth material downslope resulting from gravity.

oxidation—any chemical reaction in which a substance loses electrons (the element oxygen is often the agent, but not necessarily so).

regolith—the layer of mineral and rock fragments produced by weathering that covers the earth's surface.

slump—the downward sliding of a mass of material moving as a unit along a curved surface.

soil—the portion of the regolith containing minerals, organic matter, water, and air that supports the growth of plants.

soil profile—the succession of layers, called *horizons*, in a vertical section of soil.

speleology—the study and exploration of caves.

stream—any body of flowing water usually confined within a channel.

talus slope—a pile of loose rock fragments at the base of a rock outcrop or steep cliff, caused by frost wedging.

uniformitarianism—the geological principle that the laws of nature that operate today have always operated in the past.

valleys—empty spaces in the landscape that earlier were filled with rock.

weathering—the breakdown of rock at or near the Earth's surface by mechanical or chemical means.

ANSWER KEY

1.	c	15.	c
2.	a	16.	c
3.	b	17.	b
4.	d	18.	c
5.	c	19.	d
6.	a	20.	d
7.	c	21.	a
8.	b	22.	b
9.	b	23.	c
10.	c		
11.	d		
12.	c		
13.	b		
14.	a		

CHAPTER 7

The Atmosphere: Weather and Climate

WEATHER AND CLIMATE

Weather is defined as the state of the atmosphere at a particular time over a place on the Earth's surface, and **climate** refers to a location's weather over time—and the long-range state of the atmosphere for a particular place. Meteorology is the study of the weather, while climatology is the study of the aggregate weather for a geographic locale. Meteorology and climatology are closely allied scientific fields.

The basic variables in atmospheric conditions are precipitation, temperature, humidity, pressure, cloudiness, and wind, but weather and climate are influenced by many other factors as well, including latitude, altitude, the topography of landforms, land and water distribution, ocean currents, prevailing winds, belts of low and high atmospheric pressure, and cloud cover. For example, an area's latitude determines the length of daylight it receives and the directness of the Sun's rays that travel through the atmosphere and strike its surface. Because the Earth is a sphere, **insolation**, or incoming solar radiation, is not the same at all locations. More energy is transmitted to areas near the equator than is received in the high latitudes. **Figure 7.1** illustrates how latitude determines the angle of impact of the Sun's rays.

Figure 7.1 The energy from the Sun is greater near the equator than near the poles because the radiation is more concentrated and because it passes through less of the atmosphere.

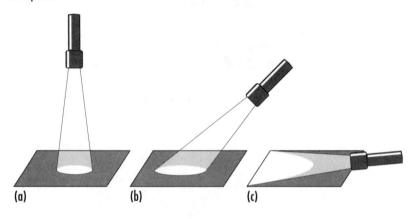

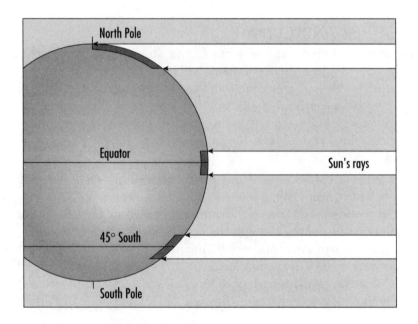

The only areas on Earth that every receive direct, vertical rays from the Sun are the **tropics**, which is the area between 23.5° north latitude (the Tropic of Cancer) and 23.5° south latitude (the tropic of Capricorn). In this region, the Earth *receives* more heat than it loses to space, whereas in the high latitudes the opposite is true: the Earth loses more heat than it receives. The temperature differences between the low and high latitudes would be much more extreme, however, if it were not for the winds and the ocean currents which continuously transfer heat from the equator toward the poles.

FACTORS INFLUENCING WEATHER AND CLIMATE

One factor that influences weather and climate is the distribution of land and water. The temperature of air over land will be hotter in the summer than the temperature of air over water at the same latitude, and colder in the winter. This is because land areas heat and cool faster than do bodies of water. But large bodies of water also have a moderating effect on the air temperatures over adjacent land areas, so that, in the summer, for instance, the farther from shore you travel, the higher the temperature.

Other major influences on climate and weather are prevailing winds and belts of low and high pressure. The uneven heating of the Earth's surface creates pressure differences that result in wind. **Wind** is the movement of air from an area of high atmospheric pressure to an area of low pressure. High pressure is due to greater air density: The atoms and molecules of colder air are closer together, or denser than the particles of warmer air. The air is hottest and the atmosphere the least dense at and around the equator. This creates a belt of low pressure known as the *doldrums*. Both to the north and south of the doldrums, between 25° and 30° latitude in each direction, lies a belt of high pressure. In this belt blow the warm, moist easterly breezes called the *trade winds*. From these latitudes to about 60° north and south are belts of low pressure known as the *subpolar lows*, where westerlies and cold easterly winds blow from polar high-pressure areas out over the Arctic Ocean and Antarctica. **Figure 7.2** illustrates the Earth's prevailing winds and high and low pressure belts. These wind and pressure patterns are modified, of course, by the arrangement of landmasses and oceans.

Figure 7.2 The entire pattern of prevailing winds and high and low pressure belts shifts northward when the northern hemisphere has its summer and southward when its summer in the southern hemisphere.

Belts of surface winds:

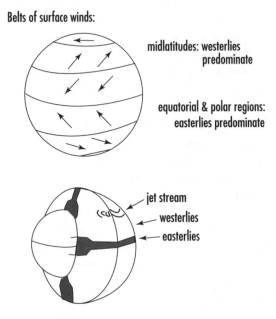

midlatitudes: westerlies predominate

equatorial & polar regions: easterlies predominate

jet stream
westerlies
easterlies

Yet another major influence on weather and climate is the pattern of currents in the oceans. Ocean currents such as the Gulf Stream and the North Atlantic Current carry warm water away from the equator and toward the North Pole. The warm Gulf Stream water flows past western Europe and moderates the climate there.

A location's altitude, or elevation, also determines its weather and climate; for instance, there is a gradual decrease in temperature with increasing altitude and it can be very cold at high elevations even in the tropics. One interesting weather phenomenon that's due to topography is that the side of a mountain that receives moisture-bearing winds usually gets more precipitation than the mountain's *leeward*, or opposite, side. This is true because when the air moves up a slope, it expands and cools, which decreases its capacity to hold moisture. Air moving down a slope becomes more dense and thus warmer, which increases its water-holding ability and reduces the likelihood of precipitation. Mountains can also block the movement of air masses. The Himalayas prevent cold air from moving out over India, and the Alps do the same for the Mediterranean coast.

Cloud cover is another important influence on weather and climate. Generally, humid places have more clouds, and places with more clouds usually experience less extreme temperatures. In the summer, a daytime cloud cover acts to resist rising temperatures, and at night (and in the winter), clouds block the Earth's loss of heat to the atmosphere.

THE ORIGIN AND EVOLUTION OF THE ATMOSPHERE

Many planets and moons in our Solar System have atmospheres, and the evolution of their atmospheres depended on where each body was positioned in the nebula when the Solar System formed. Their development also depended upon the size of the body, because a body's mass determines the strength of its gravitational field and the strength of a body's gravitational field determines the identity and amount of gases it will hold in its atmosphere.

The position of a body relative to the Sun determines how much energy it receives, and therefore its temperature. Planets close to the Sun may have had their primordial atmospheres burned off when the Sun's nuclear furnace first ignited, and their secondary atmospheres may have formed from volcanic outgassing. Internal geological processes like volcanism seem to have played a key role in the evolution of the atmospheres of Mars, Venus, Earth, and some other bodies in our Solar System.

Chemistry also plays a role in the evolution of atmospheres. In the atmosphere of Saturn's large moon, Titan, for example, large amounts of methane (CH_4) were produced by chemical reactions very early in the moon's development. Titan may now have an atmosphere that's similar to the atmosphere present on Earth when life began.

On Earth, the present atmosphere may not be the atmosphere that was present in the earliest stages of the planet; it may be a secondary atmosphere that evolved as a result of outgassing from volcanic eruptions, hot springs, the chemical breakdown of solid matter, and later, the contributions of living things. The constituents of the atmosphere today are redistributed and cycled by geological and biological processes.

The composition of the Earth's atmosphere has changed a great deal over time. The primitive atmosphere had little or no uncombined or "free" oxygen—no atomic oxygen (O), molecular oxygen (O_2), or ozone (O_3). None of the models of the early atmosphere indicate a source for any free oxygen, and even if there had been a source, other elements that were present would have rapidly combined with the oxygen. Furthermore, the presence of free oxygen in the early atmosphere would have inhibited the origin of living things by degrading the large organic molecules that were probably produced by chemical evolution.

Substantial quantities of air and water were present at the time rocks were first formed on Earth. The first sedimentary rocks began as water-born deposits, and have been dated to 3.8 billion years. For sedimentary rocks to have been produced, there had to be atmospheric gases such as carbon dioxide and water vapor to break down parent rock through weathering, and there had to have been water that transported the rock fragments and dissolved matter to the site at which they accumulated and were cemented together.

At about the time that the earliest sediments were being deposited, life was beginning on Earth. There is evidence that microscopic life colonized the floor of the Earth's first ocean as far back as 3.8–3.9 billion years ago. The earliest organisms capable of **photosynthesis** were the *cyanobacteria* (formerly called blue-green algae), which date to the same period as the earliest non-photosynthesizing life forms. But it was hundreds of millions of years after the appearance of these oxygen producing life forms before oxygen began to build up in the oceans and escape into the atmosphere. Evidence indicates that free oxygen has not been a major constituent of the Earth's atmosphere for more than half of the planet's history.

Somewhere between 1.3 and 2 billion years ago, cells with nuclei evolved. At that time, the atmosphere probably had only about one percent of its present oxygen, and more than a billion years passed before the oxygen level in the atmosphere was high enough to sustain multicellular animal life. At that time, which was nearly 700 million years ago, the atmosphere probably contained 6 to 7% of its present oxygen level.

Actual samples of Earth's early atmosphere that were trapped in ancient amber have been recovered. From these samples it appears that the atmosphere during the time of the dinosaurs was 9% *richer* in oxygen than the atmosphere today. Throughout the Earth's history there have been fluctuations in the amounts of atmospheric oxygen and other gases. Oxygen is removed and carbon dioxide is added as a result of episodes of intense volcanism or meteorite bombardment, for example. In our own times, human activities, including the widespread deforestation of the planet and the combustion of large quantities of fossil fuels, have measurably increased the carbon dioxide content of our atmosphere.

THE ATMOSPHERE'S COMPOSITION AND STRUCTURE

If the Earth were the size of an orange, the atmosphere would be as thick as the pigment layer in the orange peel. At sea level, about two tons of air is directly over our heads, and the atmosphere extends to a height of approximately one hundred kilometers.

The air that's nearest the Earth's surface is denser than the air farther up because air is compressed by its own weight. Half of the weight of the atmosphere is compressed into the lowest six and a half kilometers, and nearly 99% of the total weight of the atmosphere lies within 30 kilometers of the Earth's surface.

Gases in the lower portion of the atmosphere are circulated and continually mixed, while the outer layer is relatively unmixed. This is because the particles in this area are less dense, and collide less frequently. The boundary between these two layers, the lower **homosphere** and the upper **heterosphere**, is at a height of about 80 kilometers above sea level. **Figure 7.3** illustrates these two layers of the atmosphere.

The figure also presents another way of classifying areas of the atmosphere, based on temperature differences. The atmosphere can be divided into four major regions: the **troposphere**, the **stratosphere**, the **mesosphere**, and the **thermosphere**. The bottom-most region is the troposphere; this is the zone in which weather occurs. Temperature decreases with altitude in the troposphere, until an area is reached in which there is no change in temperature with increasing altitude. This area is called the *tropopause*. The zone above the tropopause is the stratosphere, an area of little moisture and few clouds, in which the temperature *rises* with increasing altitude. **Figure 7.3** illustrates another pause at this point, the *stratopause*, which is followed by two additional regions with another pause in-between them. The air temperature decreases in the mesosphere but rises again in the thermosphere.

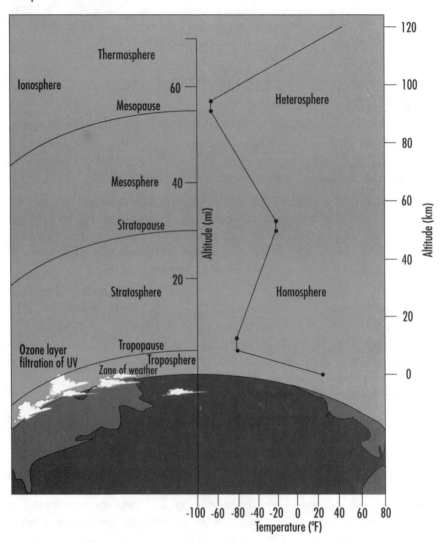

Figure 7.3 also shows the relative location of two important features of the atmosphere. The **ozone layer**, which filters ultraviolet radiation from sunlight, is located at the boundary of the stratosphere. Ultraviolet radiation is harmful to many forms of life on land, and can cause skin cancer in people. The ozone layer is thinnest around the poles, and holes have opened up there in both hemispheres, primarily due to our use of industrially produced

gases, such as the chlorofluorohydrocarbons, or CFCs. The other important feature of the atmosphere illustrated in the figure is the **ionosphere**, a region in which atmospheric particles are continually subjected to ionizing radiation from the Sun. The electrified nature of the ionosphere causes radio signals that reach this region to be reflected back to the ground.

In the lower atmosphere, where the constituent gases are completely mixed, air is mainly composed of nitrogen and oxygen, with small amounts of argon, helium, neon, hydrogen, and carbon dioxide. Water vapor generally makes up about 2 percent of the air, but this amount varies. **Figure 7.4** is a pie graph that illustrates the proportion of the atmosphere's constituent gases.

Figure 7.4 Air is a mixture of odorless gases, of which nitrogen and oxygen make up 97%. Small amounts of water vapor, argon, carbon dioxide, neon, helium, and hydrogen make up the other 3%.

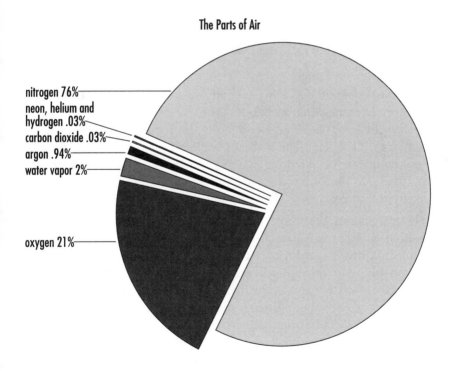

The Parts of Air

nitrogen 76%

neon, helium and hydrogen .03%

carbon dioxide .03%

argon .94%

water vapor 2%

oxygen 21%

The molecules that make up air are unimaginably tiny. A single ounce of air contains 1,000 billion, trillion atoms. The Earth's atmosphere contains a total of 1.6×10^{44} atoms, weighing 5,000 trillion tons. On average, each breath a person takes contains 8×10^{22} air particles. It has been calculated that if each particle in a single breath were the size of a grain of sand, there would be enough sand in a single exhale to cover the surface of the entire U.S. to the depth of an eight-story building!

ENERGY IN THE ATMOSPHERE

The amount of solar energy (insolation) received on a particular day at a place on the Earth is determined by the following factors:

- the *solar constant*, which depends upon the energy output of the Sun and the distance from Earth to the Sun;

- the transparency, or clearness, of the atmosphere;

- the duration of the sunlight period of the day;

- the angle at which the Sun's midday rays strike the location.

The solar constant actually isn't constant—it fluctuates slightly and may figure in some climate changes. The average solar constant for all points on the Earth is about two langleys (a langley is a gram-calorie per square centimeter). The distance between *aphelion* and *perihelion*—the points in the Earth's orbit at which it is farthest away and closest, respectively, to the Sun, results in about a 7% difference in the amount of sunlight that reaches the outer atmosphere.

The transparency of the atmosphere greatly affects the amount of insolation that reaches Earth's surface. Transparency also differs according to latitude—at higher latitudes sunlight has to pass through the atmosphere at more severe angles than in the tropics—and this makes the reflection and scattering of the rays more probable. The oblique rays of the low-angle Sun in winter are spread over a greater surface area and therefore produce less heating per unit area.

Duration of daylight also varies with latitude and season, and the longer the period of daylight, the greater the total insolation. The amount of insolation is also affected by the topography; the amount of sunlight can be greatly reduced in a valley surrounded by hills.

Earth is only large enough to intercept one two-billionths of the total energy given off by the Sun, and less than half of that actually reaches the surface. **Figure 7.5** shows that about a third of the incoming solar radiation is reflected into space by our clouds and atmospheric dust. Atmospheric gases, dust, and clouds themselves absorb about a fifth of the incoming energy, and another third is scattered and reflected by the atmosphere. Only about a fifth of the incoming radiation from the Sun directly strikes the Earth's surface and is absorbed, while another third is absorbed by the surface after having first been reflected. The absorbed energy is then reradiated into the the atmosphere, and it is this reradiated energy that heats the atmosphere nearest the Earth. The energy that reaches the surface through reflection and absorption is transformed from shortwave light to longwave infrared, or heat, radiation, which eventually warms the bottom portion of the troposphere. Weather is the mechanism by which this reradiated heat is moved from one place to another.

Four processes play a role in the distribution of heat energy through the atmosphere: **radiation, conduction, convection,** and **advection** (wind). The main source of warmth for the troposphere is the infrared energy that is absorbed, then reradiated from the Earth's surface. Some of this, about 20%, escapes back into space, but most is captured and held by water vapor, carbon dioxide, and other greenhouse gases such as methane.

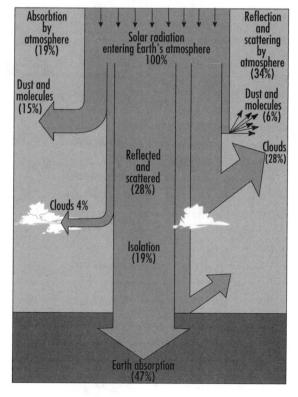

Figure 7.5 Solar energy entering the Earth's atmosphere is distributed in various ways as it encounters clouds, dust, gases, and the Earth's surface.

Absorbtion by atmosphere (19%)

Solar radiation entering Earth's atmosphere 100%

Reflection and scattering by atmosphere (34%)

Dust and molecules (15%)

Dust and molecules (6%)

Clouds (28%)

Reflected and scattered (28%)

Clouds 4%

Isolation (19%)

Earth absorption (47%)

Conduction is a process in which heat energy is transferred between two substances in contact with one another. This occurs because atmospheric and ground molecules come into contact, but it does not play a major role in moving heat throughout the atmosphere. The process of convection does play a major role, however. Convection occurs when heat is transferred by a circulating fluid (a fluid can be a liquid or a gas). Warm air rises, carrying heat energy higher into the atmosphere and displacing pockets of cooler air, which sink. Often there is a horizontal component to the rising and settling of these warm and cool air parcels, and this horizontal movement of air over the surface is called *advection*, or wind. Vertical and horizontal motions make up wheel-like convection cells, illustrated in **Figure 7.6**. The large and small-scale winds that are generated from imbalances between the rising and sinking air masses transfer heat energy around the Earth and create daily changes in the weather.

Figure 7.6 Warm masses of air rise and displace cooler, denser parcels of air, which sink. Air that moves horizontally in this process is called wind.

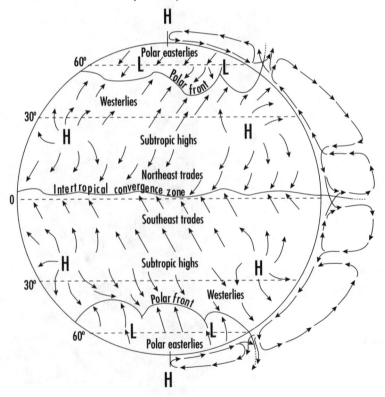

CHECK YOUR PROGRESS

1. Which of the following is NOT a major influence on weather and climate

   a. altitude
   b. topography
   c. longitude
   d. low- and high-pressure belts

2. The zone of low pressure on either side of the equator is known as

   a. the trades   **c.** the westerlies
   b. the doldrums   **d.** the easterlies

3. A cloudy sky in the summer

   a. makes the day warmer
   b. makes the day less humid
   c. prevents temperatures from falling at night
   d. makes the night cooler

4. A moisture-laden parcel of air moving up the slope of a mountain will

   a. expand, cool, and possibly produce precipitation
   b. contract, warm, and gain moisture
   c. expand and warm, leading to condensation
   d. contract and cool, leading to precipitation

5. The early Earth atmosphere probably did NOT contain

   a. carbon dioxide   **c.** hydrogen cyanide
   b. acetylene   **d.** oxygen

6. The layer in the Earth's atmosphere where the highest temperatures are reached is the

   a. thermosphere   **c.** stratosphere
   b. mesophere   **d.** troposphere

7. The reason the troposphere is warmest near the Earth's surface is because

   a. the air is most compressed there by the weight of the atmosphere
   b. the Earth's surface reradiates solar energy which heats the lower troposphere
   c. radioactive elements in the Earth's crust heat the atmosphere above the ground
   d. lightning strikes the surface which in turn heats the layer above

8. The region of the atmosphere which absorbs harmful ultra-violet radiation is the

   a. ionosphere
   b. heterosphere
   c. ozone layer
   d. thermosphere

9. The process of convection often involves replacement air flowing horizontally along the Earth's surface in a movement called

   a. conduction
   b. radiation
   c. circulation
   d. advection

10. Heat energy in the atmosphere is primarily redistributed around the atmosphere by means of

   a. convection cells
   b. conduction
   c. radiation
   d. the doldrums

AIR MASSES AND MOVEMENTS

On the whole, the air that makes up the atmosphere is quite stable. The predominant motion is a horizontal flowing; large air masses over the oceans and continents move horizontally at various speeds. An air mass may cover 16,000 kilometers horizontally without moving through more than just a few hundred meters vertically.

Vertical motions may occur in a variety of ways. The movement can be gradual, as occurs when moist air is lifted by a gradually sloping mass of underlying denser air. The movement also can be very abrupt, as occurs when rising thermals become thunderstorms. The instabilities that set off vertical motions in the atmosphere may be caused by any number of situations, including high level cooling, surface heating, or the sudden displacement of one air mass by another.

In general, the gases of the troposphere are circulated by winds caused by pressure imbalances that result from the uneven heating of the Earth's surface. Cooler, denser air masses are comparatively higher in pressure than warmer, less dense air masses. Advection occurs from areas of high to areas of low pressure. Also, the difference between the pressure of two air masses is called a *pressure gradient*, and the steeper the pressure gradient between two locations, the greater the wind generated between them.

Atmospheric pressure varies from place to place and with time, and decreases with increasing altitude, but not always at the same rate. The pressure at a place is determined by the mass of a column of air above it. Pressure also reflects the kinetic energy of the particles in the air, and is exerted in all directions. Pressure differences from place to place result mainly from temperature differences that affect the density of the air. Also, an increase in the amount of water vapor in air decreases its pressure, because water vapor is less dense than dry air.

Atmospheric scientists often refer to areas of high pressure as *ridges* and areas of low pressure as *troughs*. **Figure 7.7** illustrates the pressure and atmospheric circulation in the Northern Hemisphere. A similar pattern is found in the Southern Hemisphere. A region of low pressure, called the equatorial low, is found around the equator, where insolation is greatest. To the north of this is a high-pressure ridge called the *subtropical high*: Air descends to the subtropical high from as high up as the tropopause. North of this ridge is another low pressure area, the *subpolar low*, and above this is the *polar high*.

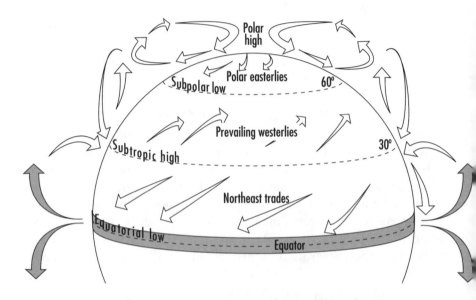

Figure 7.7 Global atmospheric circulation in the Northern Hemisphere. The ridge of subtropic high pressure generates a persistent wind system in the temperate zone: trade winds to the south and the prevailing westerlies to the north.

THE CORIOLIS EFFECT

Pressure gradients are not the only influence on motion in the atmosphere. The air that moves across the Earth's surface is also influenced by the Earth's rotation in a phenomenon called the **Coriolis effect**. The Coriolis effect can be thought of as an imaginary force that acts at right angles to the direction of the Earth. For instance, if you were in the middle latitudes of the Northern Hemisphere on a windless day and fired a rifle at a target about 150 meters away, the bullet would curve to right about a quarter of a centimeter. The curve of the path of a moving object like the bullet results from a rotating frame of reference. Different places on the Earth's surface move at different speeds as the Earth rotates; a location farthest from the axis of rotation moves a greater distance in the same amount of time and, therefore, moves faster. Quito, Ecuador moves east at about 1,600 kilometers per hour, while New York moves at 1,200 kilometers per hour, because it is at a higher latitude and is therefore closer to the Earth's axis.

The Coriolis effect influences anything that is in motion over the Earth's surface, including ocean currents. The most significant result of the Coriolis effect to us, however, is the weather. As air masses move from ridges to troughs, they take curved paths. This twist makes nearly all weather systems, such as storms, hurricanes, tornadoes, and low- and high-pressure systems, form in circular cells. High-pressure systems, or **anticyclones**, are expanding systems that form clockwise spirals in the Northern Hemisphere. Low-pressure systems (**cyclones**, hurricanes, tornadoes, and waterspouts) are contracting systems and always move counterclockwise in the Northern Hemisphere. If there were no Coriolis effect, there would be no storms. The Coriolis effect is weakest near the equator, which is a calm area of light winds mariners call the doldrums (see chapter 5).

CONSIDER THIS

Imagine a big bathtub full of water sitting in a house at the North Pole. Imagine the water is still when you pull the plug. Would you expect the water to go down the tub's drain in a particular way? As it drains out of the tub, the water will turn with the rotation of the Earth: counterclockwise. When you pull the plug, water at the edge of tub will move from the outside toward the center. As it does, the Earth's rotation underneath will cause it to drift slightly to one side, giving the water a counterclockwise spin. In the Southern Hemisphere, the reverse would occur. In an ordinary bathtub at your house, however, the Coriolis effect would provide a miniscule influence, which would be overcome by your sloshing around, your breath, the shape of your drainpipe, and so forth.

LOCAL INFLUENCES

There are also regional and local movements of air in the atmosphere. Topographic features such as mountains and valleys can affect the direction of surface winds. One of the most common local winds that develops where bodies of water and land areas are adjacent is the *sea breeze*. During the day, air moves from above cooler water, where denser air is descending, toward the warmer land, where less dense air is ascending. Conversely, after dark, because water loses heat more slowly than land, a seaward-flowing *land breeze* develops from the higher pressure over the rapidly cooling landmass. Another wind system that undergoes a daily reversal occurs in regions of mountains and valleys. At night, higher land loses heat more rapidly, cooling the air. This cool, dense air travels downslope, producing low night temperatures in valleys. On warm sunny days, the higher land is heated faster and generates an upslope flow of air called a *valley breeze*.

WINDS IN THE UPPER ATMOSPHERE

Jet streams are narrow bands of high-velocity winds in the upper troposphere near the tropopause. They follow giant, undulating paths around the Earth in the mid-latitudes. The position and extent of these flows are influenced by differential heating at the surface and by topographic features. These upper-atmosphere winds help to achieve a balance in the global circulation.

WATER IN THE ATMOSPHERE

Wind not only redistributes the heat from the Equator, it also moves moisture throughout the atmosphere. Air that comes into contact with the surface of the ocean and other bodies of water picks up evaporated moisture, and water can also be picked up from transpiring plants. An average sized tree releases some 120,000 liters of water each year, while an acre of corn transpires ten times this amount in a growing season.

On a breezy day, the rate of evaporation from a body of water is higher than it would be on a relatively windless day. The wind whisks away water vapor from above the liquid water, providing more space into which molecules can escape. The molecules that escape take heat energy with them, which cools the body of water. Try wetting your hand and then waving it in the air; it should feel cool. As the water evaporates, it removes some of the heat from your skin. This is why you feel cold when you come out of the pool or shower. Another example is the use of a hair dryer. You may have noticed that warm, fast-moving air evaporates the moisture from your hair. Energy is transferred to the water molecules in your hair, and this allows them to escape into the atmosphere more quickly.

At any one time, only a tiny fraction of the Earth's water—about 0.001 percent—is stored as clouds and vapor in the atmosphere.

The amount of water vapor the atmosphere can hold depends on the temperature of the air. The higher the temperature, the more water the atmosphere can hold. The amount of water vapor in the atmosphere is called the **humidity**, and it can vary greatly. Rain forests are usually quite high in humidity, while deserts have the least humid climates. The water vapor in the atmosphere can make up as much as 4% of its total volume, or be almost nonexistent. (Note that **relative humidity** is a different thing. It refers to the percentage of water vapor in the local atmosphere compared to the maximum that can be held by the atmosphere at that temperature. Thus the air on a muggy summer day might be at 90 to 100% relative humidity.)

At any given temperature, the amount of water vapor that a given unit or parcel of atmosphere can hold is limited. When a parcel of air is holding its capacity of water vapor it is said to be *saturated*. If a parcel of saturated air is cooled, the amount of water vapor it can hold decreases. If this happens, the extra water vapor *condenses* into very small droplets of water, and in this condensation process, it releases heat. Meteorologists have a term for this heat, **latent heat of vaporization**.

As you probably know, **condensation** is the process in which a gas changes into a liquid. If water vapor condenses above the ground, clouds and fog are formed. If the condensation occurs at the surface, *dew* and *frost* are formed. Dew is the water that appears, for instance, on the outside of a cold glass of soda on a hot summer day. The temperature at which water vapor begins to condense is called the **dew point**. The relative humidity of an air parcel at its dew point is 100%.

Dew point varies depending on the amount of water vapor present in the air and the air temperature. Water vapor begins to condense out of the air when the temperature falls to the saturation point. This often happens at night, after the heat absorbed by the ground during the day has been radiated. The air above the ground drops to the dew point temperature and dew or frost forms, the latter if the temperature drops so low that the water vapor changes directly from a gas to a solid. Air masses that have high relative humidity require only slight cooling to reach their dew points.

Water vapor that condenses above the ground often condenses on miniscule particles that are present in the air, called *condensation nuclei*. These can be salt particles from the ocean, or dust and smoke or any other type of particles. The water vapor that condenses around these particles forms fog or clouds.

Fog is basically a cloud at the ground level, but fogs and clouds are produced in different ways. Clouds form because rising air parcels expand with altitude; a parcel of air might rise because it passes over a hot surface, because it moves upward to pass over a mountain, or because it is lifted when a wedge of cooler, denser air pushes underneath it. The parcel of air expands because atmospheric pressure decreases with altitude, and in its expansion, the temperature of the parcel cools and the parcel's capacity for holding water vapor decreases. When the temperature of the parcel falls to its dew point, the excess water vapor condenses out, forming clouds.

CLOUD TYPES

A cloud is physically an *aerosol*—a suspension of water droplets or ice crystals and other particles in air. Clouds are classified on the basis of their altitude and relative stability. The most stable, or long-lasting, forms are the stratified clouds, the stratus, nimbostratus, altostratus, and cirrostratus. The low clouds are the stratus, nimbostratus, and stratocumulus. Nimbostratus are layered, rain-bearing clouds. They range from the surface to about 2 kilometers above sea level. The middle clouds are the altostratus and altocumulus. They occur from about 2 kilometers to about 6 kilometers. The high clouds are cirrus, cirrostratus, and cirrocumulus. Cirrus are wispy clouds of ice crystals, while cirrocumulus clouds form a pattern resembling fish scales and known as a "mackeral sky." They extend to a height of about 15 kilometers.

There are also clouds that develop vertically. Cumulus and cumulonimbus clouds can begin as low as 300 meters and may extend to the top of the troposphere. There are also clouds outside the troposphere, clouds that don't play a role in weather. *Nacreous* and *noctilucent* clouds occur in and above the stratosphere. Nacreous clouds range at an altitude of between 21 and 30 kilometers and noctilucent clouds at between 75 and 90 kilometers.

When clouds form, water vapor may condense out of the air to form water droplets, and these may further cool to form ice. But the vapor can also condense directly into ice crystals, and these ice crystals can serve as condensation nuclei upon which more vapor condenses. As more and more vapor molecules pile up, a snow crystal is born. Ice crystals usually freeze into the six-sided shape of hexagons because of the water molecule's structure and electrical charge. The intricate details of snow crystals arise from variations in the temperature and humidity in the cloud.

Condensation nuclei may accumulate water molecules past the point where the air's buoyancy can support them. When the resulting snow crystal or water drop falls, **precipitation** is the result. Precipitation can be rain, drizzle, sleet, hail, or snow—it qualifies as long as it falls from the atmosphere to the ground. The various kinds of precipitation form in complex, different ways that still are not completely understood by scientists. The mean annual precipitation for the Earth is about 86 centimeters, but local amounts vary greatly from place to place.

The processes of evaporation, condensation, and precipitation contribute to the **water**, or **hydrologic cycle**. The hydrological cycle can be depicted in a particular region, as is illustrated in **Figure 7.8**, or it can be thought of as a global pattern.

CONSIDER THIS

Is it possible for two snow crystals to be identical? Certainly two could be very similar, but each crystal contains many trillions of water molecules that can be arranged in different ways. So, the real question is, why *would* any two be alike?

Figure 7.8 Processes such as evaporation, transpiration, condensation, and precipitation make up the hydrologic cycle. The entire contents of the ocean are cycled through this system every two million years.

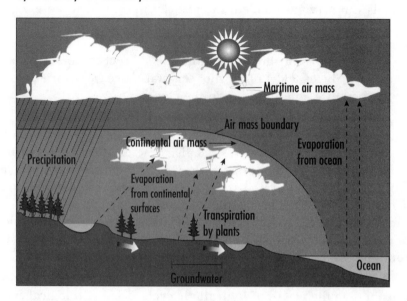

CHECK YOUR PROGRESS

11. The process by which water evaporates from plants is called

    a. transpiration   **c.** exhalation
    b. advection   **d.** vapor release

12. During a sunny summer day at the beach, the breeze is most likely to come from

    a. the south, near the equator
    b. the north, from the poles
    c. the sea, toward land
    d. the land, toward the sea

13. In the Northern Hemisphere, as a result of the Coriolis effect

    a. hurricanes spin clockwise
    b. high pressure systems form counterclockwise spirals
    c. contracting storm systems like tornadoes turn counterclockwise
    d. all weather systems rotate from the left to the right

14. If the atmospheric pressure at site A is 1,025 millibars while the pressure at site B is 1,005 m illibars, the pressure gradient will produce wind that

   a. flows parallel to the ridge and trough
   b. flows from site A toward site B
   c. flows from site B toward site A
   d. spiral to the left back toward site A

15. The most variable constituent of the atmosphere is

   a. nitrogen   c. oxygen
   b. carbon dioxide   d. water vapor

16. A parcel of air that contains one-half its capacity of water vapor is said to have a relative humidity of

   a. 200%   c. 100%
   b. 150%   d. 50%

17. A parcel of air in the atmosphere might rise to a higher elevation as the result of

   a. passing over a hot surface
   b. being pushed over a mountain
   c. being lifted by a cold, dense air mass
   d. all of the above

18. In the process of evaporation, liquid water molecules become

   a. molecules of water vapor
   b. tiny drops of water
   c. separate atoms of water
   d. atoms of hydrogen and oxygen

19. Water evaporates most readily under the following conditions

   a. hot, dry, and still
   b. hot and muggy with a lot of wind
   c. hot and dry with a lot of wind
   d. cold, wet, and still

20. The relative humidity of a parcel of air is likely to be greatest over

   a. tropical oceans   **c.** plains
   b. mountians   **d.** desert

21. The formation of fog generally occurs after the ground has lost heat by

   a. transpiration   **c.** radiation
   b. advection   **d.** evaporation

22. Which is NOT a form of precipitation:

   a. drizzle   **c.** sleet
   b. hai   **d.** frost

WEATHER PHENOMENA

An air mass is a portion of the atmosphere in which the temperature and moisture are relatively uniform. Air masses develop when large sections of air rest for a period of time over land or water areas, called *source regions*, that have fairly uniform surface conditions. Under certain conditions, an air mass over a source region will retain its characteristics when it moves away, changing only gradually in response to new surface conditions.

The temperature and humidity conditions from the bottom to top of the air mass determine its degree of stability. For example, an air mass with more cold, dry air at the bottom than at the top is relatively stable. Certain conditions reinforce this stability. Night time radiation from the surface makes such air masses even more stable. Stable air generally produces fair weather.

In the tropical and polar latitudes, air masses tend to develop and diverge away from their source regions. Consequently, in the middle latitudes, general circulation of the atmosphere results in the convergence of dissimilar air masses. When air masses that are different temperatures and humidities converge they do not mix at once, but tend to retain their boundaries for some time. Eventually, warmer, less dense air tends to be forced over colder air. The borders or surfaces between air masses are called **fronts**. Frontal boundaries can be as limited as 2 to 3 kilometers, or as extensive as 50 kilometers across.

Figure 7.9 illustrates the typical interaction of converging cold and warm fronts. In the diagram, the cold air mass pushes toward the south and under the warm air, which moves northward. Convergence and rising air along the front is accompanied by a decrease in pressure, which is why cyclones are called *lows*, or *depressions*. The pattern of air flow takes on a counterclockwise (*cyclonic*) circulation as the pressure gradient is focused toward the center. The Coriolis effect deflects the air toward the right as it moves toward the low center (it would do the opposite in the Southern Hemisphere, producing a clockwise circulation). The *warm front* is the boundary at which the advancing warm air mass is replacing colder air at the surface, and the *cold front* is to the west. Air is forced to rise when these air masses interact, and cloudiness and precipitation are often the result of this.

Mid-latitude cyclones usually travel in groups from west to east. They are circular or elongated in shape and generally have a diameter that ranges from 200 to 3,000 kilometers, though most are in-between. A typical cyclone moves at a speed of 800 to over 1,000 kilometers per day (usually moving faster in winter than in summer), and persists as long as the differences in temperature and humidity along its fronts are maintained.

Cyclones are systems in which low pressure is at the center, which causes winds to blow inward. Anticyclones, or high pressure systems, work the opposite way; pressure is highest at their centers and decreases outward. Thus, the anticyclonic wind system blows out from the center and circulates clockwise in the Northern Hemisphere (because of the Coriolis effect).

Figure 7.9 The stages in the development of a mid-latitude cyclone following the convergence of cold and warm fronts. The cold front finally overtakes the warm front, producing an occlusion. The cyclone eventually dissipates.

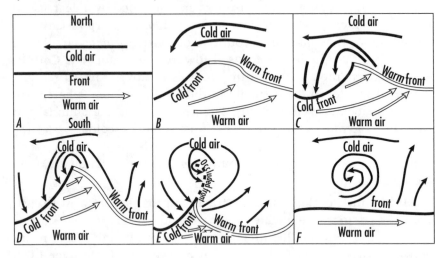

Overall, the convergence of air masses produces one of three outcomes:

1. the more dense air mass moves underneath the less dense one;

2. the lighter air mass overrides the more dense mass;

3. the two air masses remain distinct until a gradual mixing occurs.

These outcomes produce four kinds of fronts. In addition to the cold and warm fronts already discussed, there exists the *stationary front*—which is the boundary between two relatively motionless air masses, and the *occluded front*—which is formed when a warm air mass has been lifted entirely off the ground surface by an advancing cold air mass. The lifting of the warm air mass results in large-scale condensation and precipitation.

THUNDERSTORMS

Thunderstorms are caused by unstable air and vertical air motion, which produce cumulonimbus clouds. The storm's energy comes from the heat released as water condenses in rising air. A cumulonimbus cloud is a turbulent mix of particles that ranges from tiny droplets of supercooled rainwater, to ice crystals, to huge hailstones (even in the summer, the air in the upper troposphere is cold enough to freeze water). The particles most likely to lead to the formation of lightning are pea-sized pellets called *graupel*. They form when droplets of *supercooled water* (water that remains liquid at temperatures well below 0° Celsius) collide, freezing together instantly. Ice crystals then bounce off the graupel, building up charges from the friction just as you can build up static electric charges by scuffling your feet across a carpet on a dry day. The charged crystals and graupel are carried by air currents and gravity to different parts of the cloud, resulting in the separation of positively and negatively charged particles; usually the upper levels of the cloud become positively charged and the lower parts negatively charged. What happens next is like what happens to you after scuffling across the rug when you touch a doorknob: A current of electrons forms a spark from the negatively charged object (you) to the positively charged doorknob.

Lightning may occur horizontally from cloud to cloud, vertically between levels in a cloud, or from the cloud to the ground. The lightning bolt itself is an electrical discharge, which is a sudden surge of electrons. A lightning bolt is usually 5 to 6 kilometers long, but only a few centimeters in diameter. The average current in a lightning stroke is about 10,000 amperes; this flow of electrons heats the air as high as 30,000° Celsius, which is hotter than the surface of the sun. Thunder is the explosive sound that follows lightning, and is caused when heated air suddenly expands then rapidly cools and contracts.

Lightning comes in many forms: forked (multiple branches), streak (single jagged line), ribbon (parallel streaks created when wind separates the strokes of a flash), chain (a flash that breaks up into a dotted line), heat (which is too far away to hear thunder), sheet (distinct flashes too far away to be seen but the sky is illuminated), and ball (occurs rarely, floats for several seconds). Lightning strikes the Earth about 6,000 times a minute. Every year in the U.S., lightning strikes an average of a thousand people, killing more people annually than all of the tornadoes and hurricanes combined. A car provides good shelter from lightning because its metal shell makes a path for lightning to the ground (but if you are inside a car, don't touch the metal parts during a storm). If you are in your house during a thunderstorm, avoid using the phone or plumbing and electrical equipment, as the metal parts in these systems conduct electricity.

There is a simple way to judge your distance from lightning. When you see the flash, count the seconds until you hear the bang of the thunder. Three seconds is equal to a kilometer of distance (5 seconds represents a mile). For example, a flash 5 kilometers away takes 15 seconds for the sound of the thunder to reach the observer.

HURRICANES AND TORNADOES

Hurricanes are violent cyclones that only occur in the summer or early autumn and originate over tropical oceans, generally 5° to 10° from the equator. Hurricanes are generally 150 to 1,000 kilometers in diameter and typically move at 15 to 30 kilometers per hour. A hurricane's size and rate of movement are not related to its intensity or its internal wind speed. There may be a calm "eye" at the storm's center into which clear, warm air is descending, but the eye is surrounded by torrential rain and powerful, destructive winds. Internal wind speed must be at least 65 knots (33 meters per second) for a storm to be classified as a hurricane, and speeds over 130 knots have been recorded.

Some meteorologists believe hurricane numbers and intensities fluctuate over a long-term cycle. They calculate that the last several decades of the twentieth century represent a lull in the hurricane activity cycle, and that there should be a return in the next several decades to a more active phase of the cycle.

The most dangerous and violent storms on the planet are **tornadoes**. A tornado is a long, funnel-shaped cloud that emerges from an area of severe thunderstorms. It is a tight vortex that gyrates around a center of extremely low pressure and is accompanied by winds that reach speeds of over 320 kilometers per hour. Tornadoes can cause the air pressure outside a building to drop so sharply that the normal pressure inside the building pushes the walls outward with enough force to break them.

Fortunately, most tornadoes are only a few hundred meters in diameter at the ground, though diameters of up to 5 kilometers have been recorded. In North America, the regions that produce the most tornadoes are the Mississippi Valley and the interior plains, where frequent collisions occur between cold, dry air masses from Canada and warm, moist air masses from the Gulf of Mexico. At sea, tornadoes become *waterspouts*, which tend to be smaller in diameter but are similar in most other ways.

One of the most destructive natural disasters in U.S. history was Hurricane Andrew, which hit Dade County, Florida in late August, 1992 and went on to ravage Louisiana. Hurricane Andrew had winds that were recorded at 265 kilometers per hour, but may have exceeded 320 kilometers per hour. In terms of overall power, the National Hurricane Center assigned the storm the highest ranking, a *Level 5*. Some two dozen people died in the storm; the hurricane's devastation cost over $20 billion, with more than 60,000 homes severely damaged, and a quarter of a million people displaced.

FORECASTING THE WEATHER

For thousands of years people have been observing and forecasting the weather. These forecasts, however, were based on local sensory impressions. People did not begin using instruments to measure the properties of the atmosphere until after the seventeenth century, and scientific weather forecasting did not become truly useful until the mid-1800s, after the invention of the telegraph. The telegraph made it possible for meteorologists to know about the weather at a distance. The first government weather forecasts were issued in 1870 by the Army, and in 1891 the United States Weather Bureau was created. Later this agency was renamed the National Weather Service and it is now part of the National Oceanic and Atmospheric Administration (NOAA).

At regular intervals throughout the course of the day, weather stations record the local temperature, atmospheric pressure, change in pressure, precipitation, humidity, dew point, cloud type and amount of cover, visibility, ceiling, and wind direction and speed. Data from each local weather station is then transmitted so that it can be compiled and compared with data from other stations. Some properties of the atmosphere and the instruments that are used to measure them are listed in **Table 7.1**.

Weather surveillance satellites, which were first launched in the 1960s, have made it possible for us to detect weather systems as they begin. Since the 1940s, *radar* has been an important tool for meteorologists. Radar is used to measure the distance from the observer to precipitation areas and to detect and track severe weather systems such as thunderstorms, hurricanes, and tornadoes.

The *wind chill equivalent temperature*—often just referred to as the wind chill—tells you the temperature that you will *feel* outside, with the wind at the current speed, and the present temperature. The formula used by weather forecasters is based on the rate at which heat is lost by a bottle of water exposed to winds of various speeds and temperatures, but this really isn't a measure of how cold or hot a person might *feel*. *Feeling* a temperature really depends on humidity as well as the temperature and wind speed. However, in the middle latitude's winters, the wind chill index has become a popular way to communicate the day's weather picture.

The most common method for forecasting the weather makes use of weather maps and is called **synoptic forecasting**. At thousands of weather stations all over the world, weather observations are made four times a day at the same times. Forecasters then use a sequence of *synoptic charts*, or weather maps, that summarize the total weather picture at the given time. By applying what is known about the regular patterns of motion in the atmosphere, trends are deduced and used to project future weather.

Another method of forecasting the weather is **statistical forecasting**. In this method, meteorologists use mathematical equations based upon the past behavior of the atmosphere. Forecasters also work from mathematical models that are based upon the physical laws of fluid dynamics that describe the atmosphere's behavior.

Until the 1960s, weather maps were drawn by hand, but now maps are drawn by computers and used to predict temperature, humidity, and wind patterns for many levels of the atmosphere. Statistical methods are then used to map the likely minimum and maximum temperatures and precipitation.

Table 7.1. Some quantifiable properties of weather and the instruments and units to measure them.

Property	Instruments for measuring	Unit of measurement
Temperature	thermometer thermograph	degrees Celsius (° C) degrees Fahrenheit (° F)
Humidity	psychrometer hydrometer hydrograph	percent grains grams
Pressure	mercurial barometer aneroid barometer barograph	millibars inches of mercury
Precipitation	rain gauge tipping bucket	millimeters or centimeters inches
Wind	anemometer wind vane	compass direction/ meters per second/ knots miles per hour

An important aspect of weather forecasting is the prediction of the movement of fronts. The activity associated with fronts generally determines a locality's weather pattern. **Figure 7.10** shows a simplified weather map with high- and low-pressure systems and fronts charted.

Technology has provided us with new and better instruments to measure, record, and communicate data about the atmosphere, from the ground to its outer reaches, but accurate long-range forecasting is as elusive a goal as ever. The problem is that the atmosphere is a *chaotic system*, so that forecasts of weather patterns are useful for only about 6 or 7 days.

FYI

Benjamin Franklin was among the first ever to record data about large-scale patterns in the weather. As Postmaster General of the United States, he noticed that storms tend to move from place to place. From his own observations and from information about storms in letters he received from afar, he realized that weather systems pass over areas in succession.

Figure 7.10 A simple weather map might be found in a daily newspaper. With some knowledge of underlying patterns, such as the west to east flow of mid-latitude weather, you can use the newspaper map to predict weather changes yourself.

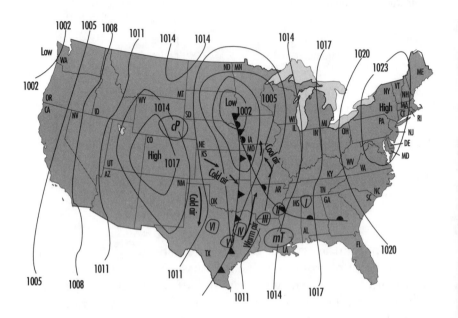

CLIMATE

Different combinations of atmospheric processes produce the different climates of Earth. A climate type is called a *climatic region* because a relatively uniform set of climatic conditions usually prevails through the area. It is important to note that the value of any classification system is dependent upon its intended use. Thus, some classification systems are more suitable for use by biologists, while others are suitable for use by weather forecasters.

The distribution of climate types is mainly based upon heat and moisture factors. The following categories are based upon the interchange of heat and moisture between the ground and the overlying air masses:

I. Climates dominated by equatorial and tropical air masses

    1. Rainy tropics (examples: Amazon Basin, Philippines)

2. Monsoon tropics (examples: west coast of India, east coast of Viet Nam)

3. Wet-and-dry tropics (examples: northern Australia, western Central America)

4. Tropical arid (desert) climate (examples: southwestern US, Sahara)

5. Tropical semiarid climate (examples: coast of Peru, lower California and Sonora)

II. Climates dominated by tropical and polar air masses

6. Dry summer subtropics (examples: Mediterranean, central California)

7. Humid subtropics (examples: southeastern US, Taiwan and southern Japan)

8. Marine climate (examples: Oregon and Washington, Britain, New Zealand)

9. Mid-latitude arid climate (examples: Nevada, southern Russia, northern China)

10. Mid-latitude semiarid climate (examples: Colorado, western and southern Argentina)

11. Humid continental warm summer climate (examples: Kansas, Danube basin in Europe)

12. Humid continental cool summer climate (examples: New England, southern Scandinavia)

III. Climates dominated by polar and arctic-type air masses

13. Taiga (also called *subarctic* or *boreal forest*; examples: western Alaska, parts of Newfoundland and Norway)

14. Tundra (north of taiga; examples: arctic coasts of Canada, Russia, a few islands in the Antarctic Ocean)

15. Polar climate (examples: Greenland, Antarctica)

IV. Climates in which altitude is the dominant factor

16. Highland climates (examples: Cascade-Sierra Nevada and Rockies in North America, Alps, Andies, Himalayas, Eastern Highlands of Africa)

This classification system is represented graphically in **Figure 7.11**. There are other classification systems that emphasize criteria in addition to heat and moisture.

Figure 7.11. Graph of temperature versus precipitation showing position of various climate types.

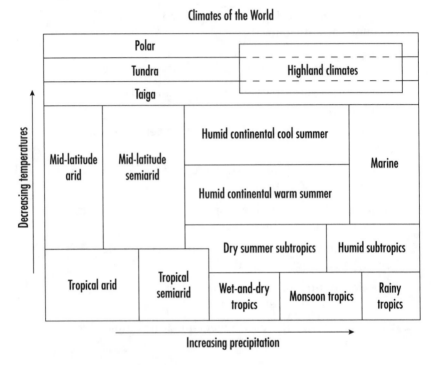

Climates of the World

What are the factors involved in determining the climate? Well, one factor relates to the distribution of land and sea, and this factor varies according to the movements of the Earth's crustal plates (see chapter 2). Currently, the Northern Hemisphere has most of the Earth's land mass, and if summers in the north are warm enough to melt the snow cover each year, ice sheets do not grow, but if they are not warm enough, snow and ice will be left over to further accumulate the next year, and glaciers will advance.

The level of warmth in the north is dependent on many variables, but a major contributing factor is the tilt of the Earth's axis. The Earth has not always been situated at an angle of 23.5°; its inclination varies over a 41,000 year cycle, and ranges between 22° and 28°.

Another variable that affects climate and is related to the Earth's rotation is what's called the 26,000 year *precession cycle* (see chapter nine). The Northern Hemisphere now tips toward the Sun in June, but in 13,000 years, the north will be tilted away from the Sun in June. When this happens, the characteristics of winter will be experienced in June in North America.

Another long-term pattern that affects climate is the periodic change in the shape of the Earth's orbit. The shape changes in a cycle of about 93,000 years, and the shape of the orbit becomes more, and then less elliptical.

All of the factors discussed above also interact with each other to enhance and inhibit weather trends, and influence the climate, and these are just a few of the many variables that influence climate change. For humans, stability in the climate is highly desirable, because many of our activities, particularly agriculture, would be greatly affected by any long-term shift in climate.

CHECK YOUR PROGRESS

23. A warm and humid air mass that moves over a warm surface is likely to

   a. remain stable, producing fair weather
   b. become more unstable, producing vertical air movement and precipitation
   c. develop subsidence and divergence, reinforcing its stability
   d. contract, increasing its rate of spin

24. Increasing the moisture in the lower layers of an air mass and adding heat energy will

   a. increase the stability of the air mass
   b. create instability
   c. cause the upper layers of air to subside
   d. create a strong horizontal air movement

25. The ability of meteorologists to forecast the weather appears mainly to be limited by

    a. the number and accuracy of synoptic observations
    b. the quality of instrumentation
    c. the power of computers
    d. the effects of chaos in the atmospheric system

26. The temperature and moisture content at a given altitude within an air mass are

    a. generally uniform throughout
    b. different between the edge and the center
    c. different in different parts of the air mass
    d. uniform or different, depending upon the time of day

27. If you hear a clap of thunder thirty seconds after seeing a flash of lightning, the distance between you and the lightning is about

    a. 90 kilometers   c. 10 kilometers
    b. 60 kilometers   d. 3 kilometers

28. Which type of cloud would be most likely associated with tornadoes?

    a. cumulus   c. stratus
    b. cumulonimbus   d. noctilucent

29. With current technology, the weather generally cannot be accurately forecast past about

    a. two weeks   c. two months
    b. one week   d. one month

30. Which of the following changes occur on a cyclical basis over time

    a. the position of the Northern Hemisphere relative to the Sun in a given month
    b. the angle of the Earth's tilt
    c. the shape of the Earth's orbit
    d. all of the above

GLOSSARY

advection—horizontally moving air, or wind.

air mass—a vast body of air exhibiting broadly similar properties throughout, particularly surface temperature and humidity.

anticyclones—an area where the atmospheric pressure is high relative the surrounding areas; a high pressure system producing a downward and outward flow of air (in the Northern Hemisphere, a clockwise circulation of air).

climate—the aggregate of the weather of a place over time, or the long-range state of the atmosphere.

condensation—the process by which a gas changes into a liquid.

conduction—the transfer of energy by two objects in contact.

convection—the vertical transfer of energy by a moving fluid.

Coriolis effect—an imaginary force which affects any body moving on a rotating surface, which acts at right angles to the body's direction of motion. It is really due to inertia.

cyclone—a low-pressure system producing an upward and inward flow of air (in the Northern Hemisphere, a counterclockwise circulation of air. The term is also used to designate a storm-like movement and also a severe type of tropical storm, like a hurricane.

dew point—the temperature to which air which is at a given pressure which has a given water vapor content must be lowered for saturation to occur. At this temperature due or frost will form.

evaporation—the process by which a liquid changes into a gas.

front—formed when air masses collide, the sloping boundary surfaces between contrasting air masses.

heterosphere—based upon composition, the outer, less-dense layer of the atmosphere where gases are relatively unmixed.

homosphere—based upon composition, the lower, denser layer of the atmosphere where gases are mixed. The homosphere extends from sea-level to about 80 kilometers.

humidity—the amount of water vapor in the atmosphere.

hydrologic cycle—a recurrent process moving water into and out of the atmosphere though living things, rocks, soils and standing bodies of water.

insolation—incoming solar radiation.

ionosphere—the electrified region of the atmosphere.

jet stream—a high speed current of air which typically flows from west to east in a wave like motion at altitudes of between 16 and 24 kilometers.

latent heat of vaporization—the energy required to evaporate water.

mesosphere—a region of the atmosphere above the stratosphere. Most of the ozone in the atmosphere is created here. The ionosphere is just above.

ozone layer—the layer of the upper atmosphere where most atmospheric ozone is concentrated—about 12 to 24 kilometers above the Earth.

photosynthesis—the process by which green plants convert carbon dioxide, water, and sunlight into carbohydrates, producing oxygen as a byproduct.

precipitation—water in liquid or solid form falling to the Earth.

relative humidity—the ratio between the amount of water vapor in the atmosphere and the highest amount of water vapor the air at that temperature could possibly hold.

stratosphere—based upon temperature, the layer of the atmosphere above the troposphere and below the mesosphere, in which the temperature rises with altitude.

statistical forecasting—a method of weather forecasting using mathematical equations based upon past behavior of the atmosphere.

synoptic forecasting—a method of weather forecasting based upon a summary of the total weather conditions at a given time. Synoptic literally "means to see at the same time"—the global pattern is constructed from observations taken at the same time.

thermosphere—The region of the atmosphere above the mesopause in which temperature increases with height.

tropics—either of two parallels of latitude, one 23° 27" north (tropic of Cancer) of the equator and one 23° 27" to its south (tropic of Capricorn). These are the two points farthest north and south that the Sun ever shines directly overhead.

troposphere—based upon temperature, the lowest layer of the atmosphere, the zone of weather.

weather—the state of the atmosphere at a particular time over any place on the Earth's surface.

wind—the movement of air parallel to the Earth's surface.

ANSWER KEY

1. c	11. a	21. c
2. b	12. c	22. d
3. c	13. c	23. b
4. a	14. b	24. b
5. d	15. d	25. d
6. a	16. d	26. a
7. b	17. d	27. c
8. c	18. a	28. b
9. d	19. b	29. b
10. a	20. a	30. d

8

The Exosphere: The Contexts of Space-time

> "I realize that Being is surrounded east, south, north and west, above and below, by wonder. Within that frame, like a little house in strange, cold, vast and beautiful scenery, is life upon this planet, of which life I am a temporary speck and impression. There is interest beyond measure within that house....Nevertheless at times one finds an urgency to go out and gaze at those enigmatical immensities."
>
> H. G. Wells.

THE SOLAR SYSTEM

Our solar system consists of the Sun, the nine planets, fifty or so moons, and numerous meteoroids, asteroids, comets, and particles of gas and dust. **Figure 8.1** illustrates some of the members of the Solar System. **Figure 8.2** illustrates the Milky Way Galaxy and shows the location of the Sun and Solar System. We cruise with the whole Solar System in a giant orbit around the galactic center. Our velocity is approximately 769,600 kilometers per hour, but even at that incredible speed, one complete orbit takes 250 million years. The last time we were situated in the Galaxy where we are now was in the Mesozoic era; the age of the dinosaurs!

Figure 8.1 The Solar System. The position of the planets can be remembered with a mnemonic, such as, My Very Extravagant Mother Just Served Us Nine Pizzas.

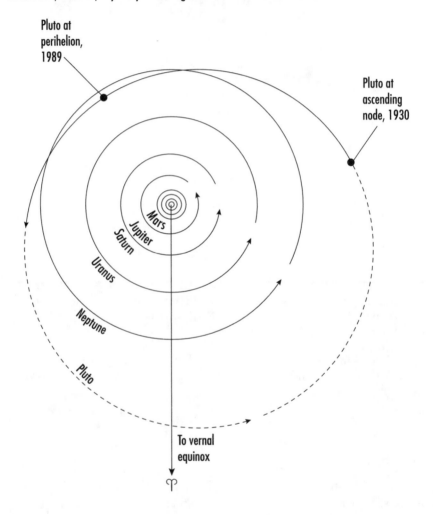

Figure 8.2 The Milky Way is about 100,000 light years in diameter and 10,000 light years thick. The Solar System is situated in the Orion Arm, about 25,000 light years from the galactic core.

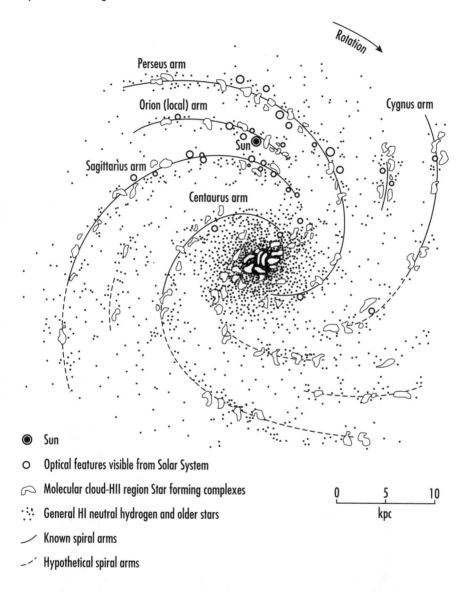

Sun

○ Optical features visible from Solar System

Molecular cloud-HII region Star forming complexes

General HI neutral hydrogen and older stars

Known spiral arms

Hypothetical spiral arms

One of the most recent surprises in astronomy was the discovery in 1996 of an icy miniplanet orbiting the Sun way out beyond Pluto in a zone called the **Kuiper Belt**. First seen by a University of Hawaii telescope and dubbed 1996TL66, the little planet has a surface area as large as Texas, with a diameter of about 480 kilometers. It revolves around the Sun once every 800 years and, at its most distant, its oblong orbit extends three times farther from the Sun than Pluto's. This miniplanet is the largest of about forty objects discovered since 1992 in the Kuiper Belt. Astronomers think that 1996TL66 is composed of the same materials as are the other objects in the outer Solar System—water, carbon dioxide, methane, and other gases—but these materials are all solidly frozen.

The Kuiper Belt, an iceberg reservoir, begins past the orbit of Neptune at about 35 to 40 **astronomical units** and stretches to a thousand AU (an astronomical unit, or AU, is the average distance between the earth and the Sun: about 150 million kilometers). **Figure 8.3** illustrates the scale of the Kuiper Belt to the Solar System. The Kuiper Belt is believed to contain anywhere from 100 million to as many as 10 billion comets. In addition to the miniplanet 1996TL66, ground-based telescopes have seen twenty-seven objects that are in the range of 100 kilometers in diameter, which is much larger than the comets that typically penetrate the inner Solar System.

Figure 8.3 The Kuiper Belt of comets in the Solar System.

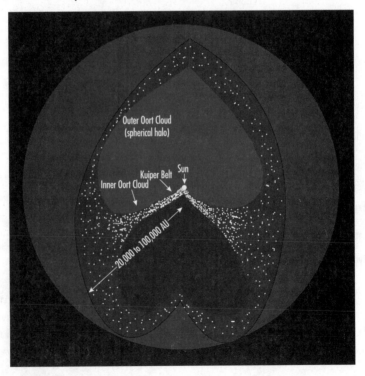

Beyond the Kuiper Belt is relatively empty space that extends for several thousand AU to the **Oort Cloud**, which contains an estimated 20 trillion or so comets. The inner Oort Cloud begins as a disk and, in a few thousand AU, expands to a complete spherical shell surrounding the Solar System (see **Figure 8.4**). At about 20,000 AU the inner merges with the outer Oort Cloud, which continues to a distance of 100,000 AU.

Figure 8.4 The Oort Cloud in the outer Solar System is a reservoir of trillions of comets.

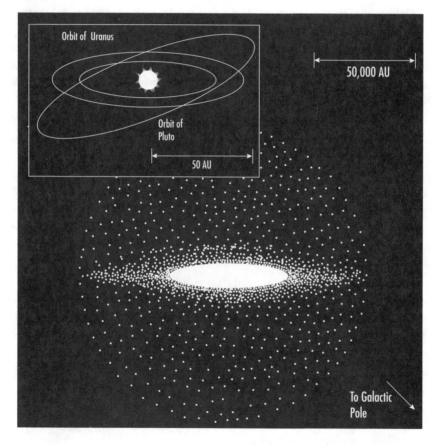

COMETS, ASTEROIDS, AND METEOROIDS

It seems likely that the impact of a comet on Earth caused the demise of the dinosaurs and many other species of animals and plants 65 million years ago. But comets also may have figured in the origin of life. Hundreds of thousands of carbon-rich comets rained on early Earth, providing both water for the earth's oceans and organic molecules to form the "primordial soup" out of which life most likely rose nearly 4 billion years ago. Numerous small, undetected comets continue to plow into the earth's atmosphere, bringing significant amounts of water and space dust to our planet.

Other objects in space include **asteroids** and **meteoroids**. Asteroids are rocky and most orbit the Sun inside the orbit of Jupiter. They number in the thousands and can be more than 700 kilometers in diameter. Most astronomers believe that asteroids are fragments that never accreted to planetary status, but another view is that they represent disintegrated planets.

In 1996, the carrot-shaped asteroid Toutatis, which is nearly 5 kilometers by 3 kilometers in size, passed within just over 5 million kilometers of Earth. Toutatis' orbit brings it near Earth every four years. In 1992, it came even closer: within 3.2 million kilometers, and it is projected that on September 29, 2004, Toutatis will cross by less than 1.6 million kilometers away from us. Objects whose orbits bring them relatively close to Earth are called *near-Earth objects* (NEOs). About 400 NEOs have been identified and tracked, of which over 200 regularly cross Earth's orbit.

Meteoroids are rocky or metallic bodies that intersect the orbits of Earth and other planets. Those that fall through the atmosphere toward us become fiery **meteors**. If the meteoroid survives its fall through the atmosphere and hits Earth, it is called a **meteorite**. Some meteorites have been found to contain carbon.

THE PLANETS AND THEIR MOONS

To most people, the most familiar objects in the Solar System are the planets and their moons. **Figure 8.5** shows the relative sizes of the planets and Earth's Moon.

Figure 8.5 The relative sizes of the planets and Earth's Moon.

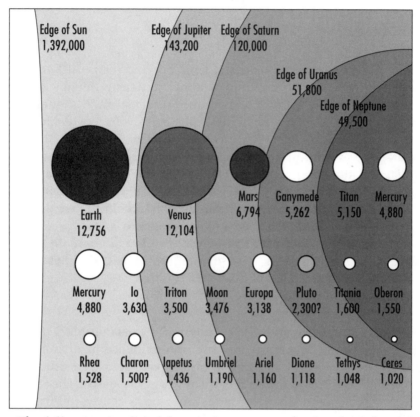

The following is a brief descriptive paragraph of each of the eight other planets in our Solar System.

MERCURY

The Scorched Planet—the second smallest of the planets and closest to the Sun. Mercury has an ancient, heavily cratered surface which resembles the Moon's, with huge cliffs (scarps) that crisscross the planet for hundreds of kilometers. The interior may have cooled and shrank, compressing the crust. Temperatures recorded by Mariner 10 ranged from 510 °C to –210 °C. Mercury's years are short (88 Earth days), but days and nights are long with a rotation period that lasts 58.6 Earth days. Mercury's crust seems to be a light, silicate rock, like Earth's. In 1991, astronomers bounced radio pulses off Mercury to discover ice at the poles. Mercury is the only planet that has no tilt to its axis so its poles never face the Sun. It has a weak magnetic field, evidence that it has or had a liquid core. The surface gravity is 0.39 times that of Earth. Multiply your weight times this to find your weight there. If you weigh 125 pounds on Earth, you would weigh nearly 49 pounds on Mercury.

VENUS

The Twin Planet—Earth's nearest neighbor and the most Earth-like of planets in size, physical composition, and density. Venus' surface is hot and dry, the surface temperature reaches 482 °C, hot enough to melt lead—this is the highest planetary surface temperature known in the Solar System. Venus has two continent-like highland areas—one in the equatorial region, which is about the size of Australia, and the other, to the north, is half the size of Africa. There appear to be two major active volcanic areas, one larger than the Hawaii-Midway chain, and containing a mountain higher than Mt. Everest. Venus' thick cloud-covered atmosphere is composed of carbon dioxide and sulfuric acid—enriched clouds circulate east to west at hurricane speeds. The surface gravity is 0.91 times that of Earth.

MARS

The Red Planet—we still don't know if life exists on Mars. Results from the Viking spacecraft indicated no evidence of organic molecules but a meteorite of Martian origin recovered from Antarctica contains structures some scientists say are microfossils. The Plain of Chryse photos show a rusty landscape and a gently rolling plain with rippled sand dunes littered with rocks. Viking data show that the weather has changed little over time. The highest temperature recorded was –21 °C, and the lowest was –124 °C. The atmosphere is largely carbon dioxide, with small amounts of nitrogen, oxygen, and argon. In Mars' atmosphere there is only 1/1,000 as much water as in Earth's atmosphere, yet clouds and even fog do form. The volcano Olympus Mons is 550 kilometers in diameter and 27 kilometers high, and dwarfs all of the mountains on Earth. Running water seems to have played a major role in the early shaping of Mar's surface; there is evidence of shorelines, gorges, riverbeds, and islands. The fact that liquid water exists on the surface indicates that Mars experienced, at one time, a warmer climate. Mars' history seems to have begun with heavy meteorite bombardment, followed by extensive volcanic activity. Phobos and Deimos are Mars' small, irregularly shaped, highly cratered moons. The surface gravity is 0.39 times that of Earth.

JUPITER

The Giant Planet—the largest planet in our Solar System—is a whirling ball of liquid hydrogen covered with a cloudy atmosphere of hydrogen and helium and small amounts of methane, ammonia, ethane, acetylene, and other compounds. Jupiter's core is iron-rich rock. The Great Red Spot on Jupiter is a hurricane-like giant storm over 40,000 kilometers long and 14,500 kilometers wide. Jupiter rotates very quickly—once every 9 hours 55 minutes—but takes twelve Earth years to complete a revolution around the Sun. Of Jupiter's sixteen satellites, four exceed 3,000 kilometers in diameter (the Galilean Moons; Io, Europa, Ganymede, and Callisto). Io is spectacularly active, volcanically. Europa appears to be entirely covered by a frozen ocean. The surface gravity of Jupiter is 2.60 times that of Earth.

SATURN

The Ringed Planet—composed mostly of hydrogen. The Pioneer 11 spacecraft discovered that Saturn's rings consist of thousands of ringlets, which are composed of particles of ice and rock of various sizes orbiting around the equator. Saturn generates more heat than it receives from the Sun. Wind speeds in its 1,000 kilometer thick atmosphere are in excess of 1,775 kilometers per hour. Titan is the largest of Saturn's seventeen moons and is similar in size to the inner planets Mercury and Mars. The surface gravity is 1.10 times that of Earth.

URANUS

Four times larger than Earth, Uranus has a thick cloud layer composed of 87% hydrogen and 13% helium. The planet appears to have a rocky core, above which is a zone of liquid water, methane, and ammonia. Uranus is the only giant planet without oval storm systems. Uranus has a magnetic field nearly as strong as Earth's. It has fifteen moons and a set of rings made of particles of ice and rock of various sizes. Because of its distance from the Sun, Uranus has a long period of revolution—eighty-four years. It is unique among the planets in that it has a backward rotation; its axis of rotation is inclined 98° from the vertical. The surface gravity is 0.88 times that of Earth.

NEPTUNE

The Blue Planet—densest of the gas giants. Neptune is similar in composition and structure to Uranus. Its atmosphere gets its blue color because of the presence of methane. Unlike Uranus, Neptune has many clouds and numerous oval storm systems in its atmosphere, including a prominent storm near the equator called the Great Dark Spot. Neptune has eight moons and several rings made of particles of ice and rock of various sizes. The largest satellite, Triton, has a very eccentric orbit. Neptune has a crust of frozen nitrogen and methane, and an atmosphere of methane. The surface gravity is 1.14 times that of Earth.

PLUTO

The Icy Planet—the smallest planet. It probably consists mostly of ice, with a surface of frozen methane. Its maximum temperature is –212 °C. Pluto's orbit is highly inclined, 17° outside the plane of the solar system. Its orbit is so eccentric that Pluto actually orbits inside Neptune's orbit for part of the time during its long, 248-year revolution around the Sun. Pluto is about the same size as Neptune's moon, Triton, and may have begun as an asteroid or a Neptunian moon that escaped. Pluto's lone moon, Charon, was discovered in 1978. Pluto has never been visited by any spacecraft. The estimated surface gravity is 0.05 times that of Earth.

Anyone for a trip to Mars?

It seems likely that someday astronauts will visit and explore the Red Planet. These astronauts may even be the first colonizers of the Solar System. A colonizer on Mars would require about 1 kilogram per day of provisions, and including all the odds and ends needed to set up an adequate habitat, each astronaut would need about half a tonne (1 tonne = 0.9842 ton) of materials per year. Thus, forty years worth of supplies would weigh about 20 tonnes per person—which is not much more than the weight of a fully fueled return vehicle, which would weigh about 34 tons per person anyway.

THE ORIGIN AND EVOLUTION OF THE SOLAR SYSTEM

Scientists still do not completely understand the origin and evolution of the Solar System, but a theoretical model can be created based on studies of young star systems. Any model for the formation of the solar system must account for the fact that all of the planets revolve in a plane, in nearly circular orbits, and in the same direction.

Evidence indicates that our Solar System began about 4.6 billion years ago. Presently there are two existing theories that account for how the Solar System formed; the *catastrophic theory* and the *nebular theory*. Both were first suggested in the mid-Eighteenth century. The catastrophic theory postulates that there was a collision or near collision between our Sun and a passing star. This would account for the fact that the Sun spins very slowly, completing one rotation every twenty-five days. If a near collision occurred, the passing star could have caused a tidal bulge on the Sun that broke away to form the members of our solar system.

According to the modern version of the nebular theory, about 5 billion years ago an enormous nebula in one of the Galaxy's spiral arms broke up into a number of spherical clouds, one of which was to become the Sun and planets. The "mother globule" was 100 thousand AU in size. The gas and dust then collapsed, perhaps in reaction to a nearby **supernova**. The contraction increased the rotational speed and the nebula flattened at the poles, forming an equatorial lens-shaped disk. As the density of the disk increased, so did the temperature.

Within the cloud, dust particles (particles larger than hydrogen and helium) condensed to create even larger particles. Closer to the **protosun** higher temperatures allowed only the heavier materials to condense, such as silicates and metals, whereas farther out, lighter particles condensed to form ice. From the revolving disk, concentric rings eventually formed. Particles collided with each other, joining to form grains, which later accreted into small solid bodies, or **planetesimals**, which were about 1 kilometer in diameter. Planetesimals gradually accreted more mass from the matter in spread out in the rings; they became larger **protoplanets**. The protoplanets separated from the contracting nebula before the developing Sun began its thermonuclear fusion.

CHECK YOUR PROGRESS

1. An "astronomical unit" is
   a. the distance light travels in a year
   b. the mass of the sun
   c. the standard unit for speed
   d. the average distance from the earth to the Sun

2. A tidal bulge in the early Sun is associated with which theory of the origin of the solar system?
   a. catastrophic theory   c. relativity theory
   b. nebular theory   d. gravitational theory

3. The only planet with two moons is
   a. Pluto   c. Mercury
   b. Mars   d. Venus

4. The Great Red Spot on Jupiter is believed to be associated with
   a. volcanic activity
   b. processes associated with irregular surface topography
   c. the infall of a moon, asteroid, or comet
   d. weather conditions in the planet's atmosphere

5. The Oort Cloud is located
   a. between the orbits of Mars and Jupiter
   b. just beyond Pluto
   c. thousands of AU from the Sun
   d. just beyond Neptune

6. Meteorites are
   a. rocky   c. can contain carbon
   b. intersect Earth's orbit   d. all of the above

7. If you weigh 100 pounds on Earth, on Mars you would weigh
   a. 39 lbs.   c. 90 lbs.
   b. 32 lbs.   d. 225 lbs.

8. If a 100 pound backpack were taken to Jupiter, it would weigh

   a. 20 lbs.   c. 160 lbs.
   b. 50 lbs.   d. 260 lbs.

9. The water that filled the early oceans on Earth may have originated from

   a. the combining of hydrogen and oxygen from the solar wind
   b. comets that hit the Earth
   c. water that vaporized from the inner planets
   d. all of the above

THE MILKY WAY: A SPIRAL JEWEL IN THE UNIVERSE

Compared with the galactic core and the ribs of the spiral arms, there are few stars in our neighborhood of the Galaxy. There are only about fifty stars within a radius of fifteen light years from our Sun, the closest being a triple star system just over four light years away in the **constellation** Centaurus and visible only from the Southern Hemisphere.

THE SUPERGIANT LIFE CYCLE

With instruments like the Hubble Space Telescope, we now can see more stars and galaxies than ever before, yet all of this visible matter appears to account for just .1 or less of the mass of the entire Universe. What makes up the rest (if there indeed is more) is highly speculative, and is one of the biggest questions in modern astronomy. But the visible portion certainly is fascinating enough. Take Betelgeuse, for example. Betelgeuse is a massive red supergiant star that's 500 light years away. It makes up the shoulder in the beautiful constellation of Orion. In 1996, the HST photographed Betelgeuse, providing us with the first direct, detailed image of any star other than the Sun. The photo shows that the supergiant star's hot outer atmosphere measures nearly 1.5 billion kilometers in diameter.

The ancient Egyptians recognized that the appearance of the star Sirius coincided with the annual flooding of the Nile. Sirius is the brightest star visible in the Northern Hemisphere and is found in the constellation Canis Major (the Big Dog), which is located near Orion. Sirius is only eight and a half light years away, making it the third closest star, after the Sun and the triple star system in Centauri. Actually Sirius is a double star—two stars orbiting each other, which astronomers call Sirius A and Sirius B. Astronomers have found that over half the known stars are actually double star systems, and roughly another third are triple star systems. Singletons like our Sun are common, but not typical.

The distance between Sirius A and Sirius B is about the same as the distance between the Sun and the planet Uranus. Sirius A is a blue hot star, a real lighthouse. Sirius B, on the other hand is a white dwarf star about the size of Earth, but 350,000 times Earth's mass. Sirius B is so dense that a cup full of its matter would outweigh a cement truck. Astronomers believe white dwarfs represent normal old age for 97% of all stars.

Massive supergiant stars like Betelgeuse go through their stellar life cycles quickly, in just millions of years, compared to average stars like our Sun, which typically endure for longer than 10 billion years. Hydrogen fuels most stars: the high temperature and pressure in the star's core fuses four hydrogen nuclei (single protons) into one helium nuclei (two protons and two neutrons), releasing enormous amounts of energy which radiates outward. The pressure of the energy radiating outward from the core counteracts the star's tendency to collapse. Eventually, the star's core consumes most of its hydrogen fuel, limiting its hydrogen fusion. With a reduction in the outward pressure of the radiation released during hydrogen fusion, the core contracts, compressing the helium "ash" so that temperature and pressure are raised. The helium fusion reaction begins to take place, producing carbon. The carbon-producing reaction continues until helium runs low, at which time the core contracts again and the temperature rises until carbon fuses to produce neon and other elements. As the carbon supply becomes exhausted, the core contracts until the neon fusion reaction commences, forming oxygen and magnesium. The fusion process later ignites the oxygen, which forms silicon and sulfur. Silicon and sulfur fuse to form members of the iron group of elements—iron, nickel, chromium and others. At this point, the core temperature is some 3.5 billion degrees and a cubic centimeter of the supergiant's core weighs some 10,000 tons.

Figure 8.6 illustrates the "stellar onion" model—what astronomers believe to be the structure of an advanced supergiant star. According to the model, the final collapse takes only a fraction of a second. As the collapse accelerates, the core temperature soars to more than a 100 billion degrees and the density increases to billions of tons per cubic centimeter. With the nuclear fuel in the core exhausted, the star's outgoing radiation ceases. Without the energy from radiation, the star's core caves in until it becomes so dense that electrons and protons are fused to form neutrons. When neutrons are formed, the core stops collapsing, but the star's outer layers continue to fall inward, compressing the core further. Soon the crushed neutron core snaps back, sending out a shock wave that blasts away the star's outer layers and triggers a new round of element-forming fusion. This event creates a visible **supernova**. Supernovae have been seen as new bright stars where none have appeared before. A naked and rapidly spinning neutron star is all that remains. The expanding rings or bubbles of gas and dust from the supernova may ultimately be recycled into one or more new stars. Supernova explosions are the source of all the natural elements heavier than iron.

The creation of a neutron star isn't the only possible death scenario for the more massive supergiant stars. When the heaviest supergiant stars become supernovae, they may end up leaving behind **black holes**.

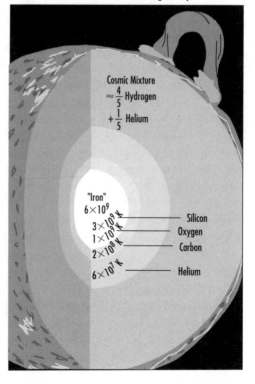

Figure 8.6 A cross section of a supergiant star on the brink of becoming a supernova.

This type of death begins, as before, with the collapse of a star's core. The ultrahigh density of the imploding core, however, transforms the electrons into negatively charged particles called **kaons.** The creation of kaons prevents the electrons from merging with the protons to form neutrons. Instead of a neutron core, a nucleon core is created that consists of a mixture of neutrons, protons, and kaons. The transformation of electrons into kaons creates a barrage of massless or nearly massless particles called neutrinos. This neutrino flood heats the nucleon core, stabilizing it long enough for the imploding outer layers to rebound off it, and this creates the supernova. After the neutrino blast fades, the core collapses into a black hole, vanishing forever from the visible universe.

Stars are born from huge nebulae that may be some three or four light years in diameter. The dust and gas of the nebula contracts, perhaps in reaction to a shock wave from a nearby supernova, or perhaps due to attracting magnetic fields. The temperature of the contracting cloud rises as particle collisions increase in the shrinking volume. When the outer layers reach a temperature of several thousand degrees, the light of the **protostar** begins to shine through.

In the Milky Way, most new stars form in dense clusters, often surrounded by massive stars. Astronomers can see disks of dust and gas around young stars in the Orion nebula, that range in size from fifty to 1,000 times the distance from the Earth to the Sun. If the gas and dust in these disks form clumps, they could become planets. However, intense ultraviolet radiation and fierce winds from the supernova of a massive star in its vicinity can disrupt a stellar nursery. Unaccreted dust and gas, which astronomers call *placental material*, is often blown away, robbing baby stars of additional matter. This limits their ultimate size and perhaps seals the fate of any developing planets. In Orion's stellar nursery, 1,500 light years from Earth, the Hubble Space Telescope has detected evidence of such a scenario. Protoplanetary disks around some young stars have sharp edges, as if they had been abruptly truncated.

The **escape velocity** is the speed necessary for a moving object to overcome the gravitational field of a celestial body. Compare the following escape velocities:

Mercury—4.2 kilometers per second (km/s)

Venus—10.3 km/s

Earth—11.2 km/s (40,000 kilometers, or 25,000 miles per hour)

Moon—2.3 km/s

Mars—5.0 km/s

Jupiter—63.4 km/s

Saturn—39.4 km/s

Uranus—21.5 km/s

Neptune—24.2 km/s

Pluto—0.3 km/s (estimated)

Sun—616 km/s

Sirius B—3,400 km/s (estimated)

A typical neutron star—200,000 km/s

THE DIMENSIONS OF SPACE-TIME

The exosphere is the entire realm of the planets and stars. On the next cloudless night, go outside and look up at the sky: the Moon and one or more planets might be visible. Venus is brighter than any star when it is visible, while Jupiter, Saturn, and Mars appear as bright stars, but they don't twinkle like stars do. Mercury can sometimes be seen just before the rising Sun, or just after sunset. None of the other planets can be seen with the unaided eye, and this is why they were the last to be discovered.

Although you may not realize it, some of what appear to be stars in a clear dark sky are actually emission nebulae. **Nebulae** are enormous clouds of gas and dust, and through good binoculars, you will see that what first appeared to be a star is actually a fuzzy patch in the sky. Astronomers now have evidence that nebulae materials sometimes contract and clump together to form stars and planets—a theory for star formation called the nebular hypothesis. If you look closely through your binoculars at the Great Nebula in the constellation Orion, visible in the evening in the Northern Hemisphere in winter, you can see at least three hot, young stars, surrounded by unaccreted dust and gas, or placental material.

Nebulae also appear at the end of a star's life cycle. In double or multiple star systems, close interaction between stars may cause an exchange of hot ionized gases, which can destabilize a star and result in an explosion of its outer layer. A star also may blow off its own outer layer as an outcome of a chain of events that begins with a shortage of hydrogen fuel in the star's core. Such expulsions of **plasma** are called novae.

FYI

Chinese and Korean astronomers first recorded the observation of a supernova in 1054. Rock paintings found in the southwestern United States suggest that it may have also been observed by Native Americans. The expanding debris from this explosion can still be observed today as the Crab nebula. There are only a seven recorded observations of supernovas in our Galaxy. The first supernova clearly visible to the naked eye since 1604 appeared in 1987. Designated as SN1987A, the star was a blue supergiant in The Large Magellanic Cloud (LMC). The explosion itself actually happened a long time ago, as the LMC is a satellite of the Milky Way 170,000 light years away.

Astronomers categorize stars based on their mass, color, size, and surface temperature. Stars vary widely in their properties. Our own Sun is a rather average star, yet its volume could hold a million Earths. If you look carefully at individual stars in the night sky, you can see that they differ in color—some are whiter than others, some appear yellow or reddish, others have a hint of blue.

The most obvious difference in stars is in their brightness. Astronomers speak of **apparent magnitude**, a system of classifying stellar objects based on their brightness that originated in the work of the Greek astronomer, Hipparchus, who lived 2,100 years ago. Hipparchus divided stars into six classes, with the brightest being first class stars, those slightly fainter, second class, and so forth. The brightest stars in a constellation, such as the orange-red star Aldebaran in the constellation Taurus, have apparent magnitudes of +1 or 0, and even brighter objects like Venus and the Moon have negative magnitudes. Most people cannot see stars that are dimmer than magnitude of +6. On a dark desert night, you might see in the sky about three thousand stars of magnitude six and brighter. Binoculars would extend your vision to dimmer magnitudes, showing you more stars, and a telescope would reveal more still.

The total number of stars in our Milky Way galaxy alone is estimated to be anywhere from 100 billion to nearly one trillion. The stars that can't be seen are either too faint or too far away, and most faraway stars inhabit one of the multitude of other galaxies in the Universe. Recently the Johns Hopkins University Space Telescope Science Institute assembled a cosmic portrait from 343 exposures taken by the Hubble Space Telescope of a tiny area of the sky. That composite photograph, representing a narrow deep core sample of the Universe, showed at least 1,500 galaxies, most so faint that they had never been seen before.

The stars are, in the words of Sir James Jean, as numerous as the grains of sand on all the beaches of all the seas in the world! And the space between the stars is equally unimaginable. Interstellar space is so vast that a collision between any of a half-dozen basketballs bouncing around inside a sphere the size of the Earth would be more probable than a collision between stars. Within our own Galaxy, for every cubic centimeter of star matter there are 1,022 cubic centimeters of space. But as vast as it is, the space between stars is not empty—just about everywhere are small bits of matter, in the form of gases and dust, including molecules such as carbon monoxide, formaldehyde and hydrogen cyanide, even amino acids.

GALAXIES GALORE

A typical galaxy is an aggregation of a trillion or so stars moving about each other in various configurations; in our Galaxy, the pattern of stars is a spiral. Smaller aggregations of stars are called dwarf galaxies, or, if they are within our Galaxy, **globular clusters**. For a long time it was thought that a fuzzy patch visible in the southern skies, the Large Magellanic Cloud, was the closest galaxy to our own, but in 1994 astronomers found a dwarf galaxy of a billion stars only 50,000 light years away from the center of the Milky Way. The dwarf had not been noticed before because it had been obscured by stars in the Milky Way. Our Galaxy's powerful gravitational pull is stretching the dwarf galaxy and ultimately will tear it apart.

FYI

The Hubble Space Telescope is the largest orbiting telescope ever built. As big as a bus, it carries a 2.4 meter (96 inch) mirror and five instruments, each the size of a telephone booth. The telescope is able to discern objects fifty times fainter than Earth-based telescopes. Without the interference of the turbulence of Earth's atmosphere, the HST is able to see objects of a given brightness up to seven times farther away and can reveal details ten times smaller than Earth-based telescopes.

Galaxies tend to be clustered together with other galaxies. Astronomers speak of "the Local Group" as being our own neighborhood cluster. The Milky Way and "M31," a similar spiral galaxy in the constellation Andromeda, are the largest galaxies in the Local Group, and our Local Group is part of an even larger grouping of galaxies called the Virgo supercluster. In such clusters, galaxies often orbit other galaxies.

CONSIDER THIS

"All over our galaxy, vast, irregular, lumpy, pitch-black, interstellar clouds are collapsing under their own gravity, and spawning stars and planets. It happens about once a month. In the observable Universe—containing as many as a hundred billion galaxies—perhaps a hundred solar systems are forming every second....The Universe is lavish beyond imagining."

Carl Sagan and Ann Druyan.
Shadows of Forgotten Ancestors
(New York: Random House, 1992) p. 13.

THE DIMENSIONS OF SPACE-TIME

Stars and galaxies and other objects stand out from their backdrop, the darkness of outer space, but space itself is more than emptiness. Most of us typically think of space as having three dimensions—length, width, and height. **Figure 8.7** depicts a representation of the coordinates of everyday three dimensional space.

However, in his theory of relativity, Albert Einstein, conceptualized four dimensions of space by adding the dimension of time. With time as an inseparable dimension, space becomes **space-time**.

The concept of 4-D space-time (three space dimensions and one of time) was one of several concepts Einstein used to arrive at relativity. Another basic concept is that matter and energy curve the geometry of space-time, and that this curvature manifests itself as **gravity**. Einstein rejected Newton's notion of a *force of gravity*. Instead, Einstein demonstrated that gravity is equivalent to *acceleration*: the "force of gravity" is due to an object's position relative to other matter in curved space. Space is not just a void between objects but has geometric properties that are dependent upon the distribution of the mass it contains. Massive objects curve or warp the geometry of space around them.

Figure 8.7 A representation of the three dimensions of space.

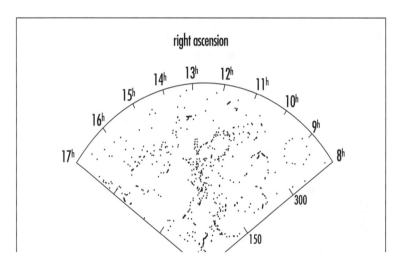

In Einstein's theory, matter moves along natural paths, called geodesics, which follow the curvature of space-time created by the distribution of mass and energy. A geodesic in the vicinity of a massive object curves in toward the center of the space the object has warped.

According to relativity theory, space and time don't exist apart from matter. As Einstein himself explained it, "It was formerly believed that if all material things disappeared out of the universe, time and space would be left. According to relativity theory, however, time and space disappear together with things."

Astronomers still don't know the shape of space-time for the Universe as a whole. Space-time could be positively curved, like a sphere, or negatively curved, like a saddle-shape, or the curve could be flat.

CHECK YOUR PROGRESS

10. Which of the following planets would NEVER be visible (to the unaided eye), even on a dark desert night?
    - a. Neptune
    - b. Mercury
    - c. Mars
    - d. Jupiter

11. "Fuzzy" looking interstellar clouds of dust and gas are known as
    - a. space-time
    - b. placentas
    - c. stellar companions
    - d. nebula

12. A theory that describes the life cycle of stars and the origin of planets is called
    - a. relativity theory
    - b. the nebular hypothesis
    - c. universal gravitation
    - d. steady-state theory

13. The Crab nebula is actually
    - a. a triple star system
    - b. the remains of a supernova
    - c. placental material where new planets are being formed
    - d. the outer region of the Oort Cloud

14. Consider three stars of apparent magnitudes of 5, 2, and –1. Rank them in order of increasing apparent brightness:
    - a. –1, 2, 5
    - b. 5, 2, –1
    - c. 2, 5, –1
    - d. 5, –1, 2
    - e. –1, 5, 2

15. The largest galaxies in our "local group" are
    a. M31 and the Orion Nebula
    b. The Milky Way and M31
    c. the Whirlpool galaxy and the Crab Nebula
    d. The Milky Way and Orion Nebula

16. Einstein's relativity theory contradicts Newton's
    a. laws of motion
    b. laws of optics
    c. mathematics of the calculus
    d. theory of gravity

17. Supernovae
    a. are rarely observed from Earth
    b. are explosions of supergiant stars
    c. have been seen in other galaxies
    d. all of the above

THE ORIGIN, EVOLUTION, AND FUTURE OF THE UNIVERSE

In the 1920s, astronomer Edwin Hubble radically altered how people thought of the Universe. Using the most powerful telescope in the world at the time, he studied M31, the Great Nebula in Andromeda. He found that what was thought to be a nebula was instead composed of stars and that they were too far away to be part of our Galaxy. In one of the greatest moments of astronomy in the century, Hubble discovered that the Milky Way was not the Universe. This dramatic shift in our understanding of the cosmos can be compared to what took place in the Middle Ages when Copernicus and later Galileo argued that the Sun and not Earth was the center of the Universe.

Hubble later photographed and classified hundreds of distant galaxies. He also found that each galaxy was moving outward at a speed directly proportional to its distance from us. The observation that all galaxies are moving away from a common point of origin would eventually be explained as the expansion of space-time from an initial event called the **Big Bang**.

THE BIG BANG THEORY

An overview of the current scientific model for the origin of the Universe is that the Big Bang began between 10 and 20 billion years ago with the simultaneous creation of time, space, and gravity. When the Universe was about a trillionth of a second old, it consisted of a hot, dense "soup" of particles such as quarks and antiquarks, positrons and electrons, photons, and various types of neutrinos. This soup did not persist for long. The Universe soon cooled down to a trillion degrees, which is cool enough for quarks to merge into protons and neutrons and other particles. By the time a single second had passed, the Universe was filled with protons and neutrons. In the next several minutes, atomic nuclei formed and a fourth of the mass of the Universe became helium while most of the rest was hydrogen.

The three-minute old Universe was a super-hot ion plasma, hotter than the center of a star and as dense as lead throughout. For another 700,000 years, the Universe continued to cool and expand, until finally it had cooled down enough for electrons to attach themselves to atomic nuclei. The atoms that formed became the basic materials for stars.

The first evidence of the Big Bang was found in the 1960s, when astronomers began using radio telescopes to probe the nonvisible parts of the electromagnetic spectrum. Many intensely luminous objects billions of light years away were discovered. These were identified as **quasars**, young galaxies with huge black holes at their centers. Galaxies formed within a couple of billion years of the Big Bang. Young galaxies are typically situated in the middle of a thick cloud of gas out of which 5 to a 100 new stars are born each year (the middle-aged Milky Way only spawns about two stars a year).

The ultimate fate of the Universe is, as yet, unknown; several scenarios are possible. The Universe could expand forever; it could expand for a while and then collapse, or it could oscillate from explosion to crunch then explosion again. If a cosmic crunch is our fate, there is nothing to worry about for another 100 billion years. One cosmologist predicts that galaxies that are today moving away from us at half the speed of light, will eventually be moving at only thirty or so centimeters every billion years.

When we look out in space, we also look back in time. Far away things are removed from us in space-time. If you extend your hand, say to a meter away, you actually see it as it was about 0.000000003 seconds ago. Light from the Sun arrives at Earth in about 8 minutes. When we look at the center of the Milky Way, we see it not as it is today, but as it was 25,000 years ago. In fact, there is no way we can see it as it is today.

If sentient alien beings inhabited a planet near the star Rigel, which is about 900 light years away, an observer there would see our Earth at about the time of William the Conqueror. An alien observer on a planet in the Andromeda galaxy, which is 2,200,000 light years away, would see Earth as it was in the Pleistocene age, before our species evolved. The most distant visible things in the sky are equivalent to looking back 13 to 15 billion years.

The future of the Universe depends upon its mass, yet scientists cannot yet account for most of the mass that they expect exists. If current cosmological thinking is accurate, nine-tenths or more of the mass of the Universe has yet to be detected. Astronomers have evidence of the gravitational effects of invisible matter on the visible stars and galaxies. However, the mass necessary to stop the expansion of the Universe is 100 times more than the mass that has thus far been detected. This invisible matter emits no radiation, so it is referred to as "dark matter." Our Solar System doesn't appear to have any dark matter, but the space within a thousand light years of us is about 50% dark matter, and the percentage grows with greater distances in space-time.

Many ideas have been proposed to account for the existence of dark matter. Ordinary gas and dust seem to be ruled out; if ordinary gas were cold, it would emit detectable radio waves; if it were hot, it would emit X-rays. Neutrinos, which were suspected to compose dark matter at first, also seem to be ruled out.

Low mass stars—called red and brown dwarfs—and Jupiter-like objects, have also been suggested as the source of the dark matter. Galaxies have dark matter halos that are ten times wider than their visible part—so huge that distant satellite galaxies are embedded in them. Using the Hubble Space Telescope, astronomers expected to find a lot of faint stars in these halos, but have not. There is evidence galactic halos contain Jupiter-sized objects, dubbed MACHOS (Massive Compact Halo Objects), but such dim, low mass objects are difficult to detect. Stars about one-fifth the mass of the Sun appear to be very abundant, a hundred times more common than sun-size stars, but that is the cut off and stars of masses less than that are very rare. Red dwarfs make up only 6% of our Galaxy's halo and 15% of the disk, and few candidates for brown dwarfs have been found at all.

Another problem with low mass stars being the missing mass is that they are made of ordinary matter: baryons (protons and neutrons). In the theory, the big bang , which produced the baryons and which successfully accounts for the proportions of light elements in the universe, cannot exceed 10% of the critical density needed to stop the expansion and close the Universe.

Another suggested source of the missing mass would be black holes. Black holes are now widely accepted as "real" and several likely ones have been identified in our own Galaxy. Black holes are not composed of baryons, either. Astronomers think massive black holes may inhabit the cores of most galaxies. Still, it is difficult to estimate how many black holes there are. So far, there is no evidence that would imply a particularly large number of black holes, but the search continues.

A final proposed nonbaryon source for the dark matter is a new, unidentified, subatomic particle. Such particles are referred to as "WIMPS" (Weakly Interacting Massive Particles) because they do not have much interaction with other kinds of matter (otherwise they would be detectable). Many types of WIMPS have been noted—photinos, gravitinos, axions, and "strange quark matter," or strangelets.

It is interesting that at the end of the millennium nothing is known about that of which nine-tenths of the Universe is made!

A LUMPY UNIVERSE

In the early eighties, most astronomers believed that the Universe was homogenous throughout—that matter was uniformly dense in every direction. However, galactic mapping of nearby space points to a surprising inconsistency in the density of matter in the Universe. Thousands of galaxies have now been mapped in both the Northern and Southern Hemispheres and these maps show a similar pattern: dense clusters of galaxies in some places, and great voids in other places (see **Figure 8.8**). Extended wall-like structures containing thousands of galaxies have been found in the skies of both hemispheres. The Northern Hemisphere's "Great Wall" of galaxies spans 500 million light years while a similar structure in the Southern Hemisphere spans 300 million light years.

The Universe seems to have begun resembling a very smooth soup, but then cooled to the point that lumps solidified out. Over the first 6 billion years since the Big Bang, the lumps grew into galaxies and galactic clusters such as the Great Wall. The recent maps that reveal a lumpy Universe cover several hundred megaparsecs of space-time (a parsec is 3.26 light years), while the known Universe covers approximately 3,000 megaparsecs.

Small Things

High energy cosmic rays are the most energetic particles in the Universe, but the source of cosmic rays is still a big mystery in astronomy. Astronomers figure the source must be outside the Galaxy because no object found thus far in the Galaxy is active enough to produce the number of cosmic rays that are observed.

In 1994, a cosmic ray was detected in the Utah desert with the record setting energy of 3×10^{20} electron volts (eV). This particle was a proton that hit our atmosphere at virtually the speed of light. Though the proton weighed only one trillionth of a trillionth of a gram, it packed the wallop of a tennis ball flying at 100 mph! Cosmic rays with energies in the range of 10^{20} eV hit the Earth rarely, about once per square kilometer per century.

CHECK YOUR PROGRESS

18. Most of the naturally occurring elements on the Earth were formed during

    a. supernovae explosions
    b. the Big Bang
    c. fusion processes within ordinary stars
    d. nuclear fission processes in stars

19. The ultimate fate of stars in their life cycle depends upon their

    a. diameter   c. composition
    b. temperature   d. mass

20. Which of the following is the LEAST likely source of the dark matter representing sufficient mass to stop the expansion and close the Universe?

    a. MACHOS   c. brown dwarfs
    b. WIMPS   d. black holes

21. Baryons are made of

    a. protons and neutrons
    b. photinos
    c. WIMPS
    d. all of the above

22. Edwin Hubble's great discovery was

    a. relativity theory
    b. that there are other galaxies and the Milky Way is not the Universe
    c. the inverse square law
    d. the Big Bang

23. The age of the Universe is closest to

    a. 4,000 years
    b. 13 million years
    c. 100 million years
    d. 10 billion years

GLOSSARY

apparent magnitude—a measure of a star's observed brightness, in contrast to its absolute magnitude (its apparent magnitude as if it were 10 parsecs from the Sun).

asteroid—any small rocky or metallic object orbiting the Sun between Mars and Jupiter and believed to be left over from the formation of the Solar System.

astronomical unit (AU)—the average distance between the Earth and the Sun (1.495 × 108 kilometers).

Big Bang—an explanation for the origin of the Universe beginning as a hot, dense atom that erupted in a burst of energy from which all matter formed.

black hole—a type of collapsed star whose gravitational field is so strong that not even light can escape.

constellation—an arbitrary formation of stars perceived as a figure or design.

escape velocity—the speed necessary for a moving object to overcome the gravitational field of a celestial body.

globular cluster—a large grouping of stars usually associated with a galaxy. About 120 globular clusters orbit the center of the Milky Way Galaxy.

gravity—the apparent attraction between two masses, explained in different ways by Newton and Einstein.

kaons—also called K-mosons, particles of matter having forms that are neutral, or positive or negative charged, with a mass nearly 1,000 times that of an electron.

Kuiper Belt—a disk beyond the orbit of Neptune encircling the Solar System, composed of comets and other material which originated during the formation of the Solar System.

meteor—a streak of light produced as an object enters the atmosphere and vaporizes.

meteorite—an object that falls to the surface of Earth without completely vaporizing in the atmosphere.

meteoroid—one of innumerable rocky or metallic objects found throughout the Solar System.

nebula—a cloud of dust or gas in interstellar space.

nova—a star that explodes or erupts, increasing greatly in brightness.

Oort Cloud—a spherical cloud of comets which begins after the Kuiper Belt and extends hundreds of thousands of AU, that was first proposed in 1950 by the Dutch astronomer, Jan Oort.

planetesimal—one of innumerable small objects believed to have surrounded the Sun as it was evolving in the early Solar System.

plasma—an ionized gas consisting of electrons and atoms missing one or more electrons.

protoplanet—a body that accreted dust and gas to form into a planet.

protostar—the original nebular material from which a star condensed.

protosun—the contracting nebula that formed the Sun.

quasar—distant, active galactic nucleus surrounded by luminous matter believed to be stars and nebulae.

space-time—a four dimensional continuum in which an event can be described, consisting of three coordinates of space and one of time.

supernova—an explosive eruption that occurs in the final stages of some massive stars. One type is caused by the core collapse of a supergiant star.

ANSWER KEY

1. d	10. a	18. a
2. a	11. d	19. d
3. b	12. b	20. c
4. d	13. b	21. a
5. c	14. a	22. b
6. d	15. b	23. d
7. a	16. d	
8. d	17. d	
9. b		

CHAPTER **9**

Earth, Moon, and Sun: A Dynamic System

GETTING SITUATED

Our Earth is roughly spherical and has a diameter of nearly 13,000 kilometers. The Moon is about 384,000 kilometers, or thirty Earth diameters, away from us and has a diameter of 3,476 kilometers. Figure 9.1 shows a comparison of the bodies to scale.

If the earth were the size of a tennis ball, the Moon to scale would be the size of a marble. At this size scale, you can approximate the distance between the two bodies by holding the tennis ball and marble two meters apart.

You can use the same tennis ball to conceptualize the scale of the earth and the Sun, except in this model, the tennis ball would represent the Sun, and the earth would be the size of the period at the end of this sentence. To correctly approximate the distance between the two bodies at this scale, the tennis ball should be about nine meters away from this page. The average distance between the earth and the Sun is about 150 million kilometers, which is almost 400 times the distance from the earth to the Moon.

Figure 9.1 Earth and the Moon, drawn to scale.

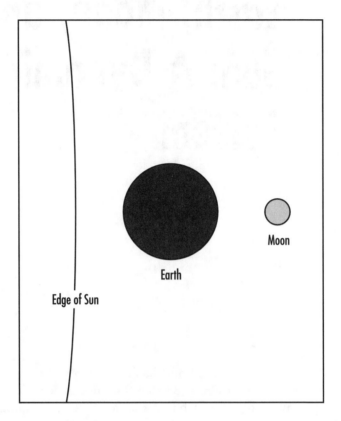

THE SUN: COMPOSITION AND STRUCTURE

The Sun is composed of a gaslike ionized form of matter called **plasma.** The composition of the solar plasma is 70% hydrogen and 27% helium. The final 3% is composed of more than sixty different heavier elements and eighteen kinds of molecules formed by combinations of elements. The Sun accounts for 99% of the mass of our entire solar system.

The heat of the Sun is produced by a process that occurs in its core called **thermonuclear fusion.** In this process, the hydrogen nuclei that make up the core fuse to become helium nuclei, releasing a small amount of energy as a result. Every second, deep within the

Sun, 500 million tons of hydrogen become helium, converting 4 million tons of mass to energy. This energy, in the form of electomagnetic radiation, is then reflected, scattered, absorbed, and reradiated as it gradually makes its way from the core to the surface. A photon of electromagnetic radiation born at the center of the Sun takes about 170,000 years to reach the surface, making the average speed of the photon through the Sun about 0.01 centimeter per year. When the photons reach the Sun's surface, there is no further resistance and they fly off at the speed of light.

The Sun's atmosphere consists of three layers. The lowest visible layer is called the **photosphere** (sphere of light) and is the visible "surface" of the Sun. It is not a solid surface; the Sun is gaseous throughout. It is from this relatively thin layer, which extends to a depth of only 500 kilometers, that we receive most of the Sun's light. The photosphere has an average temperature of 6,000° Celsius, and is mottled and granular in texture. The granular texture is created by hot rising gases; at a granule's darker boundary, cooler, less dense gases sink below the Sun's surface. Granules, which can be the size of Texas, form and dissipate several times in an hour— and there are supergranules that are bigger in diameter than the earth.

The layer above the photosphere is the **chromosphere** (sphere of color), which is about 10,000 kilometers thick. Within the chromosphere are flamelike structures of plasma called **spicules**, which appear to be generated by the strong magnetic fields at the edges of the supergranules.

The outermost layer of the Sun is the **corona**. The chromosphere and the corona are only visible during total solar eclipses. The temperature in the corona rises as you travel away from the Sun, perhaps because the plasma particles (mostly protons and electrons) are heated through interaction with the Sun's rotation and magnetic field. The outer corona is so hot that its particles stream away from the Sun in a continuous **solar wind**. The solar wind blows past the earth at an average rate between 300 and 800 kilometers per second, and its particles eventually end up beyond the solar system.

Figure 9.2 Cross section of the Sun and its atmosphere.

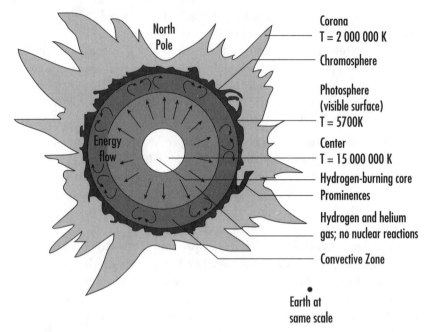

Sunspots

The Sun is a **variable star**, and is in a constant state of motion and change. An interesting transient feature of the Sun is **sunspots**, which are relatively cool, dark areas of the solar surface. The average sunspot is twice the diameter of the earth and may last for several weeks. Sunspots are formed by interacting magnetic lines of force in the solar magnetic field which become tangled as the core and outer layers rotate at different rates. The magnetic fields around sunspots are typically a thousand times stronger than the Sun's average magnetic field and act as barriers for the currents of rising hot gas underneath it. The heat in the current cannot reach the surface, which makes the sunspot cooler than its surroundings. The centers of sunspots are about one-third cooler than the surrounding photosphere, which makes them appear darker. If it were possible to observe a sunspot by itself, however, it would still be brighter than a full moon.

It was noted in the 1800s that the number of sunspots varies over the course of about eleven years, which is the duration of what we call the **sunspot cycle**. Up to 100 spots are not uncommon at a sunspot maximum, while only a few exist at the cycle's sunspot minimum. The sunspot cycle is related to the Sun's rotation and its magnetic field. Sunspots result when tangled lines of force burst through the Sun's surface. Tangles are undone when the Sun's magnetic poles reverse themselves (north becoming south and vice versa) every eleven years, thus a complete magnetic cycle is twenty-two years long.

Prominences and Flares

Surface prominences and flares are also caused by fluctuations in the Sun's magnetic field. **Prominences** are ionized gases trapped in twisted magnetic fields. Some build gradually and persist for many weeks, while others are giant arch-shaped eruptions that burst out of a twisted magnetic field around a sunspot. **Flares** are even more violent, and erupt maximally in just a few minutes, emitting large amounts of radiation in the form of X-rays, ultraviolet and visible radiation, and ionized gas particles. The electromagnetic radiation from flares reaches the earth in about eight minutes and increases ionization in the earth's upper atmosphere, which can interfere with communications. The ionized gas particles arrive days later and interact with the earth's magnetic field, generating huge electrical currents that flow down into the atmosphere and around the poles. The currents can cause magnetic storms that affect compasses and generate surges in power lines. These ionized particles can also excite atoms in the upper atmosphere, causing them to glow and become visible as **auroras.**

FYI

A violent solar flare episode occurred early in 1997. Traveling at a million miles an hour, a cloud of ionized particles that was nearly 2 million kilometers wide arrived in our atmosphere on January 10, about three days after the flare occurred. The cloud's magnetic field arrived first, causing spectacular auroras at the poles. The magnetic storm interfered with communications around the globe and is believed to have caused the failure of the Telestar satellite. The Sun is expected to gradually become more active as the turn of the century approaches, when the next maximum sunspot period occurs.

The Sun's influence in space extends out to the **heliopause**, which is the outer shell of the **heliosphere** and lies 17.6 billion kilometers from the Sun. At that point, the solar wind collides with interstellar gases and the outward pressure of the Sun's particles can no longer deflect the particle winds from other stars.

A simple sundial has two parts: a *dial plate*, which displays the hour marks, and a *gnomon*, which casts the shadow from the Sun. The gnomon can be many shapes, but is typically triangular. The gnomon's shadow will be shortest when the Sun is most directly overhead. The Sun comes closest to being overhead at solar noon, or mid-day, which usually occurs sometime around 12:00 PM. The exact time of midday can be found in an almanac or in many daily newspapers; midday is calculated as halfway between the time of sunrise and sunset. The shadow is longest when the Sun is nearest the horizon, which occurs at sunrise and sunset.

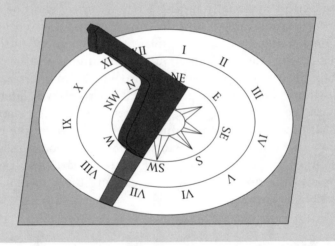

Sundials and clocks keep different time. Sundials keep local Sun Time (what astronomers call *apparent solar time*), whereas clocks keep *standard time*, which is the mean time at one of the standard meridians (by convention, the prime meridian runs through Greenwich, England, and standard meridians are set from there, one hour apart). If the sundial is aligned to mark Sun Time, there will be four days a year when the sundial and the clock agree: April 16, June 14, September 2, and December 25. Otherwise, the time between the two can differ by up to 16 minutes.

THE MOON

The Moon has a diameter of 3,476 kilometers, which is about one quarter of the diameter of Earth. Its smaller size and lower density result in a gravitational field that's about one-eighth the earth's. It would take eighty-one Moons to equal the weight of Earth and fifty Moons to fill a hollow ball the size of Earth.

The lunar surface is made up of two different kinds of regions, the lowlands and the highlands. The lowlands, called **maria**, are smooth, dark plains with few craters. Maria means "seas," and the lowlands have this name because the earliest observers of the Moon thought that these regions were oceans. Maria are regions of low elevation that repeatedly became filled with lava flows early in the Moon's history when it was volcanically active. The highlands are lighter, more heavily cratered regions that are an average of about 3 kilometers higher than the maria, and were never covered with lava.

Earth's Moon is the only celestial body that has been visited by humans. In 1969, Neil Armstrong and Buzz Aldrin set foot on the lunar surface; their footprints are still visible, and probably will be for 5 or 6 million years. Because the Moon has no atmosphere, wind and water don't disturb its surface. The only weathering on the Moon comes from micrometeorite bombardment, so it takes a very long time for even the finest surface features to be altered.

Astronauts brought back over 360 kilograms of rock samples from the Moon, including samples of solidified lava from maria that reveal the Moon's early active history. The last two Apollo missions landed in the highlands, where the astronauts collected samples of a lighter, less dense kind of rock than the lava found in the maria. These rocks have been dated to between 4.1 and 4.6 billion years.

Seismographs left on the Moon during the Apollo missions have detected moonquakes that emanate from deep below the surface, providing evidence that the Moon still has a partially molten core. However, there is no evidence that the lunar surface has ever been broken into crustal plates. The only mountains on the Moon are either the result of large meteorite impacts or volcanic eruptions early in the Moon's history.

In 1994, the unmanned satellite Clementine returned to the Moon where it found evidence of ice in the craters at the Moon's poles, which are always in shadow and where the temperature remains at −387 degrees Celsius. Clementine also found mountain peaks that rise half a mile higher than Mt. Everest, and a crater basin nearly 10 kilometers deep.

MOTIONS AND INTERACTIONS: THE CYCLES OF DAYS AND SEASONS

Most of us think of Earth as a planet orbited by its sole natural satellite, the Moon. But scientists sometimes think of the Earth and the Moon as a double planet system, because of the Moon's relatively large size compared to Earth. One fact that supports this idea is that the Moon doesn't simply revolve in its orbit around Earth. Rather, the Moon and Earth revolve around a common center of gravity, the **barycenter**, a point that is inside the earth's surface but far from its center. The Earth-Moon system moves in a complex way in its orbit around the Sun. This is illustrated in Figure 9.3.

Figure 9.3 Earth and Moon trace out an intertwining pattern as they orbit the Sun.

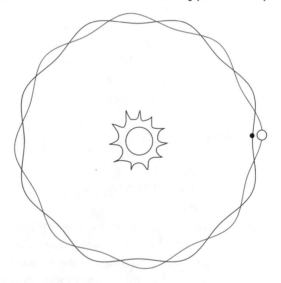

As we begin our study of the cycles of days and seasons, you will need to be familiar with the terms rotation and revolution. **Rotation** means the turning of an object about an axis while **revolution** means the path an object travels about a focus outside itself. Earth rotates on its axis every twenty-four hours (one day) and revolves around the Sun in the course of one year.

A year is the time it takes Earth to orbit the Sun: 365.2564 days, or 365 days, 6 hours, 9 minutes, and 13 seconds. This period, and the period of any planet, is related to the planet's average distance from the Sun. The closer a planet is to the Sun, the less distance it travels in orbit, and the shorter is its year. For example, Mercury orbits the

Sun in just 88 Earth days, while Pluto takes 248 Earth years for one revolution.

Imagine the Sun's path, called the *ecliptic*, as an arc that extends all the way around the Earth. Now imagine also extending the Earth's equator into the sky. This second imaginary arc is called the *celestial equator*. The ecliptic and the celestial equator are not lined up, because the earth's axis is tilted 23.5 degrees. Figure 9.3 is a diagram showing the earth in space with its tilted axis. A circle is drawn through the poles, and other circles represent the celestial equator and the ecliptic.

Figure 9.4 The curving, dashed line shows the ecliptic, the Sun's apparent path through the sky. Note that the ecliptic crosses the celestial equator at the equinoxes, the first days of spring and autumn.

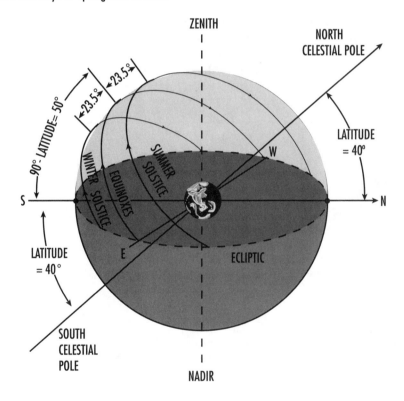

The motion of Earth around the Sun is what creates the seasons. When Earth is in that part of its orbit where the Northern Hemisphere is tilted toward the Sun, the northern half of Earth receives more direct sunlight, and therefore more heat, than the Southern Hemisphere. The northern half also receives more hours of sunlight each day. For these reasons, summer is warmer. The seasons have almost nothing to do with the closeness of the earth to the Sun, as many people erroneously believe.

Sun Day

In the middle of November in Barrow, Alaska, the Sun sets for the last time of the year. The long dark winter night begins and no Sun is seen for the next sixty-five days. In Barrow, "Sun Day" is celebrated when the Sun once again can be seen on the horizon, ending over two months of total, around-the-clock darkness. Sun Day is on or about Jan. 22; children make sun disks and go out to greet the long-awaited Sun.

Because of the earth's tilt, the Sun rises and sets just once a year at the poles. The long night and long day are not equal in length, however, because of the earth's asymmetrical shape. In the year 1995, "daytime" at the North Pole lasted 190 days.

FYI

The calendar used by the ancient Egyptians divided the year into three seasons of four months each. The Egyptian seasons were Flood Time, Winter Time, and Harvest Time. The calendar had months that were based on the lunar cycle. Each month had thirty days divided into three periods of ten days each, similar to our weeks. After twelve months, the five "leftover" days were designated for worshipping the gods. Today, we divide the year into four seasons, based upon the two equinoxes and the two solstices. The equinoxes (when day and night are of equal length) occur in the spring and autumn and the two solstices (the longest daylight period and the longest nighttime period) are at the start of summer, and the beginning of winter. The Gregorian calendar, which is used by most of the world today, was adopted in A.D. 1582. Because the year is approximately 365 and one-fourth days, an extra day is needed periodically; this day is a leap day: February 29th.

Earth's axis sweeps out in a cone shape in the sky about once every 26,000 years in a process called **precession**. Right now the north celestial pole is moving gradually closer to Polaris, but after A.D. 2100, the pole will move away from Polaris. Thirteen thousand years from now, the North Pole will have moved to a position that points to the star Vega, which will become the new pole star. Before Polaris, Thuban served this role. **Figure 9.5** illustrates this long-period change, detectable only through very careful observations.

Figure 9.5 Earth's axis now points toward Polaris, but in 13,000 years it will be pointing to within a few degrees of the bright star Vega, in the Lyre constellation.

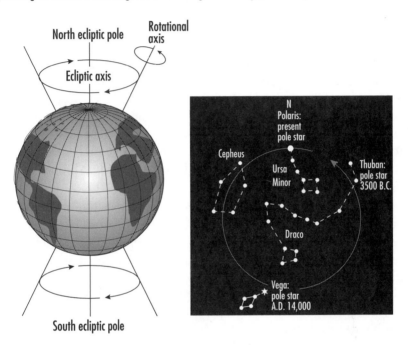

Precession is caused by the gravitational interactions of the Sun, Moon, and Earth. Because of its spin, Earth's mass tends to move outward at the equator, producing a slight bulge. The masses of the Sun and the Moon influence the earth at that 23.5° angle, tending to "right" the earth so that spin axis and orbital plane are perpendicular. This is like a tug on the axis that causes it to precess. A top behaves in a similar fashion, but in the case of the top, it's the tendency to fall that forces it to precess.

MOON PHASES

A set of perhaps more familiar motions of the Earth-Moon-Sun system involves the Moon. The Moon takes 27.322 days to orbit eastward around the earth. This is the **sidereal period**, a measure of the

Moon's orbit relative to the stars. The **lunar month** is the length of time from the appearance of one full Moon to the next: 29.53059 days, or 29 days, 12 hours, 44 minutes, and 3 seconds. The time difference between the two kinds of month occurs because while the Moon orbits Earth, Earth continues moving in its orbit around the Sun. The Moon takes two days to catch back up with the Earth. Months on the calendar, which vary from 28 to 31 days, are arbitrary divisions of the year that represent neither lunar months nor sidereal periods.

As the Moon circles the earth (the barycenter), it rotates on its axis so that the same portion of the lunar surface is always turned toward us; we recognize this view as the man-in-the-moon. Because the Moon is visible only by reflected sunlight, we only see the portion that is illuminated. At different locations in the Moon's orbit, different amounts of illuminated surface will face observers on Earth. Thus, to us, the Moon passes through a sequence of **phases**. **Figure 9.6** illustrates the relationship between the Moon's orbital position and the phases that appear to us.

At what we call the new moon, the Moon is nearly in line with the Sun and appears to set in the west with the Sun; at this point it can't be seen. After a couple of days we see the waxing, or increasing in size, crescent in the western sky just after sunset. On successive nights, the Moon will be higher above the horizon at sunset and the visible portion will be larger. First quarter is reached about a week after the new moon. The Moon progressively waxes larger, becoming the gibbous moon, and sets later and later. About two weeks after the new moon, halfway through the cycle, the Moon is full. The full moon rises in the east as the Sun sets and is visible all night. The waning phases then commence, with the visible area decreasing in size, reversing in appearance and in two weeks returning to the new moon phase. By the time the Moon reaches its third quarter, it rises at midnight. Most people miss seeing the waning phases, as the Moon is not visible in the early evening skies. Skywatching is better in the waning phases, however, as the sky is darker when the Moon is not present. Table 9.1 is an observer's guide to the Moon phases.

Figure 9.6 The relation between the Moon's orbital position and its phases. This is how the different phases of the Moon would appear to an Earth-based observer.

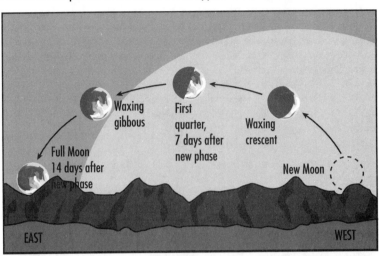

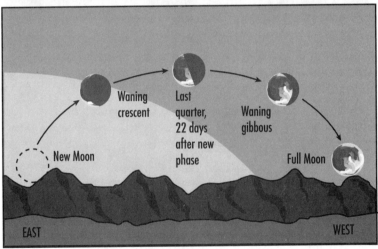

Table 9.1 An observer's guide to the Moon phases.

PHASE	MOONRISE	MOONSET
New	Dawn	Sunset
1st quarter	Noon	Midnight
Full	Sunset	Dawn
3rd quarter	Midnight	Noon

Tides are an effect of the Moon's position relative to the earth. The gravitational forces between Earth and Moon result in a distortion of the earth's shape, particularly the side facing the Moon. The **tidal forces** on the part of the earth closer to the Moon are stronger than those on the side opposite. Earth actually distorts into a slight football shape. Because they are fluid, the oceans distort three times more than solid land. Tidal bulges occur in the regions below and opposite the Moon; the water piles up to greater depths at those places. The bulge on the opposite side of the earth from the Moon may seem odd, but is the result of the fact that water is able to flow freely over the surface in such a way as to create an equilibrium that elongates the earth in those regions.

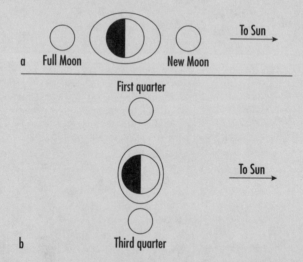

The Sun also produces tides on Earth, but is less than half as effective as the Moon because it is much farther away. When the Sun and the Moon are lined up—at new moon and full moon—the tides are higher than normal and are called *spring tides* (though they have nothing to do with the seasons). When the Moon is at first and third quarter, the Sun's influence reduces the tides. These lower than normal tides are called *neap tides*.

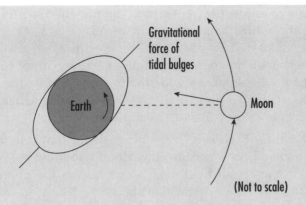

Gravitational force of tidal bulges

Earth

Moon

(Not to scale)

The patterns of tides are not all that simple, however, because there are many factors that affect the flow of ocean water. For instance, the presence of land masses provides barriers to the free flow of surface water and there is significant friction between the oceans and the ocean basin floor. Water flow is also affected by the rotation of the earth, the winds, and the varying depths of the oceans. For these reasons, the highest tide does not necessarily occur when the Moon is overhead. Thus, while observers see two high tides and two low tides daily, the times and heights of high tide vary considerably from place to place.

Another phenomenon related to the relative positions of the Sun, Moon, and Earth is that of the eclipse. There are **lunar eclipses** and **solar eclipses**, and they both have to do with the shadows cast by sunlight. A solar eclipse occurs when the Moon passes between Earth and the Sun. A shadow is cast over the Earth and our view of the Sun is blocked.

Solar eclipses can only happen when the Moon is at the new moon phase, and is directly between the Sun and Earth. **Figure 9.6** shows relative positions of the three bodies and the shadows cast by the sunlight. There is a new moon every lunar cycle, but eclipses are rare events. This is because the shadow cast by the Moon during most new moon phases does not usually fall exactly on Earth. The shadow often misses Earth because the Moon's orbital plane is tilted about 5 degrees from the plane of the ecliptic (the earth's orbital plane).

One reason that solar eclipses are such strange and special events is that the Sun and the Moon, despite being so different in actual size, have nearly equal diameters as seen from Earth. Therefore, the

Moon appears to be just the right size to completely cover the disk of the Sun (if the entire solar disk is covered, it is a total eclipse, otherwise it is a partial eclipse). Total solar eclipses are visible only to those observers who are located in the narrow path of totality, a band less than 300 kilometers wide that's swept out by the Moon's shadow. Observers just outside that path will see a partial eclipse, and those farther away will see no eclipse at all.

The total eclipse itself is a fleeting experience that lasts no more than 7.5 minutes. This is because the Moon's shadow passes by at over 1,600 kilometers an hour. The Moon covers the photosphere and allows us to see a spectacular sight; the bright gases of the chromosphere and the corona.

Figure 9.7 The relative positions of Earth, the Moon, and the Sun during a new moon in which a solar eclipse occurs.

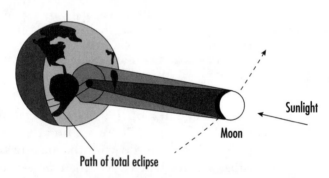

A lunar eclipse occurs when Earth's shadow blocks out all or part of the Moon. Lunar eclipses only occur during full moon phases, when Earth is between the Sun and the Moon. **Figure 9.8** shows the relative positions of the three bodies during a lunar eclipse. Once again, a lunar eclipse does not occur at every full moon because Earth's shadow seldom directly covers it. Table 9.2 below lists upcoming total eclipses of the Moon.

Figure 9.8 The relative positions of the Sun, Moon, and Earth during a typical full moon and during a full moon in which a lunar eclipse occurs.

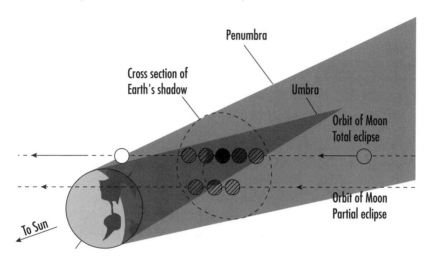

Table 9.2 Future total eclipses of the Moon. G.M.T. refers to Greenwich Mean Time, the time at Greenwich, England. Any local time can be calculated from G.M.T. (for instance, there is a five-hour difference between G.M.T. and Eastern Standard Time, so that E.S.T. = G.M.T. − 5. When it is 1:00 PM in New York City, it is 6:00 PM in Greenwich).

Date	Time of Mid-eclipse (G.M.T.)	Length of Totality (Minutes)	Length of Eclipse (Hours: Minutes)
Jan. 21, 2000	4:45	76	4:38
Jul. 16, 2000	13:57	106	5:42
Jan. 9, 2001	20:22	60	4:16
May 16, 2003	3:41	52	4:06
Nov. 9, 2003	1:20	22	3:52
May 4, 2004	20:32	76	4:38
Oct. 28, 2004	3:05	80	4:58

THE SYSTEM: PAST AND FUTURE

Astronomers did not have an acceptable theory for the origin of the Moon until the mid-1980s. Now it seems as though the Moon formed from debris that was ejected from the earth by the impact of a Mars-sized object early in the history of the solar system. It may be even more accurate to describe the event as the result of two very large protoplantets, or **planetesimals**, colliding and merging, with the larger body becoming Earth and a smaller mass of ejecta becoming the Moon. A glancing collision, instead of a direct hit, would have spun the new object rapidly and could explain the present motion of the Earth-Moon system. If the collision had occurred after the planetesimals had differentiated their iron cores and mantles, it would explain why the Moon lacks iron but is otherwise so similar in composition to the earth's mantle. Simulations of the event indicate that the iron cores of the two planetesimals would have merged in a matter of hours. The Moon today also lacks volatile elements, which this model also accounts for. These elements would have dissipated into space during the period between the collision and the consolidation of the debris into the lunar body.

FATE OF THE MOON

The ultimate fate of the Moon may be a consequence of the daily tides, which have a braking effect on the earth's rotation. The rotational speed is slowed by 0.001 of a second per day per century by the friction of the ocean waters against the sea floor. This slower rotation means the days are getting longer, which is supported by fossil evidence. Four billion years ago, the day was only six hours long.

Tidal bulges on the earth are not in a direct Earth-Moon line, and the mass these bulges contain acts on the gravitational field of the Moon in a way that pulls the Moon forward in its orbit. The result of this is that the Moon's orbit is becoming larger; it is moving away from the earth at a rate of about three centimeters a year. The overall result of tidal forces is that the Earth-Moon system itself is slowly moving in its orbit away from the Sun.

Earth rotates once on its axis each day. As that happens, a person standing somewhere on the equator, say in Quito, Equador, travels 40,234 kilometers through space, which is the Earth's circumference. That same day, the same person on the equator also travels 2,600,000 kilometers because the earth, on average, moves that distance in its orbit around the Sun.

Earth's orbit is elliptical—like an oval. We are closest to the Sun at the beginning of January and farthest away in early July. Our nearness to the Sun does not make a difference in the seasons; the seasons are due to the tilt of the earth's axis. This tilt causes the Northern Hemisphere to receive more direct rays of solar energy in the summer, and to experience longer days.

CHECK YOUR PROGRESS

1. Which distance is the greatest?

    a. the distance from the Earth to the Moon
    b. the Moon's circumference
    c. the diameter of the Sun
    d. the Sun's radius

2. The beginnings of spring and fall are called the

    a. seasonal progressions
    b. solstices
    c. equinoxes
    d. tropics of Cancer and Capricorn

3. The new moon occurs

    a. once a year   c. every week
    b. every month   d. once per century

4. Because the year is about one-fourth of a day longer than 365 days, the calendar is adjusted by

    a. adding a quarter day every four years
    b. subtracting a day every four years
    c. adding a day every four years
    d. subtracting a day at the end of each century

5. Eclipses of the Moon do not occur each month because

   a. the Moon rarely comes close enough to the earth
   b. the dark side of the Moon rarely faces the earth
   c. the earth is usually between the Moon and the Sun
   d. the Moon's orbit is at an angle to the earth's orbit around the Sun

6. When the shadow of the Moon falls on the earth, it produces a

   a. lunar eclipse   **c.** partial eclipse
   b. solar eclipse   **d.** auroras

7. If you observed the sky at 10:00 PM on a clear night during the Moon's third or last quarter, you would most likely see

   a. the quarter Moon rising in the east
   b. the quarter Moon in the western sky
   c. the quarter Moon directly overhead
   d. stars but no visible Moon

8. When the earth is in a direct line with the Sun and the Moon the tides that are produced are called

   a. flood tides   **c.** ebb tides
   b. neap tides   **d.** spring tides

9. The lowest tides occur when the Moon is in which phase?

   a. new moon
   b. full and quarter phases
   c. quarter phases
   d. gibbous phases

10. How many times each month are the Moon and the Sun at right angles to each other in relation to the earth?

    a. once   **c.** three times
    b. twice   **d.** four times

11. The Sun shines nearly vertically on the equator during the first week of

    a. spring   **c.** winter
    b. summer   **d.** all of the above

12. The longest and shortest periods of daily sunlight occur each year on

    a. the equinoxes
    b. the solstices
    c. the cross-quarter days
    d. Christmas and Easter

13. Earth's rate of rotation is gradually slowing down due to friction caused by

    a. jet stream winds
    b. winds associated with frontal systems
    c. ocean waves
    d. tides

14. Light takes about how long to travel from the Sun to the earth?

    a. 8 seconds
    b. 8 minutes
    c. 8 days
    d. light reaches the earth instantly

15. The Sun is composed mainly of

    a. hydrogen
    b. helium
    c. argon
    d. a mixture of 60 heavy elements and 18 molecules

16. Most of the light received on Earth from the Sun comes from the

    a. solar corona   c. chromosphere
    b. solar wind   d. photosphere

17. The solar wind consists of

    a. mostly protons and electrons
    b. neutrinos
    c. electromagnetic radiation
    d. all of the above

18. Scientists believe that sun spots are caused by

    a. fusion reactions in the Sun's core
    b. concentrations of heavy elements in the Sun
    c. powerful interacting magnetic fields
    d. tidal bulges in the photosphere

19. The Sun's north and south poles reverse their positions in a cycle that occurs about every

    a. 11 years   c. 220 years
    b. 22 years   d. 2,200,000 years

20. The Sun's solar wind extends outward in the Solar System to

    a. the chromosphere   c. the Oort Cloud
    b. the orbit of Pluto d. the heliopause

21. A sundial can be used to measure

    a. standard time   c. apparent solar time
    b. Greenwich Mean Time d. daylight savings time

22. Lunar mountains are most likely the result of

    a. ancient crustal plate movements
    b. early volcanic activity and meteorite impacts
    c. lava flows from the liquid lunar core
    d. rays formed from material ejected when the Moon first formed

23. A satellite in a geostationary orbit will

    a. always orbit above the same surface position
    b. always orbit from north to south over the poles
    c. always orbit over the same longitude
    d. always orbit in a fixed position relative to the stars

24. From the perspective of the stars (the sidereal period), the length of the month is approximately

    a. 27 1/3 days   c. 30 days
    b. 29 1/2   d. 31 days

GLOSSARY

auroras—the luminous phenomena seen in the sky at night in high latitudes, appearing as green or red colored rays, arcs, bands, curtains, and streamers, caused by the interaction of particles in the atmosphere with charged particles from the Sun attracted to the magnetic poles.

barycenter—the center of mass of a system, i.e., the spot in the earth around which Earth and Moon revolve.

chromosphere —the 10,000 kilometer thick layer of the Sun's atmosphere immediately above the photosphere.

corona—the outer part of the Sun's atmosphere, above the chromosphere.

flares—large eruptions of hydrogen plasma on the surface of the Sun, accompanied by bursts of radiation and followed by magnetic disturbances.

heliopause—the edge of the heliosphere.

heliosphere—the region of space over which the Sun's gases and magnetic field extend.

lunar eclipse—an obscuring of light from the Moon that occurs when the Moon passes through Earth's shadow, or umbra.

lunar month—the period of one complete revolution of the Moon around Earth, or, the interval between one new moon and the next. This is the same as the synodical month, or 29 days, 12 hours, 44 minutes, and 2.8 seconds.

maria (singular mare)—broad dark areas on the surface of the Moon.

phases of the Moon—the shapes of the illuminated surface of the Moon as they appear from Earth which result from the relative positions of the Sun, Moon, and Earth.

photosphere—the visible surface of the Sun or a star which is the source of its light.

planetesimals—any of the small, solid celestial bodies that may have existed at an early stage of development of the solar system.

plasma—a collection of charged particles, as in the atmosphere of stars, containing positive ions and electrons, exhibiting the properties of a gas but differing from a gas in being affected by magnetic fields and conducting electricity.

precession—the gradual motion of the earth's rotational axis around the ecliptic poles.

prominences—ionized gases trapped in a twisted magnetic field.

rotation—the spin of an object about an imaginary axis.

revolution—the motion of a celestial body in an orbit around another, more massive body.

sidereal period—the time required for a celestial body to make a complete revolution from the perspective of the stars.

solar eclipse—an obscuring of light from the Sun that occurs when the shadow of the Moon falls on the earth.

solar wind—a continuous flow of charged particles from the Sun's corona into space.

spicule—a relatively small, spikelike, short duration ejection of luminous material originating from the Sun's chromosphere.

sunspots—dark areas in the Sun's photosphere resulting from a relatively cooler surface temperature and believed to be caused by intense local magnetic fields that suppress convection currents bringing hot gases to the surface.

sunspot cycle—a pattern of the fluctuation of the number of sunspots that peaks every eleven years.

thermonuclear fusion—the union of atomic nuclei to form heavier nuclei, resulting in the release of energy

thermonuclear forces—the union of atomic nuclei to form heavier nuclei, resulting in the release of energy.

tidal forces—the apparent pull on a body generated by the gravitational field of another body. According to Newton's law of gravitation, the force is inversely proportional to the square of the distance, which means that the side of the earth nearest the Moon will experience a greater force than the side opposite the Moon.

variable star—a star whose brightness changes, usually in a periodic fashion.

ANSWER KEY

1. c	11. a	21. c
2. c	12. b	22. b
3. b	13. d	23. a
4. c	14. b	24. a
5. d	15. a	
6. b	16. d	
7. d	17. a	
8. d	18. c	
9. c	19. b	
10. b	20. d	

10

The Earth's History

MEASURING AND MAPPING DEEP TIME

Geological science is divided into two broad areas: physical geology and historical geology. Physical geology, which includes the fields of **geomorphology**, geophysics, geochemistry, mineralogy, petrology, crystallography, and economic geology, is the study of the materials that make up Earth and the processes that take place on and below the earth's surface. Historical geology is the study of the origin of Earth and its physical and biological changes over time. The subdivisions of the field of historical geology include **stratigraphy, paleontology,** and **geochronology**.

James Hutton, who is considered the father of modern geology, was one of the first to try to determine Earth's age from rock strata. In the early 1800s, he studied rock strata in his native Scotland and attempted to calculate the rates of weathering, erosion, and sediment redeposition.

Hutton realized that great changes were wrought on the landscape over a very long period of time by gradual, inconspicuous processes like weathering and erosion. His *principle of uniformitarianism* did not state that geological processes in the past necessarily operated at the *rate* that they do today, or that particular processes have always impacted Earth to the extent that they do today. Nevertheless, Hutton realized that Earth is quite ancient, and that no matter how much geological processes have varied in intensity, a lot of time was needed to create the planet's major geologic formations.

For instance, a road cut near the top of a mountain may reveal a layer of shale containing fossils of sea life, including trilobites, that lived over 500 million years ago, but this rock layer presently rests 300 meters above sea level. Somehow, the sediments had to be uplifted to a significant height above sea level. Yet, even if this uplift occurred as slowly as 0.2 millimeters per year, only 1.5 million years would be needed to move the fossils those 300 meters.

Hutton established two other principles that geologists continue to use in determining the sequence of events in Earth's history. First, he stated that every rock layer represents a distinct period of time, and, second, that the oldest rock layer was always on the bottom, and progressively younger layers were deposited above.

The entire geologic history of the earth is called **geological time**. Geological time is marked off by the occurrence of events that can be discerned from rocks. Besides the uplifting and erosion of mountains, geologists have found evidence of the opening and closing of seas. Remember that iron particles in magma align with the poles and then become fixed when the magma crystallizes. By studying magnetic alignment patterns on either side of the mid-Atlantic ridge, geologists have calculated that the rate of Atlantic seafloor spreading is from 1 to 6 centimeters per year in both directions. Therefore, the total growth would be from 2 to 12 centimeters a year. At this rate, it would have taken the present Atlantic Ocean from 36 to 288 million years to achieve its present width, which is a calculation that fits with the estimated occurrence of the breakup of the supercontintent, Pangaea, some 200 million years ago.

RADIOMETRIC METHODS OF DATING ROCKS

Only during the twentieth century have the ages of many rocks become fairly well established, and this is chiefly due to the discovery of **radiometric dating**. Estimates of the age of the oldest rocks on Earth are made from studying the decay of particular radioactive isotopes, which are atoms that are unstable and periodically break down into atoms of other elements, releasing energy in the process. The radioactive decay of a nucleus occurs randomly, but at a fixed rate, and is not influenced by external conditions such as pressure and temperature. Thus, chemical and geological processes do not alter the abundance or decay rate of isotopes.

The calculation of a rock's age requires three pieces of information: (1) the rate of decay of a radioactive isotope present in the rock; (2) the amount of the original element, or *parent isotope*, still remaining in the rock, and (3) the amount of the new element formed, or *daughter isotope*.

An instrument known as the **mass spectrometer** is frequently used to determine ratios of isotopes in rock samples. For instance, lead isotopes are produced by the decay of uranium isotopes. As it breaks down, a uranium-238 nucleus, which contains 92 protons and 146 neutrons, emits 6 electrons and 8 helium nuclei (2 protons and 2 neutrons, called *alpha particles*). What remains is a lead-206 nucleus that contains 82 protons and 124 neutrons. In a similar way, uranium-235, which contains 92 protons and 143 neutrons, decays to lead-207.

Ordinary lead includes the lead-204 isotope, which isn't produced by radioactive decay, and lead-208, some of which is produced by the decay of radioactive thorium. The ratio of these four lead isotopes (Pb-206, Pb-207, Pb-204, and Pb-208) at the time the earth formed is assumed to be the same as the ratio of isotopes in meteorites, so that the age of the earth has been estimated by comparing the present abundance of the lead isotopes in the rock with the amount of uranium present. In 1953, Clair Patterson and Friedrich Houtermans independently used this method to established the now widely accepted age of the earth and solar system as being close to 4.6 billion years old.

Other methods for determining the ages of ancient rocks have been used to verify the dates determined through the uranium-lead method. One method involves the decay of radioactive rubidium to strontium and another involves the decay of potassium to argon. Because potassium containing minerals are common, the potassium-argon method is widely used.

Another method for dating objects is *carbon dating*, but because the rate of production of radioactive carbon-14 has varied in the past (it is produced in the atmosphere when cosmic rays strike nitrogen atoms), the results of carbon dating must be calibrated by comparing them with ages determined by other methods. In addition, because of the more rapid decay rate of radioactive carbon, this method cannot be used to date anything older than about 70,000 years.

VARVE DATING

Varve dating is a method used in geochronology to date events that occurred in the relatively recent past, say, within a few million years. Varves are thin sedimentary layers of clays that have alternating dark and light bands that correspond to summers and winters, and are particularly common in the area of Scandinavia. Ancient varve deposits can be correlated with the annual retreat of the ice sheet during the Pleistocene glacial series. By counting the varves, scientists can establish an absolute time scale for fossils that are as old as 20,000 years.

THE GEOLOGIC TIME SCALE

The geologic time scale provides us with a way of dividing the history of the earth into manageable portions of time. In the geologic time scale, illustrated in **Figure 10.1**, the largest units of time are *eons*. The earliest eon is called the *Hadean* and is the time before the oldest known rocks: about 4 billion years ago. There is no rock record of events during this eon. The Archean eon extended from about 3.8 to 2.5 billion years ago, and was followed by the Proterozoic eon, which extended to about 570 million years ago. These eons are sometimes collectively referred to as the *Cryptozoic* or *Precambrian*. These early eons make up about 87% of geologic time.

Eons are divided into smaller units of time called *eras*, which are divided into *periods*, which are divided into *epochs*, which are divided into *ages*. Each of these spans of time represents a distinct chapter in the history of Earth. The markers between chapters are often significant tectonic events or changes in life forms, such as the rise of a mountain range or the extinction of flora and fauna that were abundant or dominant. These periods are determined from characteristics of the rock strata laid down at the time.

Figure 10.1 The geologic time scale.

TIME-ROCK UNITS OF THE GEOLOGIC COLUMN	TIME UNITS OF THE GEOLOGIC TIME SCALE (Numbers are absolute dates in millions of years before the present)				TIME RANGE OF SEVERAL GROUPS OF PLANTS AND ANIMALS
	Eon	Era	Period	Epoch	
	Phanerozoic Eon (Phaneeros = "evident"; Zoon = "life")	Cenozoic Era	Quaternary	Holocene	
				Pleistocene 2	
			Neogene	Pliocene 5	
			Tertiary	Miocene 24	
				Oligocene 37	
			Paleogene	Eocene 58	
				Paleocene	
		Mezozoic Era	Cretaceous 66		
			Jurassic 144		
			Triassic 208		
		Paleozoic Era	Permian 245		
			Pennsylvanian 286		
			Mississippian 320		
			Devonian 360		
			Silurian 408		
			Ordovician 438		
			Cambrian 505		
	Proterozoic Eon	Late		570	
		Middle		900	Precambrian compprises about 87% of the geologic time scale
		Early		1600	
	Archean Eon	Late		2500	
		Middle		3000	
		Early		3400	
	Hadean	No record		3800	

? ? ?

Origin of earth about 4.6 billion years ago

Groups shown: Invertebrates, Fishes, Land plants, Amphibians, Reptiles, Mammals, Birds

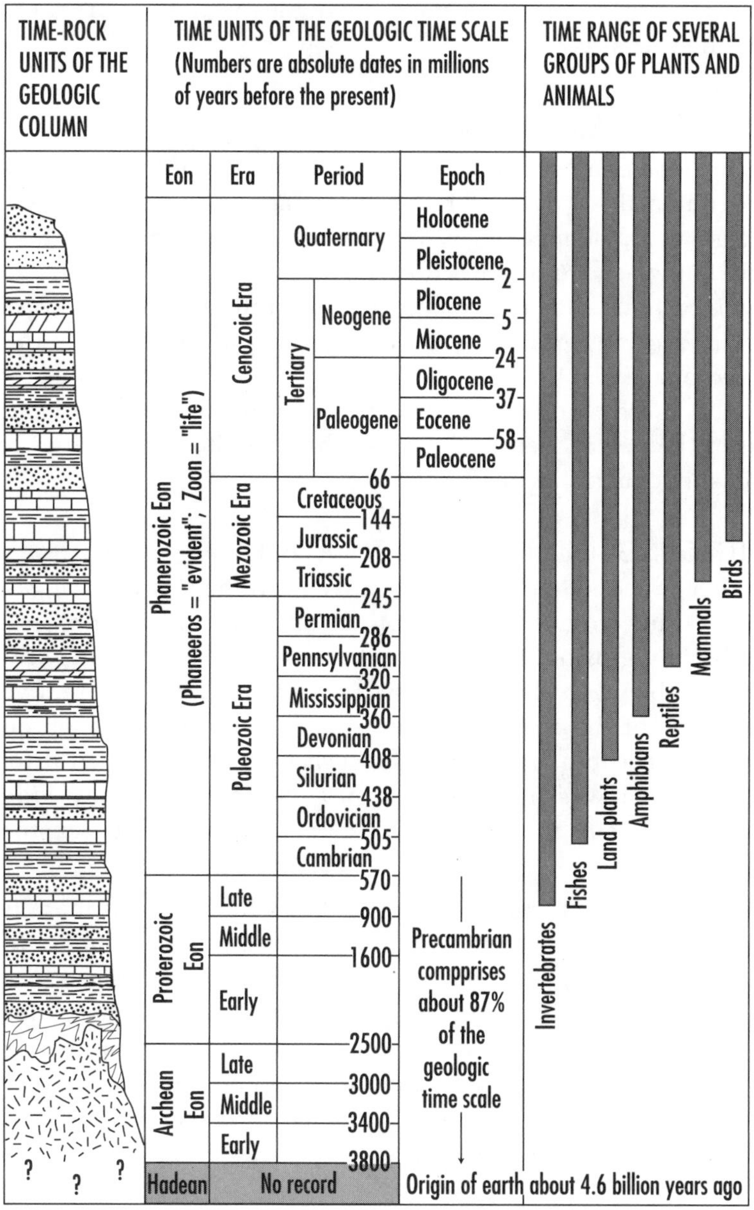

Rock units correspond to units of time in the geologic time scale: there are *rock systems* in periods, *rock series* are in epochs, and *rock stages* in ages. The rocks formed during a specified interval of time are called *time-rock units*.

THE DEVELOPING EARTH

The Hadeon eon occurred before the formation of the oldest known rocks on Earth, or over 3.8 billion years ago. Assuming that Earth is at least as old as meteorites and lunar rocks, it represents the time period between 4.6 billion and 3.8 billion years ago. Scientists have theorized that, after the coalescence of protoplanets from the solar nebula (see chapter 2), a succession of catastrophic events that involved our planet took place. Many objects collided with our planet, and the energy from these objects was transformed into heat that caused the destruction of the rocks that may have held clues to the earliest events in Earth's history.

OUTGASSING AND THE FIRST ATMOSPHERE

Another process that dominates early Earth history was *outgassing*, which occurs from the activity of volcanoes and by the processes of weathering, erosion, and sedimentation. Outgassing released water vapor, carbon dioxide and other gases into the atmosphere. Eventually, much of the carbon dioxide was removed by early photosynthetic microscopic organisms, the *cyanobacteria*, who used it for energy. Later it was incorporated into the shells of many kinds of marine organisms as calcium carbonate, and eventually transformed into limestone.

While the exact composition of Earth's initial atmosphere is unknown, scientists agree that it differed from our atmosphere today. We live in an oxygen-rich atmosphere in which things can burn (in the process of rapid **oxidation**) and food decays (slow oxidation). The early atmosphere, on the other hand, contained a higher percentage of carbon dioxide and methane and no free oxygen, and was what scientists call a *reducing environment*. It was in this environment that life arose.

CHECK YOUR PROGRESS

1. Which of the following methods of dating rocks is used by geochronologists?
   a. uranium-lead   **c.** potassium-argon
   b. rubidium-strontium   **d.** all are used

2. The dating method most useful in studying the age of artifacts from early human settlements is
   a. uranium-lead   **c.** carbon
   b. rubidium-strontium   **d.** potassium-argon

3. The commonly accepted age of Earth is
   a. 46,000,000 years   **c.** 4,500 million years
   b. 4.5 million years   **d.** 46 billion years

4. When the atoms of radioactive isotopes decay, they
   a. become atoms of a different element
   b. absorb energy from the surrounding environment
   c. combine with helium particles in the atmosphere
   d. all of the above

5. A method of dating geological events that relies on studies of summer and winter lake deposits is called
   a. rubidium-strontium dating
   b. varve dating
   c. potassium-argon dating
   d. carbon dating

6. According to the geologic time scale, which time span began approximately 570 million years ago?
   a. Cambrian period   **c.** Phanerozoic eon
   b. Paleozoic era   **d.** all of the above

7. According to the geologic time scale, the present time can be characterized as part of the
   a. Cenozoic era   **c.** Holocene epoch
   b. Quarternary period   **d.** all of the above

8. The "father of modern geology" is
   a. Stephen Jay Gould   **c.** Charles Darwin
   b. Charles Lyell   **d.** James Hutton

9. The Oswego sandstones in New York State were deposited in the Ordovician Period. This deposition would have occurred in which *era*?
   a. the Cincinnatian series
   b. the Paleocene
   c. the Paleozoic
   d. the Carboniferous

10. No rock record of the past exists for the following span of time:
   a. Crypozoic
   b. Hadeon
   c. Proterozoic
   d. Precambrian

THE ORIGIN AND EVOLUTION OF LIFE

In 1996, marine scientists at the Scripps Institute of Oceanography in San Diego found evidence that life began on Earth about 3.9 billion years ago. This evidence was in the form of isotopes of carbon found inside microscopic grains of the mineral *apatite* in a rock formation on Akilia Island, in West Greenland. The carbon deposits are not physical fossils, but scientists say they indicate that microscopic organisms lived on the floor of Earth's first ocean. The oldest known physical fossils are 3.46 billion years old.

Scientists have conducted experiments in which they simulated the early atmosphere, then injected energy into that environment by using an electric sparking device or an ultraviolet lamp. They found that elements suspected to be prevalent in the early atmosphere spontaneously combined to form organic molecules under these conditions. Some scientists suggest that life may have arisen over tens of thousands of years, a relatively brief period of time geologically.

The earliest forms of life were *anaerobes* (organisms that can live in the absence of free oxygen), and were probably single-celled and microscopic in size. They may have found sustenance by assimilating the organic molecules present in the sea water. As these organisms became abundant, food became more scarce, and at some point, some of them developed the ability to make their own food from inorganic substances. Among these first **autotrophs** were *cyanobacteria*, which are microscopic, single-celled organisms without nuclei. These organisms are capable of carrying on *photosynthesis*, and exist today.

As more and more oxygen was produced as a by-product of photosynthesis, the oxygen reacted with minerals in the seawater. After these minerals and the minerals on the land had been thoroughly oxidized, the level of oxygen increased in the atmosphere.

Eventually *aerobic* organisms appeared; these organisms use oxygen to convert food into energy.

The earliest *respirers*, or organisms that breathed oxygen, probably evolved in the seas rather than on land because, by being under water, they were protected from the toxic ultraviolet rays from the Sun. Before the land surface became hospitable to life, the ozone layer in the stratosphere had to form. This took hundreds of millions of years; the first land-dwelling respirers, the amphibians, did not evolve until about 400 million years ago.

Perhaps the most significant event during the Precambrian eon was the evolution of cells with nuclei, which are *eukaryotes*. Biologists believe that many of the parts of eukaryotic cells were once separate microorganisms that entered other cells, perhaps as parasites, then became established in a *symbiotic* relationship with their host. Eukaryotes also began reproducing sexually, so that a great variety of new genetic traits began to be passed from parent to offspring. Sexual reproduction increased the rate of evolution and, by the close of the Proterozoic eon, led to the evolution of complex multicellular animals, called **metazoans**.

By the close of this eon many new forms of life had appeared, including multicellular organisms, but because many life forms had soft bodies, they were not usually preserved as fossils. Geologists delineate the Proterozoic-Phanerozoic boundary by the relatively rapid appearance and spread of multicellular life that occurred.

THE PHANEROZOIC EON: THE PALEOZOIC ERA

At the beginning of the Paleozoic era, North America was extremely different from how it now appears. Our continent was part of a supercontinent and lay on its side relative to its situation today; what is now Washington, DC was next door to Lima, Peru, and what is today the Sahara Desert was close to the South Pole and covered by a glacier. The land that is now North America straddled the equator; it was also smaller and was dominated by a vast plain, which was the result of millions of years of weathering and erosion.

Earth in the Paleozoic era rotated more quickly, so that the days were shorter. The Moon was closer so that tidal effects were stronger. There was no vegetation on the land. At the beginning of the era Earth was recovering from an ice age, and as the climate warmed, broad, shallow seas encroached upon the interiors of the continents.

Early in the Paleozoic era, the ocean that separated North America from the supercontinent of Gondwanaland began to close; the Europe-Africa part of Gondwanaland moved westward, and a subduction zone formed beneath the eastern edge of North America. Over the long span of the Paleozoic, the plate underlying the supercontinent collided several times with North America before it was subducted. Each collision pushed up a mountain system along the eastern edge of our continent, in a process called an **orogeny**. The Appalachians contain evidence of three major orogenies. The first of these, the *Taconic orogeny*, began in the Ordovician period, and resulted in the formation of the northern Appalachians, which may have exceeded 4,000 meters in elevation at that time (see **Figure 10.2**).

Figure 10.2 The Taconic orogeny: about 550 million years ago, the lithospheric plate carrying Gondwanaland moved toward North America, closing the Lapetus Ocean, uplifting the northern Appalachians, and welding Europe to North America.

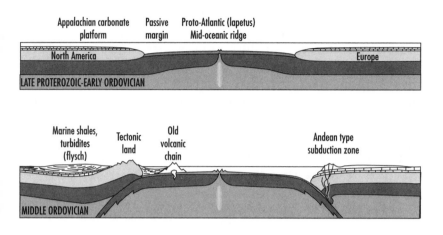

Appalachian carbonate platform   Passive margin   Proto-Atlantic (Iapetus) Mid-oceanic ridge

North America   Europe

LATE PROTEROZOIC-EARLY ORDOVICIAN

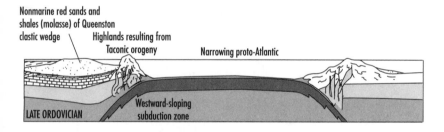

Marine shales, turbidites (flysch)   Tectonic land   Old volcanic chain   Andean type subduction zone

MIDDLE ORDOVICIAN

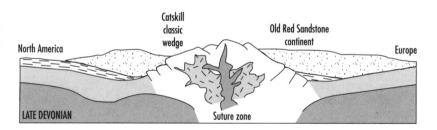

Nonmarine red sands and shales (molasse) of Queenston clastic wedge   Highlands resulting from Taconic orogeny   Narrowing proto-Atlantic

LATE ORDOVICIAN   Westward-sloping subduction zone

North America   Catskill classic wedge   Old Red Sandstone continent   Europe

LATE DEVONIAN   Suture zone

After the initial orogeny, millions of years of weathering and erosion reduced the mountains to low-lying plains, and thick wedges of clastic sediment were spread eastward and westward from the once lofty peaks. This process is illustrated in **Figure 10.3**. The Appalachians we see today are also the result of two later Paleozoic orogenies, called the *Acadian-Caledonian* and *Alleghenian orogenies*. Following the Taconic uplift, the Iapetus Ocean widened and admitted new oceanic crust along a spreading center. Meanwhile, thick sediments accumulated on the continental shelves from the erosion of the first Appalachian Mountains. This was followed by another cycle of contraction, in which the ocean gradually closed, subduction zones developed, and mountains were pushed upward. The Acadian-Caledonian orogeny occurred about 400 million years ago, at the end of the Silurian period, and formed both the Appalachian Mountains and the Caledonide Mountains of Scotland and northwestern Europe.

Figure 10.3 Sediments from the Appalachians were carried in all directions to accumulate as thick wedge-shaped deposits.

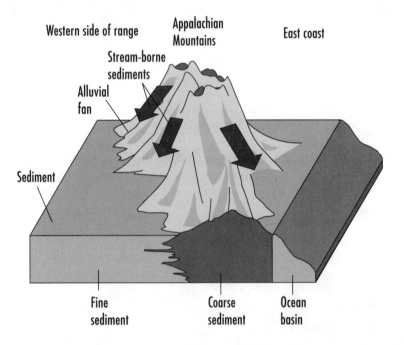

This cycle was repeated toward the end of the Paleozoic, when the North American continent again crumpled in an event called the Allegheny, or Appalachian orogeny. This was the most intense of the three events that created the Appalachians, and it affected a belt that extends over 1,600 kilometers, from southern New York to Alabama. The great folds now visible in the Ridge and Valley Province were created when the southern part of the depositional basin was crushed by the northern margin of Gondwanaland (northwestern Africa and South America). As Gondwanaland shoved North America from the south, what is now the coastal region (from Newfoundland to easternmost Connecticut) was moved from off the coast of Georgia to its present location. The same push glued Florida and southern Georgia, which were originally part of Africa, onto North America, and, during this collision, the landscape across southeastern Oklahoma and west-central Arkansas was crumpled and the Ouachita Mountains were formed, and the Yucatán peninsula, a separate terrane, was shoved between Alabama and Texas.

Also during the Paleozoic era, the Siberian plate (Northern Asia) collided with eastern Europe to form the Ural Mountains. The collision of these plates resulted in the formation of the supercontinent *Pangaea*, meaning "all land." Pangaea was surrounded by a single world ocean—the *Panthalassa*, which means "all seas." Some 75 million years later Pangaea broke up; North America separated from Africa and began its migration toward its present position.

A map of the physiographic provinces of the Appalachian region is shown in **Figure 10.4**. **Figure 10.5** shows a map of the general features of North America at the end of the Paleozoic era.

Figure 10.4 The physiographic provinces of the Appalachian region with a cross section showing the structural relationships.

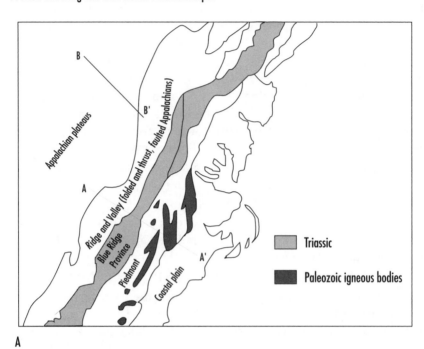

Triassic

Paleozoic igneous bodies

A

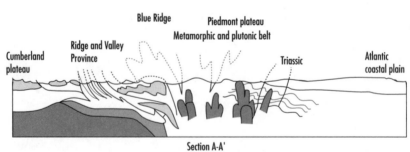

Cumberland plateau

Ridge and Valley Province

Blue Ridge

Piedmont plateau
Metamorphic and plutonic belt

Triassic

Atlantic coastal plain

Section A-A'

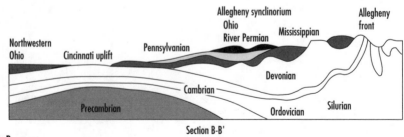

Northwestern Ohio

Cincinnati uplift

Pennsylvanian

Allegheny synclinorium
Ohio
River Permian

Mississippian

Allegheny front

Devonian

Cambrian

Precambrian

Ordovician

Silurian

Section B-B'

B

Figure 10.5 How North America might have looked during the Permian period at the end of the Paleozoic era. Note that Africa and Europe abutted North America to the east, forming the ancient supercontinent, Pangaea.

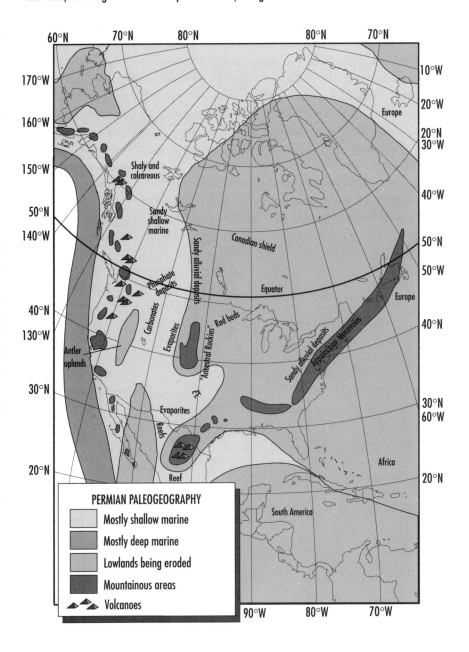

PERMIAN PALEOGEOGRAPHY

- Mostly shallow marine
- Mostly deep marine
- Lowlands being eroded
- Mountainous areas
- Volcanoes

Life in the Paleozoic Era

A variety of multicellular animals inhabited the world's oceans during the Paleozoic era, from relatively simple jellyfish and sponges to more complex trilobites, snails, worms, and shellfish. Those that had shells left behind a rich fossil record of this period, the first such record in the earth's history. The Cambrian explosion of multicellular life included the invasion of sea life onto continents, which provided new habitats and opportunities for diversification. The proliferation of shell-bearing animals was a result of the protection and support that shells provided the soft tissues and organs of the animals. Collectively, these animals are called **invertebrates**, some have abundant living descendants, other invertebrates became extinct by the end of the era, including the trilobites, which are arthropods distantly related to the crab. Still other ancient invertebrates survive today in relatively small numbers; these "living fossils" include the *crinoids* and *brachiopods* (see **Figure 10.6**).

Figure 10.6 Typical marine invertebrate life during the Paleozoic era. Crinoids are often called "sea lilies" and even look plant-like, but they were related to today's starfish and sand dollars. Trilobites are believed to be the first animals to look upon the world; their compound eyes are the most ancient visual system known.

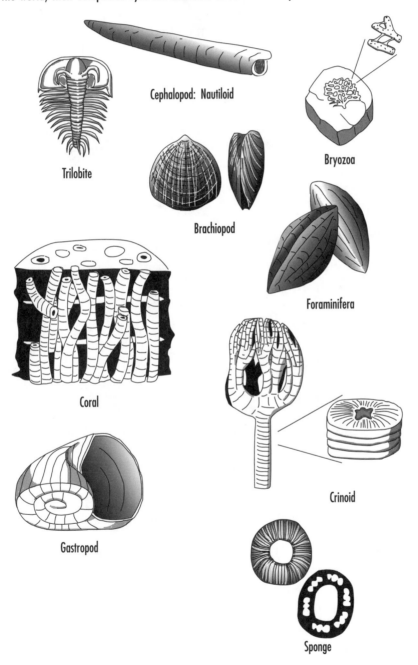

Cephalopod: Nautiloid

Trilobite

Brachiopod

Bryozoa

Foraminifera

Coral

Crinoid

Gastropod

Sponge

The first animals with internal backbones, the **vertebrates**, also evolved during the Paleozoic era. Fossils of the earliest known *chordates*, or animals that have notochords (internal supportive rods) and nerve cords, date to the Cambrian period. The earliest vertebrates were fish; they appeared in the Ordovician period and, by the Devonian, had become so abundant that paleontologists call the latter period the *Age of Fishes*. Representatives of this class of animals are shown in **Figure 10.7**.

Figure 10.7 Typical fish of the Devonian period, the *Age of Fishes*.

Amphibians also appeared during the Paleozoic. During the Silurian period, which began about 440 million years ago, enough oxygen had accumulated in the atmosphere to enable respirers to live on the land. The first invaders were distant relatives of today's frogs and **arthropods**, the group that includes crabs, centipedes, millipedes, and insects.

Plants also evolved extensively in the Paleozoic era. Early in the era, single-celled algae and bacteria dominated. They left few fossils but one type of algae left behind large layered structures called *stromatolites,* and the *receptaculids* (a lime-secreting algae) left behind fossils that are often mistaken for coral. By the end of the Silurian period some plants also developed the ability to survive on land, and by the Devonian period, vast forests of ferns and cone-bearing trees were common. In order to grow into large structures like trees, plants had to develop tubes that moved fluids from one part of the plant to another, that is, they needed a *vascular system.* The vascular system enabled part of a plant to live above ground, where there is light for photosynthesis but an unreliable supply of water, and part of the plant to live underground, where there is usually a supply of moisture, but no light.

The Paleozoic era ended with the *Permian extinction,* which was one of the greatest losses of species in the history of life on Earth. Paleontologists estimate that between 77% and 96% of all marine animal species were lost. The cause is not known, but scientists believe that the extinction may have been a result of a global climate cooling initiated by landmass movements.

MIDDLE TIME: THE MESOZOIC ERA

The Mesozoic era spanned over 180 million years and is divided into three periods, the Triassic, Jurassic, and Cretaceous. The most prominent geological event in the Mesozoic era was the breakup of the supercontinent, Pangaea. The breakup began in the Triassic period, when North America separated from Gondwanaland. Pangaea's dismemberment took 150 million years to complete.

Major orogenies occurred during this era, especially in western North America. The *Nevadan* orogeny resulted in the appearance of many large **batholiths**, massive magma bodies that include the Sierra Nevada batholith of California (see **Figure 10.8**). Batholiths form when plumes of magma migrate upward from the earth's mantle, intrude into the crust, cool, and crystallize. They are frequently associated with subduction zones. About 120 million years ago, during mid-Cretaceous time, the Sierra Nevada and Andes mountains were created by the subduction of Pacific crust under western North and South America. Later in the Cretaceous period, the Laramide orogeny resulted in the initial uplift of the Rocky Mountains (which have since been worn down and uplifted twice again).

In the middle of the Cretaceous period, Earth became much warmer; the average global temperature increased more than 10°C

Figure 10.8 Batholiths in western North America. These enormous igneous bodies arose from the earth's mantle during an event geologists' describe as the Cretaceous superplume episode.

and stayed at that temperature for 20 million years. During this time, the entire globe grew lush with green plants—ferns grew near the North Pole and dinosaurs roamed the entire planet. No one knows what caused this extraordinary climatic change, but the most plausible explanation is that extra carbon dioxide was released into the earth's atmosphere, perhaps from massive volcanic eruptions; in fact, there is evidence that, on average, about ten Mt. St. Helens-sized volcanoes erupted every month during this period. Scientists hypothesize that this increased volcanic activity was initiated by an enormous magma plume that originated deep in the Earth at the core-mantle boundary.

Earth's mantle normally receives heat that radiates out from the core. Heat percolates through the core-mantle boundary by conduction and becomes trapped just above the boundary in the lowermost 100-200 kilometers of solid silicate mantle rock. As heat accumulates here, the buoyancy of overheated, less dense lower-mantle material eventually overcomes the viscosity of the overlying rock, and huge magma blobs, or *plumes* of mantle material rise nearly 3,000 kilometers through the mantle and create volcanic eruptions.

Climate conditions did vary greatly during the Mesozoic; at times much of western North America was the site of a vast desert, but at other times, it was invaded by marine waters, known as the *Sundance Sea* (see **Figure 10.9**). Worldwide marine transgressions occurred during the Mesozoic's warm spell, as the sea level rose to 250 meters higher than it is today.

Figure 10.9 Map of the North American plate approximately 150 million years ago, showing the extent of the Sundance Sea, a shallow marine incursion into the continent.

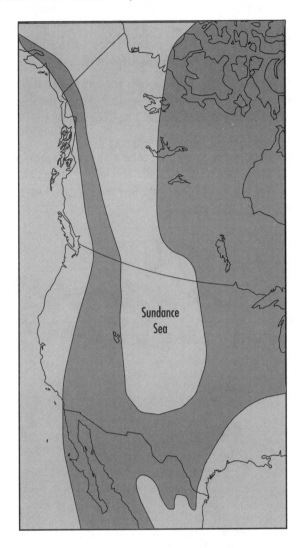

Sundance
Sea

Mesozoic Life

The Mesozoic era is most familiar as the *Age of the Dinosaurs*; these magnificent creatures appeared, reigned for 100 million years, and then disappeared. The dinosaurs were a very diverse group that inhabited land, sea, and air; some dinosaurs were warm-blooded, formed social groups, and protected their young. Some dinosaurs, such as *Ultrasaurus*, which may have weighed up to 100 tons, were the largest animals that have ever walked the earth (see **Figure 10.10**), while other dinosaur species, such as *Compsognathus*, were as small as chickens. Compsognathus was about 20 centimeters tall and weighed only about 2 kilograms. Paleontologists group dinosaurs into two groups based on their pelvic bone structure. **Figure 10.11** shows a family tree for both groups of dinosaurs.

The Mesozoic is also the time when mammals evolved; mammals and dinosaurs alike evolved from reptiles. However, mammals did not diversify and expand very much until the dinosaurs were extinct.

Figure 10.10 Dinosaurs came in all sizes. Some were much larger than elephants, while the *heterodontosaurus* was about the size of a turkey. *Heterodontosaurus* were plant-eaters who lived in desert environments; they are thought to have used burrows much like modern ground squirrels.

Figure 10.11 Evolution of the dinosaurs. Dinosaurs are divided into two groups based on their hip structures.

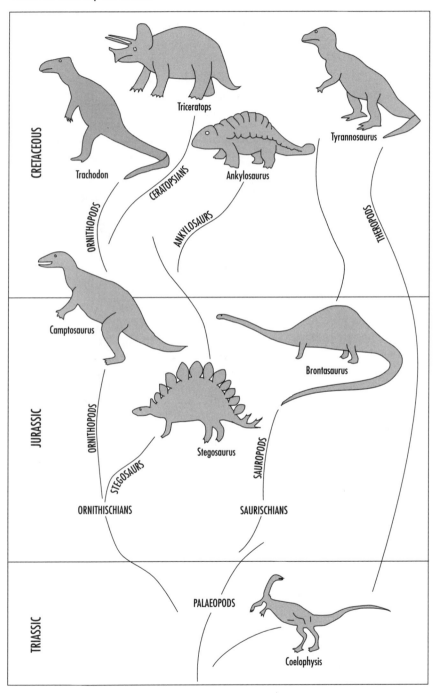

CRETACEOUS

Triceratops

Trachodon

CERATOPSIANS

ORNITHOPODS

ANKYLOSAURS

Ankylosaurus

Tyrannosaurus

THEROPODS

JURASSIC

Camptosaurus

Brontasaurus

ORNITHOPODS

STEGOSAURS

Stegosaurus

SAUROPODS

ORNITHISCHIANS

SAURISCHIANS

TRIASSIC

PALAEOPODS

Coelophysis

The Mesozoic era was also an important time for plant evolution. Paleobotanists call this era the *Age of Cycads*. The cycads are non-flowering seed plants. During this era, the **angiosperms** appeared and became diverse and widespread; these plants had flowers and produced seeds that were enclosed in fruits. The angiosperms include most of the trees, shrubs, grasses, crop plants, and flowering plants that are familiar to us today. The evolution of insects, reptiles, birds, and mammals in the Mesozoic was greatly influenced by the appearance and success of the angiosperms.

The Extinction of the Dinosaurs

There have been many hypotheses to account for the Cretaceous extinctions. Geologist Walter Alvarez proposed, in 1980, that dinosaurs became extinct primarily due to an asteroid colliding with Earth. In 1989, evidence was found of a huge impact crater north of Chicxulub on the Yucatán Peninsula (see **Figure 10.12**). Since then more evidence has been collected: drilled core samples of the Atlantic Ocean floor 100 meters beneath the seafloor off the east coast of Florida contain remnants of an asteroid impact, and one brownish section in the core samples, called the fireball layer, contains vaporized bits of the asteroid itself. The layer *beneath* this fireball layer shows fossils of abundant ocean life, but *above* this is a layer with small green glass pebbles: evidence that the materials on the ocean bottom were instantly melted by the impact of the asteroid. Much of the asteroid was probably vaporized and expelled into the atmosphere. The fireball layer has a high content of iridium, an element more abundant in asteroids than in the earth's crust. Above the layer that contains the beads is a 5 centimeter thick layer of gray clay, which contains some small fossils of the few survivors. The thickness of the gray clay layer in the core samples represents the thousands of years that passed after the disaster before marine life began to diversify again.

According to paleontologists' reconstruction of the events after the meteor impact, huge waves washed completely across Florida, depositing debris in the Atlantic. Waters in the Gulf of Mexico were agitated so much that there was little deposition there, and debris washed all the way to Arkansas. Hot fragments of the asteroid started fires that may have consumed a quarter of the world's plant life. The asteroid fall may not have been the only factor involved, but whatever the cause, the dinosaurs, pterosaurs, ammonites in the seas, and three-fourths of the species of marine plankton all died out 65 million years ago.

Figure 10.12 Map of the Yucatán. The asteroid that struck here 65 million years ago left a crater nearly 300 kilometers wide. The size of the asteroid has been estimated at between 6 and 16 kilometers across; its impact released as much energy as would 200 million hydrogen bombs. There is evidence that there was a second impact; the asteroid may have split apart before it stuck.

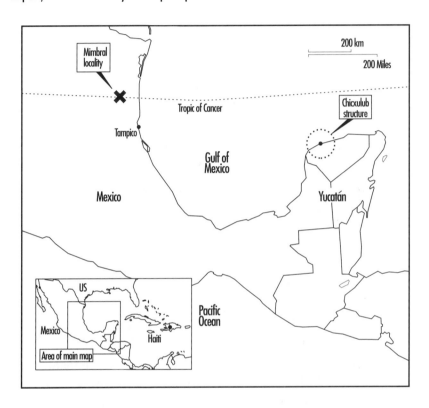

RECENT TIME: THE CENOZOIC ERA

There was little orogenic activity in eastern North America during the Cenozoic era, which began 65 million years ago. On the other side of the continent, however, the Rocky Mountains were eroded and then reelevated twice, and abundant sediment deposits were spread eastward across the Great Plains. One of the layers of this sediment formed the Ogallala Sandstone, which is the aquifer that stores underground water in the West. In the Great Basin region (see **Figure 10.13**), fault-block mountain ranges were created when the continental crust was stretched apart, probably because plate motions along the continent's western margin changed. The Coast Ranges in the Pacific Northwest also developed during the Cenozoic, as did the volcanic cones of the Cascade Range. In fact, volcanic activity has been high in this era; the extensive plateaus east of the Cascades attests to this. They are composed of piled up layers of basaltic lava, some of which is as thick as three kilometers.

Figure 10.13 The Great Basin in North America.

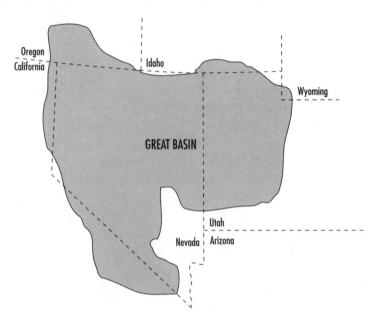

Another area that was greatly altered during the Cenozoic is the Gulf Coast. The Gulf coastal plain contains the best record of Cenozoic strata on the continent. During this era, this region experienced eight major transgressions and regressions of marine waters, and one transgression brought the sea as far north as southern Illinois. The wedge of sediments found in the Gulf coastal plain thickens seaward and has been measured in places at 10,000 meters.

Among the most spectacular geologic events in the Cenozoic era was the uplift of the Pyrenees, the Atlas Mountains, and the Alps; they rose from pressure produced by the northward movement of the African plate. The Mediterranean Sea also dried up for a time, about 5.5 million years ago, and may have been like the present Death Valley region of California. This event was not related to plate movements, but to the sudden expansion of the Antarctic ice sheet, which lowered the sea level by as much as 50 meters. As a result, the

Mediterranean became isolated from the ocean and its water gradually evaporated.

The Great Ice Age

The climate cooled gradually during the Cenozoic era. This change in climate reduced the range of the tropical forests and provided for the spread of grasslands in the middle latitudes. The Great Ice Age occurred during the latter part of the era, the Pleistocene epoch. Between one and two million years ago, ice accumulated at the Poles in great quantities, flowing outward from its weight to form an extensive continental glacier. The four advances and retreats of Pleistocene glaciers dramatically changed the land surface, created the Great Lakes, and determined the position of major river systems, including the Missouri and Ohio. Glaciation is discussed further in chapter 4.

Life in the Cenozoic

The Cenozoic era began with the great extinction of the dinosaurs and their replacement by the mammals. Evolutionary biologists believe that mammals evolved during the Mesozoic era from a type of reptile called the *therapsids*. The Cenozoic is referred to as the *Age of Mammals* because mammals diversified explosively during this time, and came to dominate Earth much as the dinosaurs had done during the Mesozoic era.

In the Pleistocene epoch, our own species appeared in Africa. Fossils of humanlike species have been dated to more than four million years of age, but fossils of our particular species, *Homo sapiens sapiens*, date only to hundreds of thousands of years. Humans differ from other members of the group to which we belong, the primates, in that we are fully *bipedal*, meaning capable of walking upright on two feet.

When the Great Ice Age was at its peak, about 11,000 years ago, the Northern Hemisphere supported a varied and abundant fauna of large mammals, including colossal ground sloths, giant beavers, woolly mammoths and mastodons, elk, the ponderous *perissodactyls*, and rhinoceroses, including the giant *Baluchitherium*, which is the largest land mammal thus far discovered. All of these beasts declined rapidly and became extinct around 8,000 years ago. The cause of their extinctions is not known, but scientists hypothesize that the extinctions may have been related to the milder climate that began to develop, or to over-predation by humans.

CONSIDER THIS

"We speak of an 'age of invertebrates' followed by an 'age of fishes, reptiles, and mammals,' all capped by an 'age of man.'...But invertebrates have always dominated the world of multicellular animal life in numbers of species and prospects for long-term success, while *Homo sapiens* is one tiny twig on life's exuberantly branching bush. This is not the 'age of man'; it is not even the 'age of insects'—a proper designation if we wish to honor multicellular animal life. As it was in the beginning, is now, and ever shall be until the sun explodes, this is the 'age of bacteria.'...Bacteria span a broader range of biochemistries and live in a wider range of environments; [and] they overwhelm all else in frequency and variety; the number of *E. coli* in the gut of any human exceeds the count of all humans that have lived since our African dawn."

Stephen Jay Gould

CHECK YOUR PROGRESS

11. The "Age of the Dinosaurs" belongs to which span of geologic time?

   a. Paleozoic era   **c.** Mesozoic era
   b. Cenozoic era   **d.** Archaeozoic era

12. According to the geologic time scale, which of the following organisms has persisted the longest on Earth?

   a. mammals   **c.** invertebrates
   b. land plants   **d.** birds

13. The organisms that evolved during the "Age of Amphibians" would be most closely related to today's

   a. marsupial mammals
   b. snakes
   c. toads
   d. crocodiles

14. Which of the following animals is most closely related to dinosaurs?

   a. birds
   b. fish
   c. whales
   d. bats

15. Living things invaded the earth's land habitats during the

   a. Precambrian
   b. Paleozoic
   c. Mesozoic
   d. Cenozoic

16. For respiring organisms to survive on land

   a. the atmosphere's ozone layer had to develop
   b. at least 5% of the atmosphere had to be oxygen
   c. fins had to evolve into walking limbs
   d. lungs had to develop

17. The supercontinent Pangaea broke up during this era of geologic time

   a. Precambrian
   b. Proterozoic
   c. Paleozoic
   d. Mesozoic

18. Animals possessing internal support rods are called

   a. chordates
   b. invertebrates
   c. crinoids
   d. arthropods

19. Humans are most closely related to which of the following organisms?

   a. fish
   b. trilobites
   c. crustaceans
   d. cyanobacteria

20. An important geologic event which occurred in the Mesozoic era was

   a. the reign of the dinosaurs
   b. the intrusion of the Sierra Nevada batholith
   c. the Appalachian orogeny
   d. the formation of Pangaea

21. As far as is presently known, humans evolved
    a. in Africa in the Pleistocene
    b. in Africa in the Permian
    c. in Asia in the Pleistocene
    d. in Asia in the Permian

22. Dinosaurs
    a. became extinct following the impact of a large meteorite
    b. developed warm-bloodedness
    c. formed social groups and protected their young
    d. all of the above

23. Paleontologists classify dinosaurs based upon
    a. features of the jaw
    b. size
    c. hip structure
    d. warm or cold bloodedness

Refer to **Figure 10.14** to answer questions 24 through 27.

Figure 10.14 A hypothetical cross section of the earth's crust, showing strata and igneous intrusions.

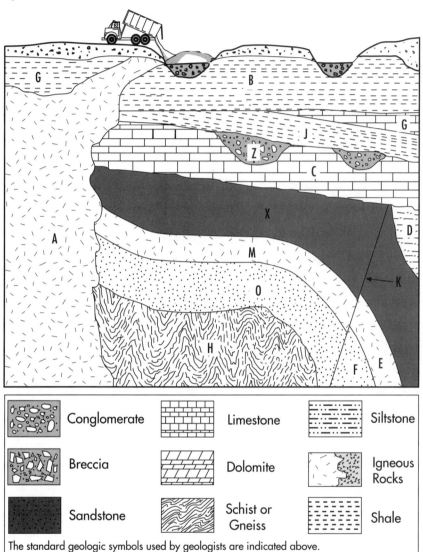

The standard geologic symbols used by geologists are indicated above.

24. The geologic cross section in **Figure 10.14** illustrates a portion of the earth's crust in which no overturning has occurred. Which letter represents an igneous intrusion into layers of rock strata?

a. A   c. C
b. B   d. D

25. Which of the layers in **Figure 10.14** represents the *oldest* of the layers shown?

a. B   c. E
b. C   d. F

26. Which of the layers in **Figure 10.14** would most likely be a site for the formation of a cave as the result of chemical weathering?

a. A   c. C
b. E   d. F

27. In **Figure 10.14**, which rock layer on the right is most likely the same age as Layer G on the left?

a. B   c. D
b. C   d. E

GLOSSARY

angiosperms—the flowering plants. Angiosperms produce seeds enclosed in fleshy fruits.

arthropods—a group of invertebrate animals comprising over one million species that are characterized by an outer body layer, a segmented body usually with specialized body regions (e.g., head, thorax, and abdomen), and usually hardened, jointed appendages. This group includes the arachnids (spiders, scorpions, mites, ticks), crustaceans (crabs, barnacles, shrimp), centipedes and millipedes, and the insects.

autotrophs—a type of nutrition in which organisms synthesize the organic materials they require from inorganic sources, such as carbon dioxide and nitrates. Green plants are *photoautotrophic*.

batholith—a massive, discordant pluton (igneous rock) that intrudes through existing rock layers.

geochronology—the study of time as applied to Earth and planetary history.

geological time—a time scale that covers the earth's history from its origin to the present, covering some 4.6 billion years. The chronology is divided into a hierarchy of time intervals.

geomorphology—the study of the origin and development of landforms.

invertebrates—animals without internal backbones.

mass spectrometer—a laboratory instrument used to measure the amount of an element in a sample. The sample is vaporized inside a chamber where it is bombarded with electrons, leaving only ions. The ion stream is passed through charged plates where the ions become deflected in proportion to their masses.

metazoans—multicellular animals that possess more than one kind of cell and have their cells organized into tissues and organs.

orogeny—the process of mountain building. Orogenesis is the process by which mountain belts are formed.

oxidation—originally, a chemical reaction with oxygen. The reverse process, loss of oxygen, is *reduction*. Now, oxidation more widely includes any loss of electrons by a substance, while reduction is a gain of electrons.

paleontology—the study of, the structure, environment, evolution, and distribution of extinct organisms through their fossil remains. Subfields include paleobotany, paleoecology, and paleozoology.

radiometric dating—methods of determining the age of an object by studying the decay of particular radioactive isotopes.

stratigraphy—the study of the origin, composition, sequence, and correlation of rock strata.

varve—thin layers of clay sediments, common in regions such as Scandinavia, that have alternating dark and light bands that correspond to summer and winter deposition.

vertebrates—animals with internal backbones.

ANSWER KEY

1. d
2. c
3. c
4. a
5. b
6. d
7. d
8. d
9. c
10. b
11. c
12. c
13. c
14. a
15. b
16. a
17. d
18. a
19. a
20. b
21. a
22. d
23. c
24. a
25. d
26. c
27. a

Practice Exams

PRACTICE EXAM ONE

Directions (1-55): For *each* statement or question, select the word or expression that, of those given, best completes the statements or answers the questions.

1. The map below shows the elevation field for a 30-by-50-meter section of a parking lot on which a large pile of sand has been dumped, The isolines show the height of the sand above the surface of the parking lot in meters.

    Which map represents the most likely elevation field for the same area after several heavy rainstorms?

    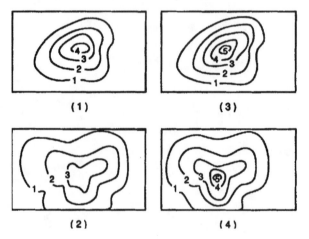

2. The Earth's actual shape is most correctly described as
    1. a circle   3. an oblate sphere
    2. a perfect sphere   4. an eccentric ellipse

3. According to the *Earth Science Reference Tables*, where are atmospheric pressure readings of 10^{-2} atmosphere found?
    1. stratosphere   3. mesosphere
    2. troposphere   4. thermosphere

4. The diagram below shows the altitude of Polaris above the horizon at a certain location.

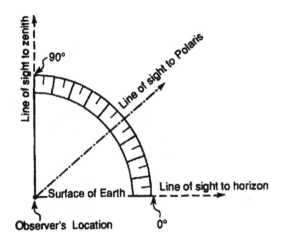

What is the latitude of the observer?
1. 10°N   2. 40° N
3. 50° N   4. 90° N

5. In the Northern Hemisphere, during which season does the Earth reach its greatest distance from the Sun?
   1. winter   3. summer
   2. spring   4. fall

6. The Coriolis Effect provides evidence that the Earth
   1. has a magnetic field
   2. has an elliptical orbit
   3. revolves around the sun
   4. rotates on its axis

7. During the warmest part of a June day, breezes blow from the ocean to shore at a Long Island beach. Which statement best explains why this happens?
   1. Winds usually blow from hot to cold areas.
   2. Winds never blow from the shore toward the ocean.
   3. Air pressure over the ocean is higher than air pressure over the land.
   4. Air pressure over the land is higher than the air pressure over the ocean.

Base your answers to questions 8 and 9 on the diagram below which repre-sents the apparent daily path of the Sun across the sky in the Northern Hemisphere on the dates indicated.

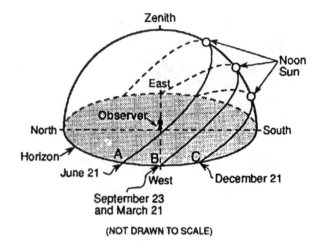

(NOT DRAWN TO SCALE)

8. At noon on which date would the observer cast the longest shadow?
   1. June 21
   2. September 23
   3. March 21
   4. December 21

9. Which observation about the Sun's apparent path at this location on June 21 is best supported by this diagram?
   1. The Sun appears to move across the sky at 1° per hour.
   2. The Sun's total daytime pattern is shortest on this date.
   3. Sunrise occurs north of east.
   4. Sunset occurs south of west.

10. At which temperature would an object radiate the *least* amount of electromagnetic energy?
    1. the boiling point of water (100°C)
    2. the temperature of the stratospause(0°C)
    3. the temperature of the North Pole on December 21 (−60°F)
    4. room temperature (293 K)

11. Infrared radiation is absorbed in the atmosphere mainly by
    1. nitrogen and oxygen
    2. argon and radon
    3. ice crystals and dust
    4. carbon dioxide and water vapor

12. The diagram below shows part of the electromagnetic spectrum.

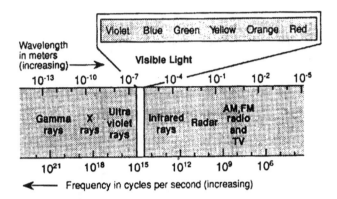

Which form of electromagnetic energy shown on the diagram has the lowest frequency and the longest wave length?
1. AM radio   3. red light
2. infrared rays   4. gamma rays

13 The factor that contributes most to the seasonal temperatures during one year in New York state is the changing
    1. speed at which the Earth travels in orbit around the Sun
    2. angle at which the Sun's rays strike the Earth's surface
    3. distance between the Earth and the Sun
    4. energy given off by the Sun

14. The tilt of the Earth on its axis is a cause of the Earth's
    (1) uniform daylight hours
    (2) changing length of day and night
    (3) 24-hour day
    (4) $365\frac{1}{4}$-day year

15. Which process most directly results in cloud formation?
    1. condensation   3. precipitation
    2. transpiration   4. radiation

16. An air mass originating over north central Canada would most likely be
    1. warm and dry   3. cold and dry
    2. warm and moist   4. cold and moist

17. Which graph best represents the relationship between the moisture holding capacity (ability to hold moisture) of the atmosphere and atmospheric temperature?

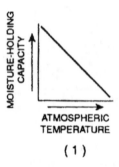

(1)

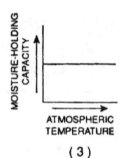

(3)

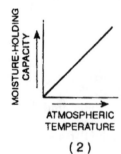

(2)

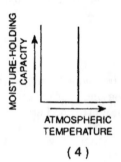

(4)

18. In the diagram of a mountain below, location *A* and location *B* have the same elevation.

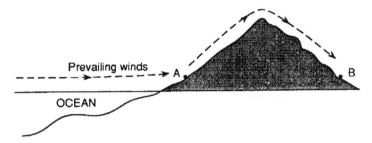

Compared to the climate location *A*, the climate at location *B*, will be

1. warmer and drier
2. cooler and drier
3. warmer and wetter
4. cooler and wetter

19. The graph below shows the air temperature and dewpoint temperature at one location at four different times during the morning.

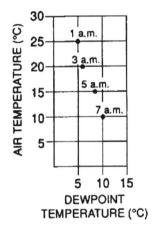

At what time was the chance of precipitation the greatest?

1. 1 a.m.
2. 5 a.m.
3. 3 a.m.
4. 7 a.m.

20. According to the *Earth Science Reference Tables,* what is the approximate dewpoint temperature when the dry-bulb temperature is 18°C and the wet-bulb temperature is 14.5°C?

1. 8.0°C
2. 10.°C
3. 11°C
4. 12°C

21. Which earth material covering the surface of a landfill would permit the *least* amount of rainwater to infiltrate the surface?

1. silt
2. clay
3. sand
4. pebbles

22. Two coastal cities have the same latitude and elevation, but are located near different oceans. Which statement best explains why the two cities have different climates?

1. They are at different longitudes.
2. They are near different ocean currents.
3. They have different angles of insolation.
4. They have different numbers of daylight hours.

23. Which graph best represents the relationship between soil permeability rate and infiltration when all other conditions are the same?

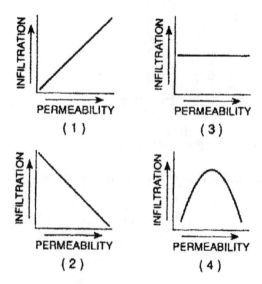

24. What most likely will happen to soil moisture when precipitation is greater than potential evapotranspiration?
    1. Soil-moisture storage may decrease.
    2. Soil-moisture deficit may increase.
    3. Soil-moisture may be recharged.
    4. Soil-moisture may be used.

25. In which type of climate does chemical weathering usually occur most rapidly?
    1. hot and dry
    2. hot and wet
    3. cold and dry
    4. cold and wet

26. A sample of rounded quartz sediments of different sizes is dropped into a container of water. Which graph best shows the settling time for these particles?

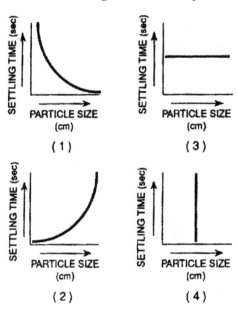

27. Where is metamorphic rock frequently found?
    1. on mountaintops that have horizontal layers containing marine fossils
    2. within large lava flows
    3. as a thin surface layer covering huge areas of the continents
    4. along the interface igneous intrusions and sedimentary bedrock

28. The map below shows the top view of a meandering stream as it enters a lake.

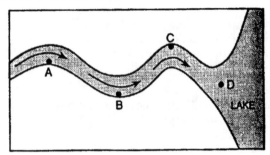

At which points along the stream are erosion and deposition dominant?
1. Erosion is dominant at A and D, and deposition is dominant at B and C.
2. Erosion is dominant at B and C, and deposition is dominant at A and D.
3. Erosion is dominant at A and C, and deposition is dominant at B and D.
4. Erosion is dominant at B and D, and deposition is dominant at A and C.

29. The particles in a sand dune deposit are small and very well-sorted and have surface pits that give them a frosted appearance. This deposit most likely was transported by
1. ocean currents   3. gravity
2. glacial ice   4. wind

30. The diagram below represents a sedimentary rock outcrop.

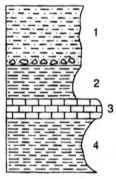

Which rock layer is most resistant to weathering?
1. 1   3. 3
2. 2   4. 4

31. Which property is most useful in mineral identification?
    1. hardness
    2. color
    3. size
    4. texture

32. The diagrams below represent four rock samples. Which rock took the longest time to solidify from magma deep within the Earth?

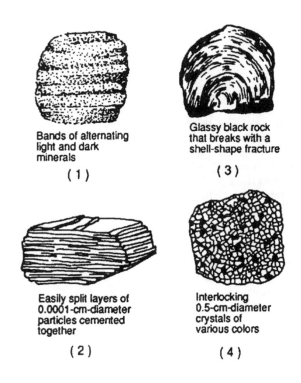

Bands of alternating
light and dark
minerals
(1)

Glassy black rock
that breaks with a
shell-shape fracture
(3)

Easily split layers of
0.0001-cm-diameter
particles cemented
together
(2)

Interlocking
0.5-cm-diameter
crystals of
various colors
(4)

33. According to the *Earth Science Reference Tables*, which two elements make up the greatest volume of the Earth's crust?
    1. silicon and potassium
    2. silicon and iron
    3. iron and nickel
    4. oxygen and potassium

34. The recrystallization of unmelted material under high temperature and pressure results in
    1. metamorphic rock   3. igneous rock
    2. sedimentary rock   4. volcanic rock

35. According to the *Earth Science Reference Tables*, which sedimentary rock would be formed by the compaction and cementation of particles 1.5 centimeters in diameter?
    1. shale   3. conglomerate
    2. sandstone   4. siltstone

36. Fossils of organisms that lived in shallow water can be found in horizontal sedimentary rock layers at great ocean depths. This fact is generally interpreted by most Earth scientists as evidence that
    1. the cold water deep in the ocean kills shallow water organisms
    2. sunlight once penetrated to the deepest parts of the ocean
    3. organisms that live in deep water evolved from species that once lived in shallow waters
    4. sections of the Earth's crust have changed their elevations relative to sea level

37. Earthquakes generate compressional waves (*P*-waves) and shear waves (*S*-waves). Compared to the speed of shear waves in a given earth material, the speed of compressional waves is
    1. always slower
    2. always faster
    3. always the same
    4. sometimes faster and sometimes slower

38. A *P*-wave reaches a seismograph station 2,600 kilometers from an earthquake epicenter at 12:10 p.m.. According to the *Earth Science Reference Tables*, at what time did the earthquake occur?
    1. 12:01 p.m.   3. 12:15 p.m.
    2. 12:05 p.m.   4. 12:19 p.m.

39. The elevation of a certain area was measured for many years, and the results are recorded in the data table below.

Year	Elevation (m)
1870	102.00
1890	102.25
1910	102.50
1930	102.75
1950	103.00

If the elevation continued to increase at the same rate, what was most likely the elevation of this area in 1990?
1. 103.25 m   3. 103.75 m
2. 103.50 m   4. 103.00 m

40. The cross-sectional diagram below of the Earth shows the path of seismic waves from an earthquake. Letter X represents the location of a seismic station.

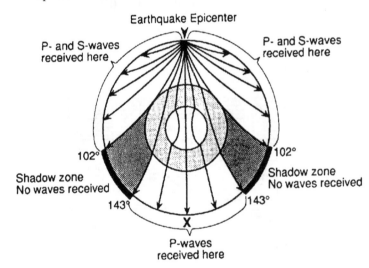

Earthquake Epicenter

P- and S-waves received here

P- and S-waves received here

102°

102°

Shadow zone No waves received

Shadow zone No waves received

143°

143°

X

P-waves received here

Which statement best explains why station X received only P-waves?
1. S-waves traveled too slowly for seismographs to detect them.
2. Station X is too far from the focus for S-waves to reach.
3. A liquid zone within the earth stops S-waves.
4. P-waves and S-waves are refracted by the Earth's core.

41. Geologists have subdivided geologic time into periods that are based on
    1. carbon dating
    2. rock types
    3. fossil evidence
    4. landscape regions

42. An ancient bone was analyzed and found to contain carbon 14 that had decayed for nearly two half lives. According to the *Earth Science Reference Tables* how old is the bone?
    1. 1,400 years
    2. 2,800 years
    3. 5,600 years
    4. 11,000 years

43. According to the *Earth Science Reference Tables* studies of the rock record suggest that
    1. the period during which humans existed is very brief compared to geologic time
    2. evidence of existence of humans is present over much of the geologic past
    3. humans appeared at the time of the intrusion of the Palisades sill
    4. the earliest humans lived at the same time of the dinosaurs

44. The diagram below shows a cross-sectional view of part of the Earth's crust

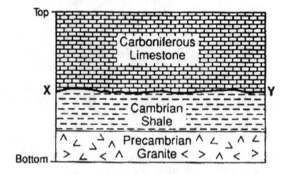

What does the unconformity (buried erosional surface) at line *XY* represent?
    1. an area of contact metamorphism
    2. a time gap in the rock record of the area
    3. proof that no deposition occurred between the Cambrian and Carboniferous rock layers
    4. overturning of the Cambrian and Carboniferous rock layers

45. The diagram below shows a cross section of the Earth's crust. line *XY* is a fault.

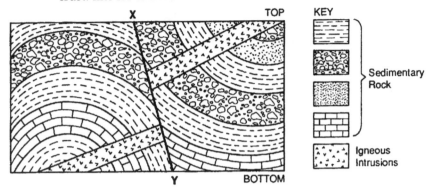

Which sequence of events, from oldest to youngest, has occurred in this outcrop?

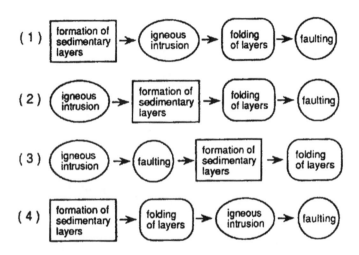

(1) formation of sedimentary layers → igneous intrusion → folding of layers → faulting

(2) igneous intrusion → formation of sedimentary layers → folding of layers → faulting

(3) igneous intrusion → faulting → formation of sedimentary layers → folding of layers

(4) formation of sedimentary layers → folding of layers → igneous intrusion → faulting

46. Which geologic evidence best supports the inference that a continental ice sheet once covered most of New York State?
   1. polished and smooth pebbles; meandering rivers; V–shaped valleys
   2. scratched and polished bedrock; unsorted gravel deposits; transported boulders
   3. sand and silt beaches; giant swamps; marine fossils found on mountaintops
   4. basaltic bedrock; folded, faulted, and tilted rock structures, lava flows

47. The boundaries between landscape regions are usually indicated by sharp changes in
 1. bedrock structure and elevation
 2. weathering rate and method and deposition
 3. soil association and geologic age
 4. stream discharge rate and direction of flow

48. According to the *Earth Science Reference Tables*, which type of landscape region is found at 44° North latitude and 75° West longitude.
 1. plains   3. lowlands
 2. plateaus   4. mountains

49. The diagram below represents a partial cross section of a model of the Earth. The arrows show inferred motions within the Earth.

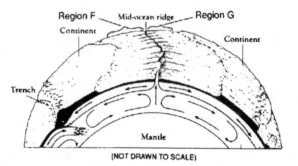

(NOT DRAWN TO SCALE)

Which property of the oceanic crust in regions *F* and *G* is a result of these inferred motions?
 1. The crystal size of the rock decreases constantly as distance from the mid-ocean ridge increases.
 2. The temperature of the basaltic rock increases as distance from the mid-ocean ridge increases.
 3. Heat-flow measurements steadily increase as distance from mid-ocean ridge increases,
 4. The age of the igneous rock increases as distance from the mid-ocean ridge increases.

50. The diagram below shows an example of conglomerate rock.

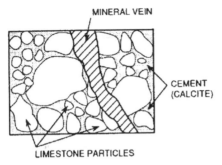

MINERAL VEIN

CEMENT (CALCITE)

LIMESTONE PARTICLES

The oldest part of the sample is the
1. conglomerate rock sample
2. calcite cement
3. limestone particles
4. mineral vein

51. The map below shows the drainage pattern of a volcanic region.

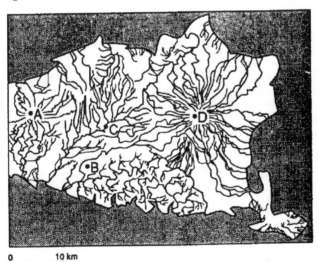

0   10 km

Which two locations are most likely volcanic mountain peaks?
1. *A* and *B*   3. *A* and *D*
2. *B* and *C*   4. *B* and *D*

52. The map below shows average annual temperatures in degrees Fahrenheit across the United States.

Which climate pattern is most important in determining the pattern shown in the eastern half of the United States?
1. ocean currents
2. mountain barriers
3. elevation above sea level
4. latitude

Note that questions 53 through 55 have only three choices.

53. The diagram below shows an area where sea level gradually dropped over a period of a thousand years. A continuous sandy beach deposit stretching from A to B was created.

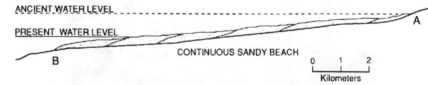

Which statement about the beach deposit would most likely be true?
1. It is older at A than B.
2. It is older at B than A.
3. It is the same age at A and B.

54. As warm, moist air moves into a region, barometric pressure readings in the area will generally
    1. decrease
    2. increase
    3. remain the same

55. As surface runoff in a region increases, stream discharge in that region will usually
    1. decrease
    2. increase
    3. remain the same

Base your answers to questions 56 through 60 on the *Earth Science Reference Tables*, the contour map below, and your knowledge of earth science. Points *A*,*B*,*Y*, and *Z* are reference points on the map. Note that portions of the map are incomplete.

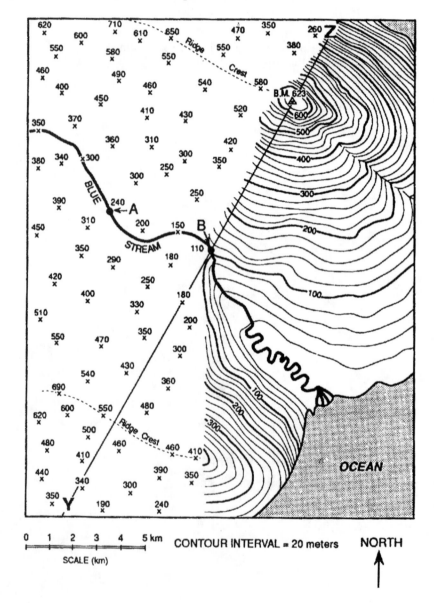

0 1 2 3 4 5 km   CONTOUR INTERVAL = 20 meters   NORTH

SCALE (km)

56. Which diagram best represents the profile along line *YZ*?

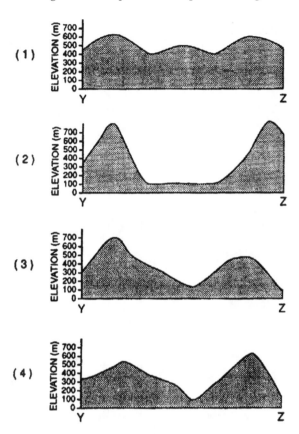

57. A benchmark (B.M. 623) located at the top of the hill is shown. What is the elevation of the contour line that is closest to this benchmark?
    1. 600 m   3. 620 m
    2. 610 m   4. 630 m

58. In which general direction is Blue Stream flowing?
    1. east   3. northwest
    2. west   4. southeast

59. The gradient of Blue Stream between point *A* and point *B* is approximately
    1. 26 m/km   3. 130 m/km
    2. 70 m/km   4. 350 m/km

60. On which map is the 300-meter contour line completed correctly?

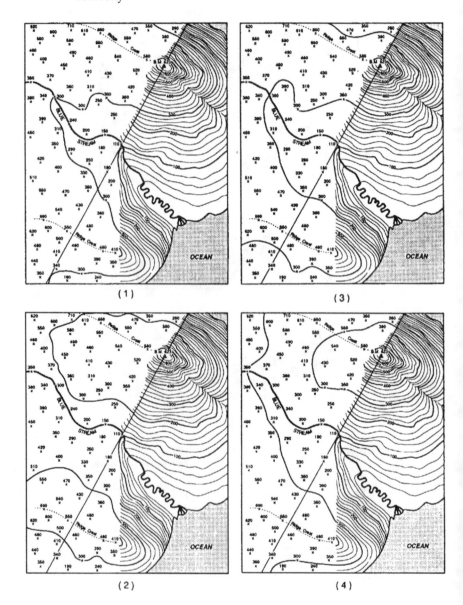

(1)

(3)

(2)

(4)

Base your answers to questions 61 through 65 on the *Earth Science Reference Tables*, the diagram below and your knowledge of earth science. The diagram represents a model of a moon in its orbit. Point F_1 and F_2 are focal points of the orbit.

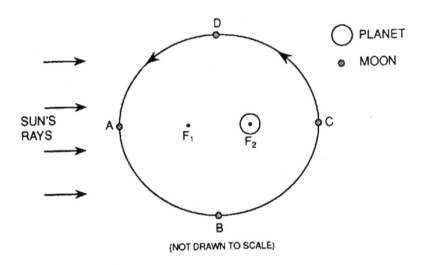

(NOT DRAWN TO SCALE)

61. If the moon takes 6.8 days to move fom point *A* to point *B*, the best estimate of the time required for one complete revolution is
    1. 20 days   3. 34 days
    2. 27 days   4. 41 days

62. When viewed from the planet, the moon has the greatest apparent diameter at point
    1. *A*   3. *C*
    2. *B*   4. *D*

63. If the distance from F_1 to F_2 is 42,000 kilometers and the distance from *A* to *C* is 768, 000 kilometers, what is the eccentricity of the moon's orbit?
    1. 0.055   3. 0.81
    2. 0.18   4. 0.94

64. For an observer on the planet which position in the moon's orbit does the full-moon phase occur?
    1. *A*   3. *C*
    2. *B*   4. *D*

65. As the moon moves in its orbit from point *D* to point *B*, the force of gravitational attraction between the moon and the planet
    1. increases, only
    2. decreases, only
    3. increases, then decreases
    4. decreases, then increases

Base your answers to questions 66 through 70 on the *Earth Science References Tables,* the diagrams below, and your knowledge of earth science. The diagram shows the steps used to determine the amount of heat held by equal masses of iron, copper, lead, and granite.

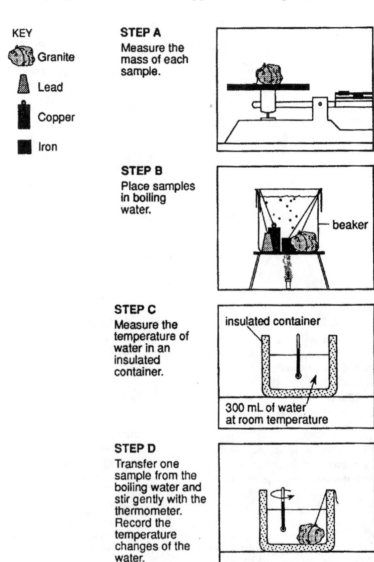

KEY

Granite

Lead

Copper

Iron

STEP A
Measure the mass of each sample.

STEP B
Place samples in boiling water.

beaker

STEP C
Measure the temperature of water in an insulated container.

insulated container

300 mL of water at room temperature

STEP D
Transfer one sample from the boiling water and stir gently with the thermometer. Record the temperature changes of the water.

STEP E
Repeat steps C and D with each sample.

66. This method of determining the amount of heat absorbed by substances assumes that the energy lost by a heat source is
   1. refracted by a heat sink
   2. reflected by a heat sink
   3. absorbed by a heat sink
   4. scattered by a heat sink

67. Which substance has the highest specific heat?
   1. copper   3. iron
   2. granite   4. lead

68. Why must the water be kept boiling in step B?
   1. All samples must be heated to the same high temperatures.
   2. Boiling changes the melting point of the materials being tested.
   3. The samples must be heated above 100° C.
   4. Less energy is lost during a phase change.

69. The granite sample is transferred from the boiling water. Why is the total heat lost by the granite greater than the total heat gained by the room-temperature water?
   1. The granite sample has less volume than the other samples.
   2. The granite sample lost some heat to the air as it was being transferred.
   3. Water gained heat from the insulated container.
   4. Water has a lower specific heat than the granite sample.

70. The movements of water molecules that transfer heat from one place to another within the water are called
   1. radiation waves
   2. transverse waves
   3. conduction collisions
   4. convection currents

Base your answers to questions 71 through 75 on the *Earth Science Reference Tables*, the diagrams and graph below, and your knowledge of earth science. The diagrams show the general effect of the Earth's atmosphere on insolation from the Sun at middle latitude during both clear-sky and cloudy-sky conditions. The graph shows the percentage of insolation reflected by the Earth's surface at different latitudes in the Northern Hemisphere in winter.

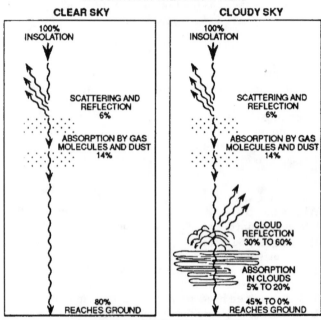

INSOLATION IN THE ATMOSPHERE

CLEAR SKY

100% INSOLATION

SCATTERING AND REFLECTION 6%

ABSORPTION BY GAS MOLECULES AND DUST 14%

80% REACHES GROUND

CLOUDY SKY

100% INSOLATION

SCATTERING AND REFLECTION 6%

ABSORPTION BY GAS MOLECULES AND DUST 14%

CLOUD REFLECTION 30% TO 60%

ABSORPTION IN CLOUDS 5% TO 20%

45% TO 0% REACHES GROUND

EARTH'S SURFACE (45° NORTH LATITUDE)

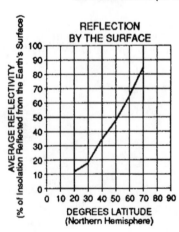

REFLECTION BY THE SURFACE

AVERAGE REFLECTIVITY (% of Insolation Reflected from the Earth's Surface)

DEGREES LATITUDE (Northern Hemisphere)

71. Approximately what percentage of insolation actually reaches the ground at 45° North latitude on a clear day?
   1. 100%   3. 60%
   2. 80%   4. 45%

72. Which factor keeps the greatest percentage of insolation from reaching the Earth's surface on cloudy days?
   1. absorption by cloud droplets
   2. reflection by cloud droplets
   3. absorption by clear-air gas molecules
   4. reflection by clear-air gas molecules

73. According to the graph, on a winter day at 70° North latitude, what approximate percentage of the insolation is reflected by the Earth's surface?
   1. 50%   3. 85%
   2. 65%   4. 100%

74. Which statement best explains why, at high latitudes, reflectivity of insolation is greater in winter than in summer?
   1. visible-light radiation
   2. infrared radiation
   3. ultraviolet radiation
   4. radio-wave radiation

75. The radiation that passes through the atmosphere and reaches the Earth's surface has the greatest intensity in the form of
   1. visible-light radiation
   2. infrared radiation
   3. ultraviolet radiation
   4. radio-wave radiation

Base your answers to questions 76 through 80 on the *Earth Science Reference Tables*, the weather map below showing part of the United States, and your knowledge of earth science. Letters A through E represent weather stations.

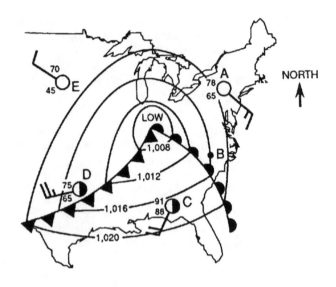

76. At which weather station is the barometric pressure reading most likely to be 1,018.0 millibars?
   1. *A*   3. *C*
   2. *B*   4. *D*

77. Which weather station model best represents weather conditions at station *B*?

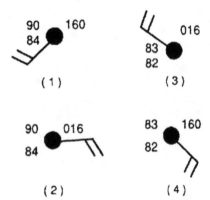

78. Which station's weather has been influenced most recently by the passage of a cold front?
    1. E
    2. B
    3. C
    4. D

79. At which weather station is precipitation most likely occurring at the present time?
    1. A
    2. B
    3. E
    4. D

80. If the low-pressure center follows a normal storm track, it will move toward the
    1. southeast
    2. southwest
    3. northeast
    4. northwest

Base your answers to questions 81 through 85 on the *Earth Science Reference Tables,* the information and diagrams below, and your knowledge of earth science. A mixture of colloids, clay, silt, sand, pebbles, and cobbles is put into stream I at point *A*. The water velocity at point *A* is 400 centimeters per second . A similar mixture of particles is put into stream II at point *A*. The water velocity in stream II at point *A* is 80 centimeters per second.

STREAM I

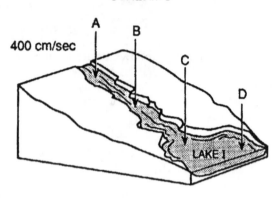

400 cm/sec

STREAM II

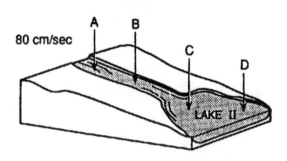

80 cm/sec

81. Which statement best describes what happens when the particles are placed in the streams?
1. Stream I will move all particles that are added at point *A*.
2. Stream II will move all particles that are added at point A.
3. Stream I cannot move sand.
4. Stream II cannot move sand.

82. Which statement is the most accurate description of conditions in both streams?
    1. The greatest deposition occurs at point *B*.
    2. Particles are carried in suspension and by bouncing along the bottom.
    3. The particles will have a greater velocity than the water in the stream.
    4. The velocity of the stream is the same at point *B* as at point *C*.

83. If a sudden rainstorm occurs at both streams above point *A*, the erosion rate will
    1. increase for stream I, but not for stream II.
    2. increase for stream II, but not for stream I.
    3. increase for both streams.
    4. not change for either stream.

84. What will most likely occur when the transported sediment reaches lake II?
    1. Clay particles will settle first.
    2. The largest particles will be carried.
    3. The sediment will become more angular because of abrasion.
    4. The particles will be deposited in sorted layers

Note that question 85 has only three choices.

85. In lake I, as the stream water moves from point *C* to point *D*, its velocity
    1. decreases.
    2. increases.
    3. remains the same.

───────────────

Base your answers to questions 86 through 90 on the *Earth Science Reference Tables*. The diagram represents three cross sections of the earth at different locations to a depth of 50 kilometers below sea level. The measurement given with each cross section indicates the thickness and the density of the layers.

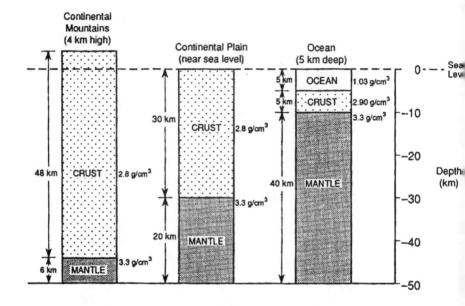

86. In which group are the layers of the Earth arranged in order of increasing average density?
    1. mantle, crust, ocean water
    2. crust, mantle, ocean water
    3. ocean water, mantle, crust
    4. ocean water, crust, mantle

87. Which material is most likely to be found 20 kilometers below sea level at the continental mountain location?
    1. basalt   3. shale
    2. granite   4. limestone

88. Which statement about the Earth's mantle is confirmed by the diagram?
    1. The mantle is liquid.
    2. The mantle has the same composition as the crust.
    3. The mantle is located at different depths below the Earth's surface.
    4. The mantle does not exist under continental mountains.

89. Compared with the oceanic crust, the continental crust is
    1. thinner and less dense.
    2. thinner and more dense.
    3. thicker and less dense.
    4. thicker and more dense.

90. The division of the Earth's interior into crust and mantle, as shown in the diagram, is based primarily on the study of
    1. radioactive dating.
    2. seismic waves.
    3. volcanic eruptions.
    4. gravity measurements.

Base your answers to questions 91 through 95 on the *Earth Science References Tables,* the graph below, and your knowledge of earth science. The graph shows the development, growth in population, and extinction of the six major groups of trilobites, labeled *A* through *F.*

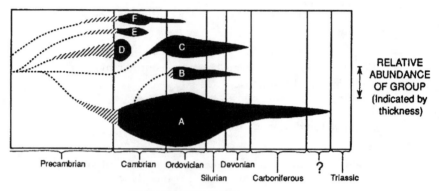

RELATIVE
ABUNDANCE
OF GROUP
(Indicated by
thickness)

Precambrian   Cambrian   Ordovician   Devonian   ?

Silurian   Carboniferous   Triassic

GEOLOGIC TIME ZONES

KEY TO SYMBOLS:

■ Population based on fossil record

▨ Population presumed: fossil evidence rare

········ Assumed evolutionary relationship

91. The fossil evidence that forms the basis for this graph was most likely found in
    1. lava flows of ancient volcanoes.
    2. sedimentary rock that formed from ocean sediment.
    3. granite rock that formed from former sedimentary rocks.
    4. metamorphic rock that formed from volcanic rocks.

92. Which group of trilobites became the most abundant?
    1. *A*   3. *C*
    2. *B*   4. *D*

93. During which period did the last of these trilobite groups become extinct?
    1. Cretaceous   3. Permian
    2. Triassic   4. Carboniferous

94. Which interference is best supported by graph?
    1. All trilobites evolved from group *A* trilobites.
    2. The trilobites groups became most abundant during the Devonian Period.
    3. Precambrian trilobite fossils are very rare.
    4. Trilobites could exist in present-day marine climates.

95. The diagrams below represent rock outcrops in which the rock layers have not been overturned. Which rock outcrop shows a possible sequence of the trilobite fossils?

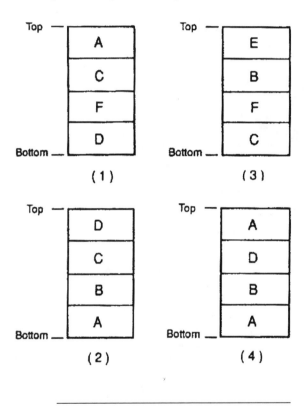

Base your answers to questions 96 through 100 on the *Earth Science Reference Tables*, the diagrams below, and your knowledge of earth science. Diagram I shows a map of Niagara Falls and part of the Niagara River Gorge and the past locations of the edge of the Horseshoe Falls as it receded (eroded upstream) due to weathering and undercutting. Diagram II shows a geologic cross section of the rock layers at the edge of the Niagara River Gorge.

DIAGRAM I

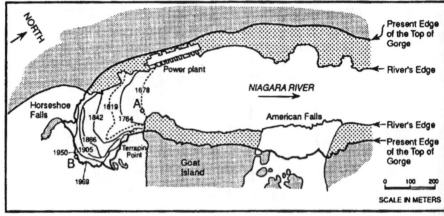

DIAGRAM II

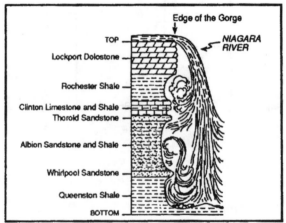

96. According to the map and scale, what is the approximate rate at which the Horseshoe Falls receded upstream from point *A* in 1678 to point *B* in 1969?
1. 1 meter per year
2. 0.1 meter per year
3. 10 meters per year
4. 200 meters per year

97. According to the geologic cross section (diagram II), the top rock layer at Niagara Falls consists of
1. marine-derived sediments compacted and cemented together.
2. crystalline minerals resulting from melting and solidification.
3. banded and distorted layers due to extreme pressure.
4. metamorphosed clay, sand, and volcanic ash.

98. Most scientists believe that the Niagara River started flowing at the end of the last ice age. During which geologic epoch did this ice age occur?
1. Early Triassic   3. Miocene
2. Paleocene   4. Pleistocene

99. In which New York State landscape region is Niagara Falls located?
1. Appalachian Plateau
2. Tug Hill Plateau
3. Erie-Ontario Lowlands
4. St. Lawrence Lowlands

100. What is the age of the surface bedrock at Niagara Falls, New York?
1. Devonian   3. Ordovician
2. Silurian   4. Cambrian

Base your answers to questions 101 through 105 on the *Earth Science Reference Tables* and your knowledge of earth science.

101. A barometric pressure reading of 28.97 inches is equal to
    1. 981 mb
    2. 984 mb
    3. 1,006 mb
    4. 1,008 mb

102. A student incorrectly converted 20° C to 64° F instead of 68°F. What is the student's approximate percent error?
    1. 44%
    2. 5.9%
    3. 6.3%
    4. 4%

103. A fine-grained igneous rock contains 11% plagioclase, 72% pyroxene, 15% olivine, and 2% amphibole. This rock would most likely be classified as
    1. granite
    2. rhyolite
    3. gabbro
    4. basalt

104. What do the tropopause, stratopause, and mesopause all have in common?
    1. Each is a point of maximum temperature in its layer of the atmosphere.
    2. Each is an interface between two layers of the atmosphere.
    3. Each is a region of increasing pressure within the atmosphere.
    4. Each is a zone of decreasing water vapor content within the atmosphere.

105. Which relative concentrations of elements are found in a felsic rock?
    1. a high concentration of aluminum and a low concentration of iron
    2. a high concentration of iron and a low concentration of aluminum
    3. a high concentration of magnesium and a low concentration of iron
    4. a high concentration of magnesium and a low concentration of aluminum

ANSWER KEY

1.	2	11.	4	21.	2	31.	1
2.	3	12.	1	22.	2	32.	4
3.	1	13.	2	23.	1	33.	4
4.	2	14.	2	24.	3	34.	1
5.	3	15.	1	25.	2	35.	3
6.	4	16.	3	26.	1	36.	4
7.	3	17.	2	27.	4	37.	2
8.	4	18.	1	28.	2	38.	2
9.	3	19.	4	29.	4	39.	2
10.	3	20.	4	30.	3	40.	3

41.	3	51.	3	61.	2	71.	2
42.	4	52.	4	62.	3	72.	2
43.	1	53.	1	63.	1	73.	3
44.	2	54.	1	64.	3	74.	2
45.	4	55.	2	65.	4	75.	1
46.	2	56.	4	66.	3	76.	3
47.	1	57.	3	67.	2	77.	4
48.	4	58.	4	68.	1	78.	4
49.	4	59.	1	69.	2	79.	2
50.	3	60.	1	70.	4	80.	3

81.	1	91.	2	101.	1
82.	2	92.	1	102.	2
83.	3	93.	3	103.	4
84.	4	94.	3	104.	2
85.	1	95.	1	105.	1
86.	4	96.	1		
87.	2	97.	1		
88.	3	98.	4		
89.	3	99.	3		
90.	2	100.	2		

PRACTICE EXAM TWO

Directions (1-55): For *each* statement or question, select the word or expression that, of those given, best completes the statements or answers the questions.

1. Which statement about a mineral sample found in a field in New York State is most likely an inference?
   1. The sample was transported by a glacier.
   2. The sample is white in color.
   3. The sample is rectangular, with sharp, angular corners.
   4. The sample is 8 cm long, 5 cm wide, and 3 cm high.

2. The use of a triple-beam balance to determine the mass of a rock is an example of measuring by using
   1. all of the five senses
   2. inferences and interpretations
   3. a direct comparison with a standard
   4. a combination of dimensional quantities

3. Which graph best represents the relationship between the latitude of an observer and the observed altitude of Polaris above the northern horizon?

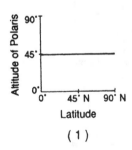

(1)

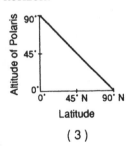

(3)

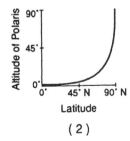

(2)

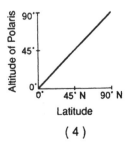

(4)

4. According to the *Earth Science Reference Tables*, as altitude increases from the tropopause to the mesopause, the atmospheric temperature will
   1. decrease, only
   2. increase, only
   3. decrease, then increase
   4. increase, then decrease

5. Which diagram best illustrates the heat transfer movement in fluids?

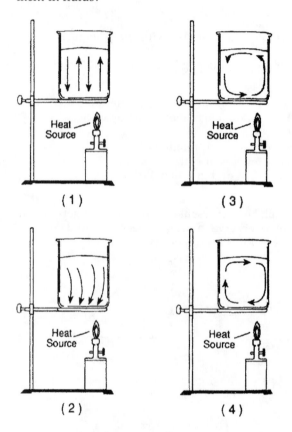

6. The diagrams below represent fossils found at different locations.

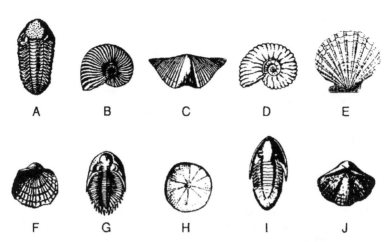

A   B   C   D   E

F   G   H   I   J

When classified by similarity of structure, which three fossils should be grouped together?
1. *A, F* and *H*
2. *C, F* and *J*
3. *E,G* and *H*
4. *B, D* and *I*

7. From which set of polar and equatorial diameters can the actual shape of the Earth be inferred?
   1. polar diameter = 12,714 km
      equatorial diameter = 12,714 km
   2. polar diameter = 12,756 km
      equatorial diameter = 12,756 km
   3. polar diameter = 12,714 km
      equatorial diameter = 12,756 km
   4. polar diameter = 12,756 km
      equatorial diameter = 12,714 km

8. The best evidence that the distance between the Moon and the Earth varies is provided by the apparent change in the Moon's
   1. shape   3. altitude
   2. diameter   4. phase

9. Earth's atmospheric winds are deflected in a predictable manner because of the Earth's
   1. rotation   3. gravity
   2. revolution   4. inclination

10. Approximately how many hours of daylight are received at the North Pole on June 21?
    1. 0
    2. 12
    3. 18
    4. 24

11. In general, good absorbers of electromagnetic radiation are also good
    1. refractors
    2. radiators
    3. reflectors
    4. convectors

12. An increase in latent heat can cause liquid water to
    1. melt
    2. condense
    3. freeze
    4. evaporate

13. The average air temperature on Earth may increase as a result of the ability of carbon dioxide and water vapor to absorb
    1. visible light
    4. radio waves
    3. gamma radiation
    4. infrared radiation

14. According to the *Earth Science Reference Tables*, an air pressure of 29.47 inches of mercury is equal to
    1. 996 mb
    2. 998 mb
    3. 1,002 mb
    4. 1,014 mb

15. The Graph below shows the changes in height of ocean water over the course of 2 days at one Earth location.

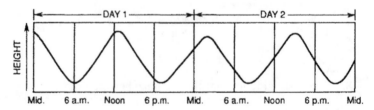

Which statement concerning these changes is best supported by the graph?
    1. The changes are cyclic and occur in predictable time intervals.
    2. The changes are cyclic and occur at the same time every day.
    3. The changes are noncyclic and occur at sunrise and sunset.
    4. The changes are noncyclic and may occur at any time.

16. On which map of temperatures across the United States is the 60°F isotherm drawn correctly?

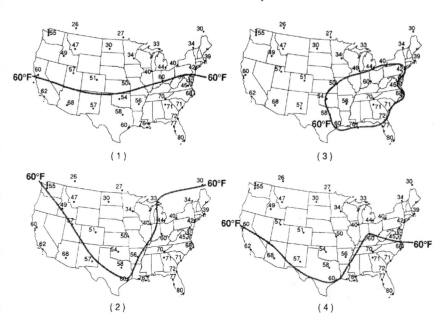

(1)   (3)

(2)   (4)

17. The diagram below shows the apparent paths of the Sun in relation to a house in New York State on June 21 and December 21.

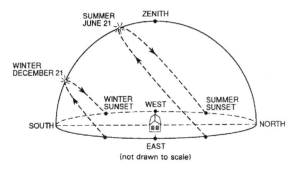

(not drawn to scale)

Which statement best explains the cause of this apparent change in the Sun's path?
1. The sun's orbital velocity changes as it revolves around the Earth.
2. The Earth's orbital velocity changes as it revolves around the Sun.
3. The Earth's axis is tilted $23\frac{1}{2}°$.
4. The Sun's axis is tilted $23\frac{1}{2}°$.

18. In the Northern Hemisphere, what is the direction of surface wind circulation in a high-pressure system?
    1. clockwise and outward from center
    2. clockwise and toward the center
    3. counterclockwise and outward from the center
    4. counterclockwise and toward the center

19. Which abbreviation indicates a warm air mass that contains large amounts of water vapor? [Refer to the *Earth Science Reference Tables.*]
    1. cP   3. mT
    2. cT   4. mP

20. Which gas in the atmosphere has the most influence on day-to-day weather changes?
    1. ozone   3. water vapor
    2. oxygen   4. carbon dioxide

21. Which condition most likely exists when precipitation is greater than potential evapotranspiration and soil water storage is at the maximum?
    1. usage   3. recharge
    2. runoff   4. drought

22. Which station model represents an atmospheric pressure of 1,009.2 millibars and a temperature of 75°F?

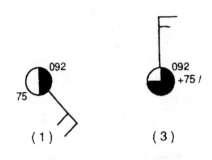

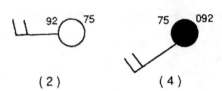

23. The diagram below represents snow falling on the Tug Hill Plateau in New York State.

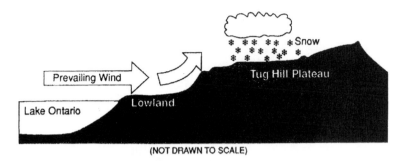

(NOT DRAWN TO SCALE)

The best explanation for the formation of snow under these conditions is that
1. dry air rises and warms
2. moist air rises and cools
3. moist air rises and warms
4. dry air sinks and cools

24. The diagram below represents the Earth's orbital path around the Sun. The Earth takes the same amount of time to move from A to B as from C to D.

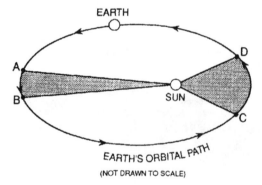

(NOT DRAWN TO SCALE)

Which values are equal within the system?
1. The shaded sections of the diagram are equal in area.
2. The distance from the Sun to the Earth is the same at point A and at point D.
3. The orbital velocity of the Earth and the Sun at point B is the same as the gravitational force at point C.
4. The gravitational force between the Earth and the Sun at point B is the same as the gravitational force at point D.

25. The graph below represents the average temperature of a city for each month of the year.

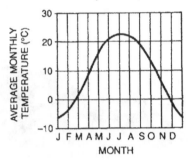

Where is this city most likely to be located?
1. inland in the Northern Hemisphere, in a middle latitude
2. inland in the Southern Hemisphere, in a middle latitude
3. on a coast near the Equator
4. on a coast in the Antarctic

26. According to the *Earth Science Reference Tables*, which element is most abundant by mass in the Earth's crust?
1. nitrogen   3. silicon
2. oxygen   4. iron

27. The photograph below shows a fan-shaped accumulation of sediment.

The accumulation of sediment is the direct result of
1. weathering of bedrock
2. erosion by wind
3. deposition by running water
4. transport by glaciers

28. What is the best explanation for the two statements below?
   • Some mountains located near the Earth's Equator have snow-covered peaks.
   • Icecaps exists at the Earth's poles.
   1. High elevation and high latitude have similar effects on climate.
   2. Both mountain and polar regions have arid climates.
   3. Mountain and polar regions receive more energy from the Sun than other regions do.
   4. An increase in snowfall and an increase in temperature have a similar effect on climate.

29. During winter, Lake Ontario is generally warmer than adjacent land areas. The primary reason for this temperature difference is that
   1. water has a higher specific heat than land has
   2. water reflects sunlight better than land does
   3. land is more dense than water is
   4. winds blow from land areas toward the water

30. As a particle of sediment in a stream breaks into several smaller peices, the rate of weathering of sediment will
   1. decrease due to a decrease in surface area
   2. decrease due to an increase in surface area
   3. increase due to a decrease in surface area
   4. increase due to an increase in surface area

31. When mineral are dissolved, how are the resulting ions carried by rivers?
   1. by precipitation
   2. by tumbling and rolling
   3. in suspension
   4. in solution

32. The relative hardness of a mineral can best be tested by
   1. scratching the mineral across a glass plate
   2. squeezing the mineral with calibrated pliers
   3. determining the density of the mineral
   4. breaking the mineral with a hammer

33. The diagrams below show how plant materials are changed into the three forms of coal by natural processes.

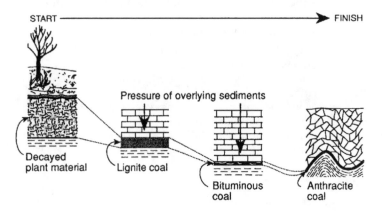

By which process is anthracite coal formed from bituminous coal? [Refer to *Earth Science Reference Table.*]

1. solidification   3. deposition
2. metamorphosis   4. intrusion

34. In the diagram below, the arrow shows the direction of stream flow around a bend.

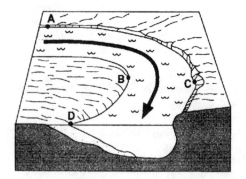

At which point does the greatest stream erosion occur?

1. *A*   3. *C*
2. *B*   4. *D*

35. Which is an accurate statement about rocks?
   1. Rocks are located only in continental areas of the Earth.
   2. Rocks seldom undergo change.
   3. Most rocks contain fossils.
   4. Most rocks have several minerals in common.

36. The size of the mineral crystals found in an igneous rock is directly related to the
   1. density of the minerals
   2. color of the minerals
   3. cooling time of the molten rock
   4. amount of sediment cemented together

37. Which statement best explains why the direction of some seismic waves changes sharply as the waves travel through the Earth?
   1. The Earth is spherical.
   2. Seismic waves tend to travel in curved paths.
   3. The temperature of the Earth's interior decreases with depth.
   4. Different parts of the Earth's interior have different densities.

38. The diagram below represents a cross section of a portion of the Earth's crust and mantle. Letters A, B, C, D and X identify locations within the crust.

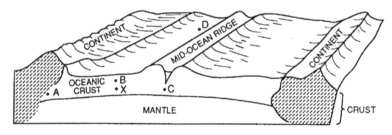

The age of oceanic crust increases along a line between location X and location

1. A	3. C
2. B	4. D

39. In a soil sample, the particles have the same shape but different sizes. Which graph best represents the relationship between particle size and settling time when these particles are deposited in a quiet body of water?

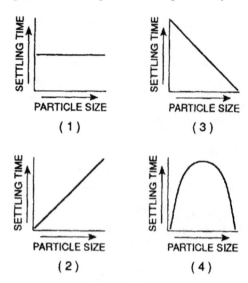

40. The best evidence of crustal uplift would be provided by
    1. marine fossils in the Rocky Mountains
    2. sediment in the Gulf of Mexico
    3. trenches in the Pacific Ocean floor
    4. igneous rock deep within the Earth

41. According to the *Earth Science Reference Tables*, what is the approximate total distance traveled by an earthquake's *P*-wave in its first 9 minutes?
    1. 2,600 km   3. 7,600 km
    2. 5,600 km   4. 12,100 km

42. Which evidence supports the theory of ocean floor spreading?
    1. The rocks of the ocean floor and continents have similar origins
    2. In the ocean floor, rocks near the mid-ocean ridge are cooler than rocks near the continents
    3. The pattern of magnetic orientation of rock is similar on both sides of the mid-ocean ridge.
    4. The density of oceanic crust is greater than the density of the continental crust.

43. A layer of volcanic ash may serve as a time marker because the ash is
   1. generally deposited only on land
   2. composed of index fossils
   3. deposited rapidly over a large area
   4. often a distinct color

44. One similarity between uranium-238 and carbon-14 is that both
   1. decay at a predictable rate
   2. have the same half life
   3. are normally found in large quantities in living matter
   4. are found in granite

45. The diagram below represents a series of brachiopod fossils showing progressive changes during the Early Mississippian Epoch. The fossils are drawn to scale

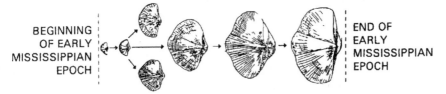

BEGINNING OF EARLY MISSISSIPPIAN EPOCH

END OF EARLY MISSISSIPPIAN EPOCH

One explanation for this process of change is the theory of
   1. superposition
   2. evolution
   3. dynamic equilibrium
   4. fossilization

46. What is the best interpretation of the two statements below?
   • Corals are marine animals that live in warm ocean water
   • Fossil corals are found in surface bedrock in areas of New York State.
   1. Corals once lived on land.
   2. Corals have migrated northward.
   3. Parts of New York State are now covered by warm ocean water.
   4. Parts of New York State were once covered by warm ocean water.

47. Which feature often indicates a boundary between landscape regions?
   1. a highway cutting through a mountain region
   2. resistant bedrock composed of more than one type of mineral
   3. a long, meandering stream flowing across a large, level region
   4. a change in slope between adjoining bedrock types with different structures

48. According to the *Earth Science Reference Tables*, when did the intrusion of the Palisades Sill occur?
   1. before the Appalachian Orogeny
   2. during the late Triassic period
   3. during the Paleozoic Era
   4. after the extinction of dinosaurs and ammonites

49. According to the *Earth Science Reference Tables*, what are the respective decay products of uranium, potassium, and rubidium?
   1. lead (Pb), argon (Ar), and strontium (Sr)
   2. carbon (C), oxygen (O), and nitrogen (N)
   3. hydrogen (H), lithium (L), and helium (He)
   4. silicon (Si), oxygen (O), and aluminum (Al)

50. According to *Earth Science Reference Tables*, at which location could a geologist find shale containing eurypterid fossils?
   1. Old Forge   3. New York City
   2. Syracuse   4. Long Island

51. The advance and retreat of continental ice sheets produced deposits of sands and gravels during the Pleistocene Epoch. According to the *Earth Science Reference Tables*, in which New York State landscape region were such sands and gravels deposited over Cretaceous and Tertiary materials?
   1. Atlantic Coastal Plain
   2. Erie-Ontario Lowlands
   3. Adirondack Mountains
   4. Tug Hill Plateau

52. According to the *Earth Science Reference Tables,* in which type of landscape region is Elmira, New York, located?
    1. mountains
    2. plain
    3. plateau
    4. lowlands

53. The block diagrams below show a river and its landscape during four stages of erosion.

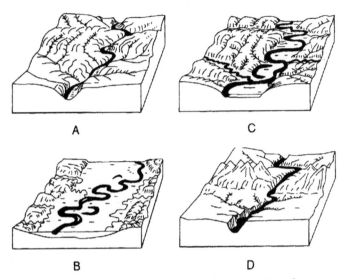

A   C

B   D

In which order should the diagrams be placed to show the most likely sequence of river and landscape development?
    1. *A, D, B, C*
    2. *B, D, C, A*
    3. *C, B, A, D*
    4. *D, A, C, B*

54. Which condition is characteristic of a landscape region in dynamic equilibrium?
    1. a balance between uplifting and erosion
    2. a balance between weathering and erosion
    3. more erosion than uplifting
    4. more uplifting than erosion

Note that question 55 has only three choices.

55. A person in New York State observes a star that is due
    east and just above the horizon. During the next hour,
    the distance between the star and the horizon will
    appear to
    1. decrease
    2. increase
    3. remain the same

Base your answers to questions 56 through 60 on the *Earth Science Reference
Tables,* the contour map below and your knowledge of earth science. Letters A through K represent locations in the area. Hachure lines (   ) show
depressions.

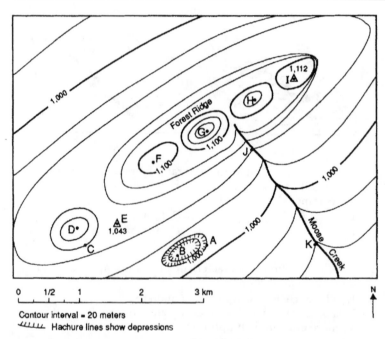

0   1/2   1   2   3 km
L__I__I__I_____I_____I

Contour interval = 20 meters
⌐⌐⌐⌐⌐ Hachure lines show depressions

56. Which hilltop could have an elevation of 1,145 meters?
    1. D   3. G
    2. F   4. H

57. Toward which direction does Moose Creek flow?
    1. southeast   3. southwest
    2. northeast   4. northwest

58. Which graph best represents the map profile along a straight line from point C through point A to point K?

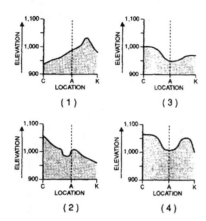

(1)   (3)

(2)   (4)

59. Which equation would be used to determine the stream gradient along Moose Creek between points J and K?

1. gradient $= \dfrac{1.8km}{80m} \times 100$

2. gradient $= \dfrac{0.8km}{60m}$

3. gradient $= (1{,}040 \text{ m} - 960 \text{ m}) \times 20 \text{ m}$

4. gradient $= \dfrac{80m}{1.8km}$

60. What is the *lowest* possible elevation of point B?
1. 981 m   3. 961 m
2. 971 m   4. 941 m

Base your answers to questions 61 through 65 on the *Earth Science Reference Tables*, the diagram below, and your knowledge of Earth Science. nhe diagram shows the Earth's position in its orbit around the Sun at the beginning of each season. The moon is shown at various positions as it revolves around the Earth.

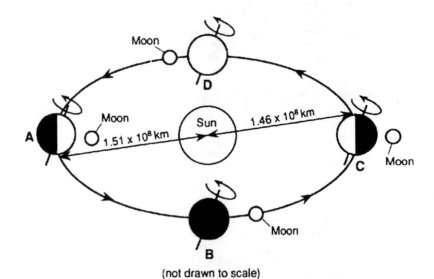

(not drawn to scale)

61. What is most likely represented by the symbol ⟲ near the Earth's axis at each position?
   1. the direction of Earth's rotation
   2. the path of the Sun through the sky
   3. the changing tilt of Earth's axis
   4. convection currents in the atmosphere

62. The Earth's orbit around the Sun is best described as
   1. a perfect circle
   2. an oblate spheroid
   3. a very eccentric ellipse
   4. a slightly eccentric ellipse

63. Which position of the Earth represents the beginning of the winter season for New York State?
    1. *A*   3. *C*
    2. *B*   4. *D*

64. Which position of the Earth shows the Moon located where its shadow may sometimes reach the Earth?
    1. *A*   3. *C*
    2. *B*   4. *D*

65. As the Earth moves from position *B* to position *C*, what change will occur in the gravitational attraction between the Earth and the Sun?
    1. It will decrease, only.
    2. It will increase, only.
    3. It will decrease, then increase.
    4. It will remain the same.

Base your answers to questions 66 through 70 on the *Earth Science Reference Tables,* the weather map of the United States below, and your knowledge of earth science.

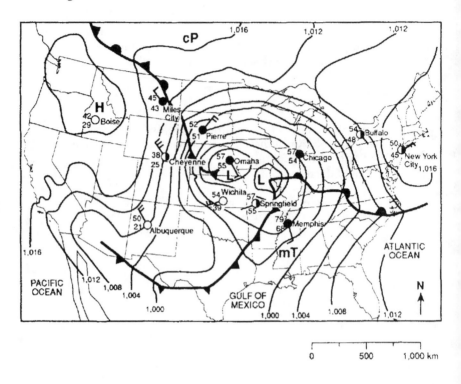

66. Which kind of frontal sysytem is located northwest of Miles City, Montana?
   1. cold front   3. stationary front
   2. warm front   4. occluded front

67. The air mass over Memphis, Tennessee, most likely originated in
   1. the Noth Pacific
   2. central Canada
   3. the central United States
   4. the Gulf of Mexico

68. According to the map, at which city is precipitation most likely occurring?
    1. Boise, Idaho
    2. Omaha, Nebraska
    3. Albuquerque, New Mexico
    4. New York City

69. If the low-presssure systems follow the paths of most weather system in the United States, in which direction will they move?
    1. northwest
    2. southwest
    3. northeast
    4. southeast

70. The weather front west front west of Memphis, Tennessee, is moving at a speed of 50 kilometers per hour. What is the most likely weather forecast for Memphis for the next 12 hours?
    1. showers followed by clearing skies and cooler temperatures
    2. showers followed by warm, humid conditions
    3. cleariing skies followed by warm, dry conditions
    4. a continuation of the present weather conditions

Base your answer to questions 71 through 75 on the *Earth Science Reference Tables*, the data table below, and your knowledge of earth science. The table shows the time of sunrise and sunset and the total amount of insolation received on the Earth's surface for four locations, *A, B, C* and *D*, at the beginning of the season. The locations have the same longitude, but are at different latitudes. Data were collected on clear, sunny days.

Location A – 66° North Latitude

Date	Sunrise	Sunset	Total Insolation (cal/cm^2)
March 21	6:00 a.m.	6:00 p.m.	373
June 21	12:51 a.m.	11:09 p.m.	1,014
September 23	5:48 a.m.	6:12 p.m.	393
December 21	11:06 p.m.	12:54 a.m.	1

Location B – 43° North Latitude

Date	Sunrise	Sunset	Total Insolation (cal/cm^2)
March 21	6:00 a.m.	6:00 p.m.	674
June 21	4:24 a.m.	7:36 p.m.	1,023
September 23	5:54 a.m.	6:06 p.m.	682
December 21	7:33 a.m.	4:27 p.m.	284

Location C – 0° Latitude

Date	Sunrise	Sunset	Total Insolation (cal/cm^2)
March 21	6:00 a.m.	6:00 p.m.	923
June 21	6:00 a.m.	6:00 p.m.	814
September 23	6:00 a.m.	6:00 p.m.	909
December 21	6:00 a.m.	6:00 p.m.	869

Location D – 23° South Latitude

Date	Sunrise	Sunset	Total Insolation (cal/cm^2)
March 21	5:57 a.m.	6:03 p.m.	851
June 21	6:42 a.m.	5:18 p.m.	545
September 23	6:00 a.m.	6:00 p.m.	827
December 21	5:15 a.m.	6:45 p.m.	1,044

71. Which location received the greatest total insolation on June 21?
   1. A   3. C
   2. B   4. D

72. From which location would an observer see the Sun in the northern sky at noon on March 21?
   1. A   3. C
   2. B   4. D

73. A comparison of the times of sunrise and sunset in New York State on December 21 and June 21 shows that, in December, the Sun
   1. rises later and sets earlier
   2. rises earlier and sets later
   3. rises and sets earlier
   4. rises and sets later

74. Which statement best explains why surface temperatures are higher at 43° N than at 66° N on June 21?
   1. At 66° N, there is complete darkness.
   2. At 66° N, winter is beginning.
   3. At 43° N , summer is ending.
   4. At 43° N, the angle of insolation is greater.

75. Why are the times of sunrise and sunset for March 21 and September 23 nearly the same at each location?
   1. The Sun's altitude at noon is the same everywhere on these days.
   2. The Earth is at its closet and farthest points from the Sun on these days.
   3. The Sun's insolation reaches its maximum intensity on these days.
   4. The Sun is directly above the Equator on these days.

Base your answers to questions 76 through 80 on the *Earth Science Reference Tables,* the diagram below, and your knowledge of earth science. The diagram of the particles is given below each diagram. All soil samples consist of solid spherical particles.

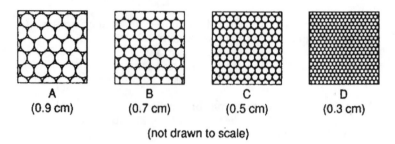

A
(0.9 cm)

B
(0.7 cm)

C
(0.5 cm)

D
(0.3 cm)

(not drawn to scale)

76. Particles of the size shown are classified as
    1. cobbles   3. sand
    2. pebbles   4. silt

77. Which graph best represents the capillarity of these soil samples?

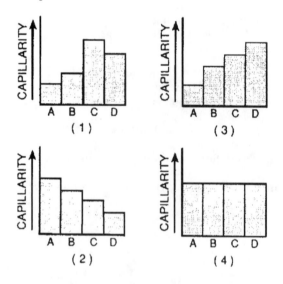

78. Water can infiltrate these soils if they are
    1. saturated and impermeable
    2. saturated and permeable
    3. unsaturated and impermeable
    4. unsaturated and permeable

79. Which sample has the greatest permeability?
    1. *A*   2. *C*
    2. *B*   4. *D*

Note that question 80 has only three choices.

80. Some particles from sample *D* are mixed with particles from sample *A*. Compared to the original porosity of sample A, the porosity of the resulting mixture will be
    1. less
    2. greater
    3. the same

Base your answers to questions 81 through 85 on the *Earth Science Reference Tables*, the diagram below, and your knowledge of earth science. The diagram represents a profile of a stream. Points *A* through *E* are locations along the stream.

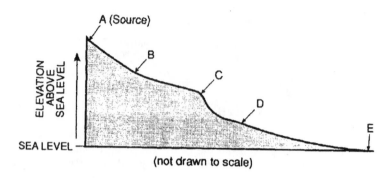

81. The primary force responsible for the flow of water in this stream is
    1. solar energy   3. wind
    2. magnetic fields   4. gravity

82. Between which two points is potential energy changing to kinetic energy most rapidly?
    1. *A* and *B*   3. *C* and *D*
    2. *B* and *C*   4. *D* and *E*

83. The largest particles of sediment transported by the stream at location *C* are sand particles. What is the approximate velocity of the stream at location *C*?
    1. 50 cm/sec   3. 300 cm/sec
    2. 200 cm/sec   4. 600 cm/sec

84. In what way would a sediment particle most likely change while it is being transported by the stream?
    1. It will become more dense.
    2. It will become more angular.
    3. Its size will decrease.
    4. Its hardness will increase.

85. At which location would the amount of deposition be greatest?
    1. *A*   3. *E*
    2. *B*   4. *D*

Base your answers to questions 86 through 90 on the *Earth Science Reference Tables*, the diagrams below of five rock samples, and your knowledge of Earth science.

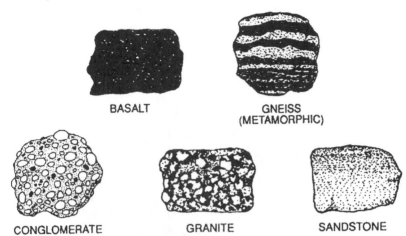

BASALT

GNEISS
(METAMORPHIC)

CONGLOMERATE

GRANITE

SANDSTONE

86. Which sample is composed of sediments 0.006 centimeter to 0.2 centimeter in size that were compacted and cemented together?
   1. conglomerate   3. gneiss
   2. sandstone   4. granite

87. If granite were subjected to intense heat and pressure, it would most likely change to
   1. conglomerate   3. gneiss
   2. sandstone   4. granite

88. The basalt was most likely formed by
   1. heat and pressure
   2. melting and solidification
   3. compaction and cementation
   4. erosion and deposition

89. Which sample would most likely contain fossils?
   1. gneiss   3. sandstone
   2. granite   4. basalt

90. Which sample is igneous and has a coarse texture?
   1. sandstone   3. basalt
   2. conglomerate   4. granite

Base your answers to questions 91 through 95 on the *Earth Science Reference Tables*, the diagram below, and your knowledge of earth science. The diagram shows a cross section of bedrock where the Niagara Rivers flows over Niagara Falls

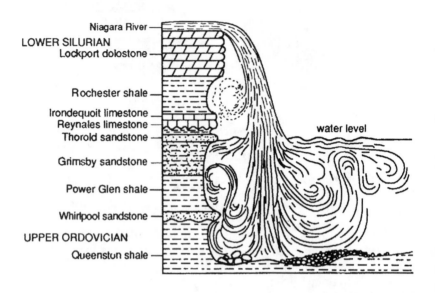

91. The Niagara River begins at
    1. the Genesee River
    2. Niagara Falls
    3. Lake Erie
    4. the St.Lawrence River

92. Which is the youngest rock unit?
    1. Lockport dolostone
    2. Whirlpool shale
    3. Rochester sandstone
    4. Thorold shale

93. Which rock layers appear to have weathered and eroded most?
   1. Irondequoit limestone and Whirlpool sandstone
   2. Power Glen shale and Queenston shale
   3. Lockport dolostone and Reynales limestone
   4. Thorold sandstone and Rochester shale

94. A sedimentary layer resembling the Rochester shale is located in another section of New York State. The best way to correlate these two rock units would be to compare the
   1. thickness of layers
   2. index fossils contained in the layers
   3. minerals cementing the sediments
   4. color of the layers

95. Which rock unit was most likely formed from chemical precipitates?
   1. Lockport dolostone
   2. Whirlpool sandstone
   3. Rochester shale
   4. Thorold sandstone

Base your answers to questions 96 through 100 on the *Earth Science Reference Tables*, the map and information below, and your knowledge of earth science.

The map shows the location of major islands and coral reefs in the Hawaiian Island chain. Their ages are given in million of years.

The islands of the Hawaiian chain formed from the same source of molten rock, called a hot plume. The movement of the Pacific Plate over the Hawaiian hot plume created a trail of extinct volcanoes that make up the Hawaiian Islands. The island of Hawaii (lower right) is the most recent island formed. Kilauea is an active volcano located over the plume on the island of Hawaii.

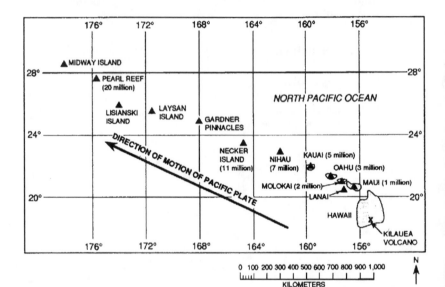

96. Approximately how far has the Pacific Plate moved since Necker Island was located over the plume at X?
1. 300 km
2. 1,100 km
3. 1,9000 km
4. 2,600 km

97. What is the location of Lisianski Island?
1. 26° N 174° E
2. 26° N 174° W
3. 26° S 174° E
4. 26° S 174° W

98. Approximately how long will it take the noon Sun to appear to move from Kauai to Pearl Reef?
    1. 1 hour
    2. 2 hours
    3. 15 minutes
    4. 45 minutes

99. What kinds of animals were common in New York State 20 million years ago, when Pearl Reef was forming?
    1. primitive humans
    2. early reptiles
    3. dinosaurs and ammonites
    4. grazing mammals

100. Which graph shows the general relationship between the age of individual islands in the Hawaiian chain and their distance from the hot plume?

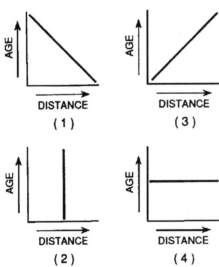

Base your answers to questions 101 through 105 on the *Earth Science Reference Tables* and your knowledge of earth science.

101. Which radioactive element has a half-life of 4.5 x 10 years?

1. carbon–14.
2. rubidium–87
3. uranium–238
4. potassium–40

102. Students calculated the circumference of a globe to be 60 centimeters. The actual circumference of the globe is 63. centimeters. The percent deviation of the students' calculation was

1. 0.48%
2. 4.8%
3. 5.0%
4. 21%

103. In the Earth's interior, which zone has a temperature higher than its melting point?

1. crust
2. stiffer mantle
3. inner core
4. outer core

104. What is the dewpoint temperature when the dry-bulb temperatures is 22° C and wet-bulb temperatures is 15°C?

1. 7° C
2. 10° C
3. 12° C
4. 14° C

105 A pebble has a mass of 35 grams and volume of 14 cubic centimeters. What is its density?

1. 0.4 g/cm³
2. 2.5 g/cm³.
3. 490 g/cm³
4. 4.0 g/cm³

ANSWER KEY.

1.	1	11.	2	21.	2	31.	4
2.	3	12.	4	22.	4	32.	1
3.	4	13.	4	23.	2	33.	2
4.	4	14.	2	24.	1	34.	3
5.	3	15.	1	25.	1	35.	4
6.	2	16.	4	26.	2	36.	3
7.	3	17.	3	27.	3	37.	4
8.	2	18.	1	28.	1	38.	1
9.	1	19.	3	29.	1	39.	3
10.	4	20.	3	30.	4	40.	1

41.	2	51.	1	61.	1	71.	2
42.	3	52.	3	62.	4	72.	4
43.	3	53.	4	63.	3	73.	1
44.	1	54.	1	64.	1	74.	4
45.	2	55.	2	65.	2	75.	4
46.	4	56.	3	66.	4	76.	2
47.	4	57.	1	67.	4	77.	3
48.	2	58.	2	68.	2	78.	4
49.	1	59.	4	69.	3	79.	1
50.	2	60.	3	70.	1	80.	1

81.	4	91.	3	101.	3
82.	3	92.	1	102.	2
83.	1	93.	2	103.	4
84.	3	94.	2	104.	2
85.	3	95.	1	105.	2
86.	2	96.	2		
87.	3	97.	2		
88.	2	98.	1		
89.	3	99.	4		
90.	4	100.	3		

Earth Science Reference Tables

1994 EDITION
The University of the State of New York
THE STATE EDUCATION DEPARTMENT
Albany, New York 12234

This edition of the Earth Science Reference Tables should be used in the classroom beginning in the 1993–94 school year. The first examination for which these tables will be used is the June 1994 Regents Examination in Earth Science.

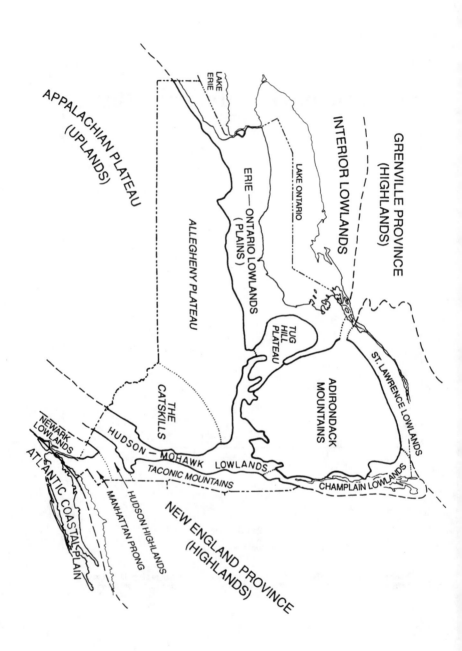

figure 02

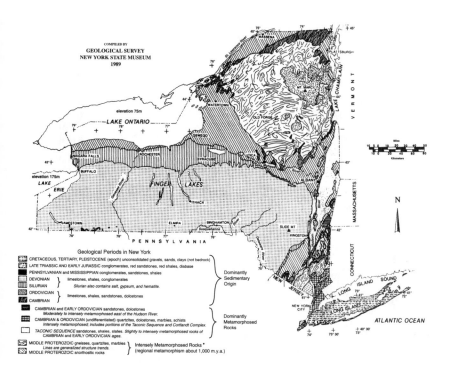

COMPILED BY
GEOLOGICAL SURVEY
NEW YORK STATE MUSEUM
1989

elevation 75m

—LAKE ONTARIO—

elevation 175m
LAKE ERIE

FINGER LAKES

P E N N S Y L V A N I A

V E R M O N T

LAKE CHAMPLAIN

MASSACHUSETTS

CONNECTICUT

LONG ISLAND SOUND

NEW JERSEY

NEW YORK CITY

LONG ISLAND

ATLANTIC OCEAN

N

Geological Periods in New York

CRETACEOUS, TERTIARY, PLEISTOCENE (epoch) unconsolidated gravels, sands, clays (not bedrock)
LATE TRIASSIC AND EARLY JURASSIC conglomerates, red sandstones, red shales, diabase
PENNSYLVANIAN and MISSISSIPPIAN conglomerates, sandstones, shales
DEVONIAN } limestones, shales, conglomerates
SILURIAN } Silurian also contains salt, gypsum, and hematite.
ORDOVICIAN } limestones, shales, sandstones, dolostones
CAMBRIAN }

Dominantly Sedimentary Origin

CAMBRIAN and EARLY ORDOVICIAN sandstones, dolostones
   Moderately to intensely metamorphosed east of the Hudson River.
CAMBRIAN & ORDOVICIAN (undifferentiated) quartzites, dolostones, marbles, schists
   Intensely metamorphosed; includes portions of the Taconic Sequence and Cortlandt Complex.
TACONIC SEQUENCE sandstones, shales, slates. Slightly to intensely metamorphosed rocks of
   CAMBRIAN and EARLY ORDOVICIAN ages.
MIDDLE PROTEROZOIC gneisses, quartzites, marbles
   Lines are generalized structure trends.
MIDDLE PROTEROZOIC anorthositic rocks

Dominantly Metamorphosed Rocks

Intensely Metamorphosed Rocks *
(regional metamorphism about 1,000 m.y.a.)

figure 03

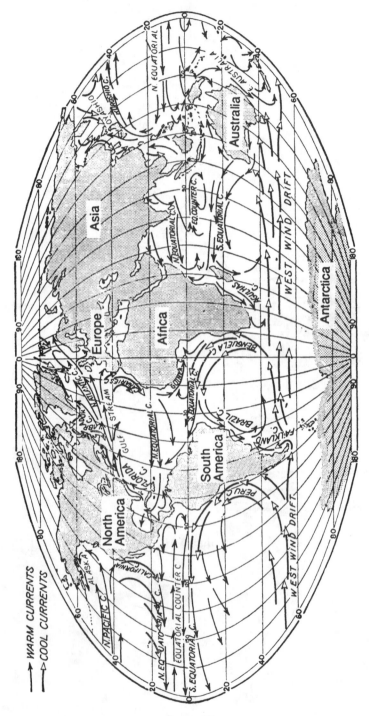

figure 04

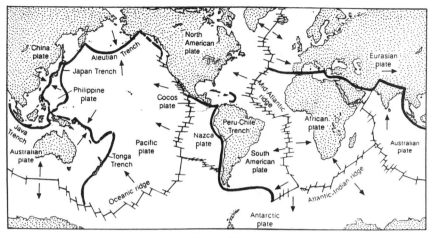

figure 05

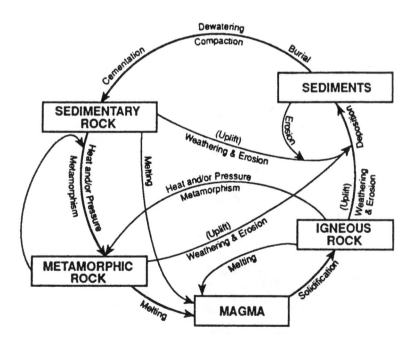

figure 06a

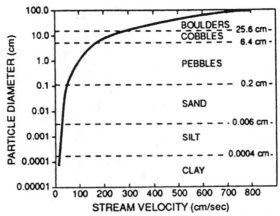

*This generalized graph shows the water velocity needed to maintain, but not start movement. Variations occur due to differences in particle density and shape.

figure 06b

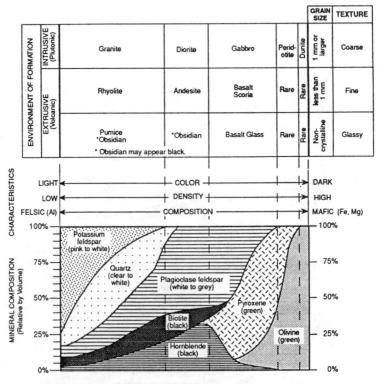

Note: The intrusive rocks can also occur as exceptionally coarse-grained rock, Pegmatite.

figure 06c

INORGANIC LAND-DERIVED SEDIMENTARY ROCKS

TEXTURE	GRAIN SIZE	COMPOSITION	COMMENTS	ROCK NAME	MAP SYMBOL
Clastic (fragmental)	Mixed, silt to boulders (larger than 0.001 cm)	Mostly quartz, feldspar, and clay minerals; May contain fragments of other rocks and minerals	Rounded fragments	Conglomerate	
			Angular fragments	Breccia	
	Sand (0.006 to 0.2 cm)		Fine to coarse	Sandstone	
	Silt (0.0004 to 0.006 cm)		Very fine grain	Siltstone	
	Clay (less than 0.0006 cm)		Compact; may split easily	Shale	

CHEMICALLY AND/OR ORGANICALLY FORMED SEDIMENTARY ROCKS

TEXTURE	GRAIN SIZE	COMPOSITION	COMMENTS	ROCK NAME	MAP SYMBOL
Nonclastic	Coarse to fine	Calcite		Chemical Limestone	
	Varied	Halite	Crystals from chemical precipitates and evaporites	Rock Salt	
	Varied	Gypsum		Rock Gypsum	
	Varied	Dolomite		Dolostone	
	Microscopic to coarse	Calcite	Cemented shells, shell fragments, and skeletal remains	Fossil Limestone	
	Varied	Carbon	Black and nonporous	Bituminous Coal	

figure 07a

TEXTURE	GRAIN SIZE	COMPOSITION	TYPE OF METAMORPHISM	COMMENTS	ROCK NAME	MAP SYMBOL
FOLIATED — Slaty	Fine	CHLORITE MICA / QUARTZ FELDSPAR AMPHIBOLE GARNET PYROXENE	Regional	Low-grade metamorphism of shale	Slate	
FOLIATED — Schistose	Medium to coarse			Medium-grade metamorphism; mica crystals visible from metamorphism of feldspars and clay minerals	Schist	
FOLIATED — Gneissic	Coarse		(Heat and pressure increase with depth, folding, and faulting)	High-grade metamorphism; mica has changed to feldspar	Gneiss	
NONFOLIATED	Fine	Carbonaceous		Metamorphism of plant remains and bituminous coal	Anthracite Coal	
	Coarse	Depends on conglomerate composition		Pebbles may be distorted or stretched; often breaks through pebbles	Meta-conglomerate	
	Fine to coarse	Quartz	Thermal (including contact) or Regional	Metamorphism of sandstone	Quartzite	
		Calcite, Dolomite		Metamorphism of limestone or dolostone	Marble	
	Fine	Quartz, Plagioclase	Contact	Metamorphism of various rocks by contact with magma or lava	Hornfels	

figure 07b

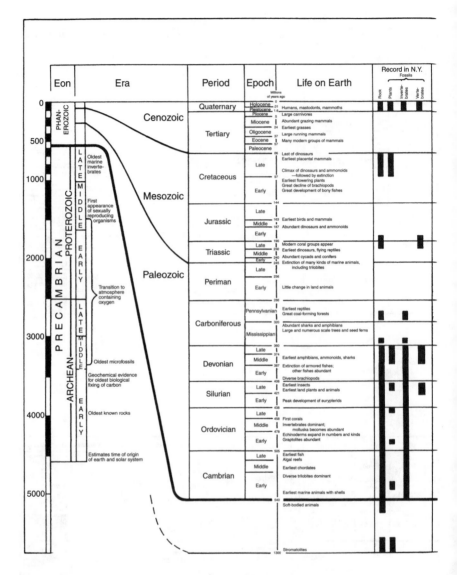

figure 08

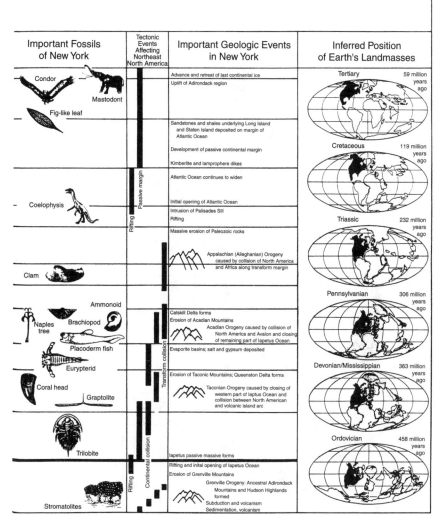

Important Fossils of New York	Tectonic Events Affecting Northeast North America	Important Geologic Events in New York	Inferred Position of Earth's Landmasses
Condor		Advance and retreat of last continental ice	Tertiary 59 million years ago
Mastodont		Uplift of Adirondack region	
Fig-like leaf			
		Sandstones and shales underlying Long Island and Staten Island deposited on margin of Atlantic Ocean	
	Passive margin	Development of passive continental margin	Cretaceous 119 million years ago
		Kimberlite and lamprophere dikes	
		Atlantic Ocean continues to widen	
Coelophysis	Rifting	Initial opening of Atlantic Ocean	
		Intrusion of Palisades Sill	
		Rifting	Triassic 232 million years ago
		Massive erosion of Paleozoic rocks	
Clam		Appalachian (Alleghanian) Orogeny caused by collision of North America and Africa along transform margin	
Ammonoid			Pennsylvanian 306 million years ago
Naples tree	Brachiopod	Catskill Delta forms	
		Erosion of Acadian Mountains	
	Transform collision	Acadian Orogeny caused by collision of North America and Avalon and closing of remaining part of Iapetus Ocean	
Placoderm fish		Evaporite basins; salt and gypsum deposited	
Eurypterid		Erosion of Taconic Mountains; Queenston Delta forms	Devonian/Mississippian 363 million years ago
Coral head		Taconian Orogeny caused by closing of western part of Iaptus Ocean and collision between North American and volcanic island arc	
Graptolite			
Trilobite	Continental collision	Iapetus passive massive forms	Ordovician 458 million years ago
	Rifting	Rifting and inital opening of Iapetus Ocean	
		Erosion of Grenville Mountains	
		Grenville Orogeny: Ancestral Adirondack Mountains and Hudson Highlands formed	
Stromatolites		Subduction and volcanism	
		Sedimentation, volcanism	

figure 09

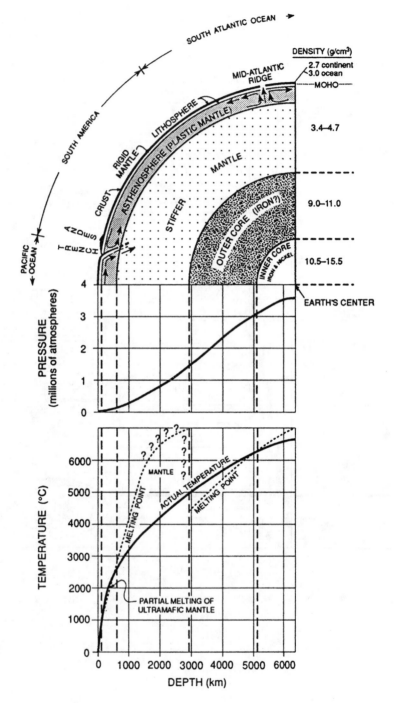

figure 10

ELEMENT (symbol)	CRUST		HYDROSPHERE	TROPOSPHERE
	Percent by Mass	Percent by Volume	Percent by Volume	Percent by Volume
Oxygen (O)	46.40	94.04	33	21
Silicon (Si)	28.15	0.88		
Aluminum (Al)	8.23	0.48		
Iron (Fe)	5.63	0.49		
Calcium (Ca)	4.15	1.18		
Sodium (Na)	2.36	1.11		
Magnesium (Mg)	2.33	0.33		
Potassium (K)	2.09	1.42		
Nitrogen (N)				78
Hydrogen (H)			66	

figure 11a

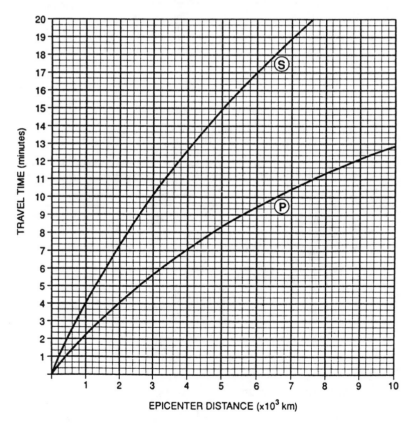

figure 11b

Dewpoint Temperatures

Dry-Bulb Temperature (°C)	Difference Between Wet-Bulb and Dry-Bulb Temperatures (°C)														
	1	2	3	4	5	6	7	8	9	10	11	12	13	14	15
-20	-33														
-18	-28														
-16	-24														
-14	-21	-36													
-12	-18	-28													
-10	-14	-22													
-8	-12	-18	-29												
-6	-10	-14	-22												
-4	-7	-12	-17	-29											
-2	-5	-8	-13	-20											
0	-3	-6	-9	-15	-24										
2	-1	-3	-6	-11	-17										
4	1	-1	-4	-7	-11	-19									
6	4	1	-1	-4	-7	-13	-21								
8	6	3	1	-2	-5	-9	-14								
10	8	6	4	1	-2	-5	-9	-14	-28						
12	10	8	6	4	1	-2	-5	-9	-16						
14	12	11	9	6	4	1	-2	-5	-10	-17					
16	14	13	11	9	7	4	1	-1	-6	-10	-17				
18	16	15	13	11	9	7	4	2	-2	-5	-10	-19			
20	19	17	15	14	12	10	7	4	2	-2	-5	-10	-19		
22	21	19	17	16	14	12	10	8	5	3	-1	-5	-10	-19	
24	23	21	20	18	16	14	12	10	8	6	2	-1	-5	-10	-18
26	25	23	22	20	18	17	15	13	11	9	6	3	0	-4	-9
28	27	25	24	22	21	19	17	16	14	11	9	7	4	1	-3
30	29	27	26	24	23	21	19	18	16	14	12	10	8	5	1

figure 12a

Relative Humidity (%)

Dry-Bulb Temperature (°C)	Difference Between Wet-Bulb and Dry-Bulb Temperatures (°C)														
	1	2	3	4	5	6	7	8	9	10	11	12	13	14	15
-20	28														
-18	40														
-16	48	0													
-14	55	11													
-12	61	23													
-10	66	33	0												
-8	71	41	13												
-6	73	48	20	0											
-4	77	54	32	11											
-2	79	58	37	20	1										
0	81	63	45	28	11										
2	83	67	51	36	20	6									
4	85	70	56	42	27	14									
6	86	72	59	46	35	22	10	0							
8	87	74	62	51	39	28	17	6							
10	88	76	65	54	43	33	24	13	4						
12	88	78	67	57	48	38	28	19	10	2					
14	89	79	69	60	50	41	33	25	16	8	1				
16	90	80	71	62	54	45	37	29	21	14	7	1			
18	91	81	72	64	56	48	40	33	26	19	12	6	0		
20	91	82	74	66	58	51	44	36	30	23	17	11	5	0	
22	92	83	75	68	60	53	46	40	33	27	21	15	10	4	0
24	92	84	76	69	62	55	49	42	36	30	25	20	14	9	4
26	92	85	77	70	64	57	51	45	39	34	28	23	18	13	9
28	93	86	78	71	65	59	53	47	42	36	31	26	21	17	12
30	93	86	79	72	66	61	55	49	44	39	34	29	25	20	16

figure 12b

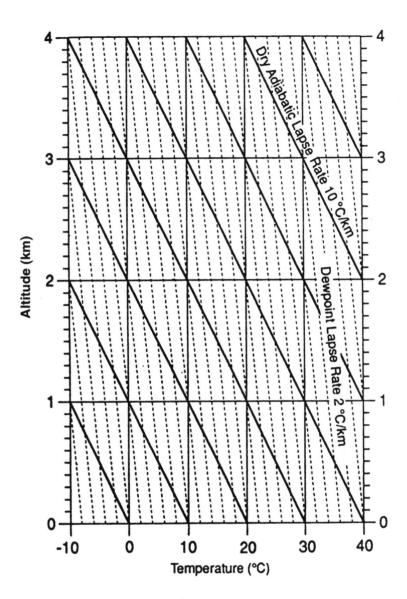

figure 13a

FAHRENHEIT   CELSIUS   KELVIN

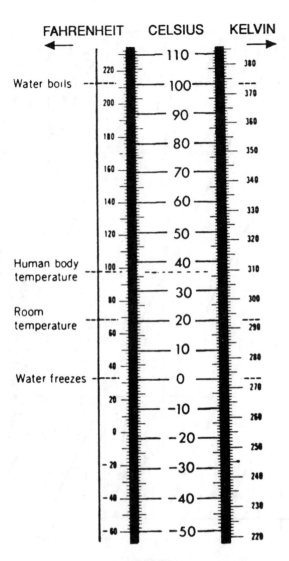

figure 13b

STATION MODEL

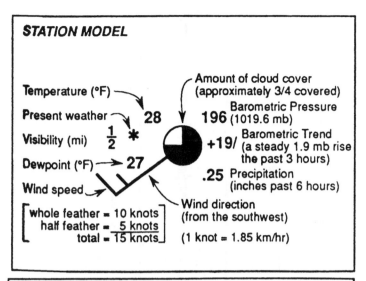

Temperature (°F)
Present weather — **28**
Visibility (mi) $\frac{1}{2}$ ✳
Dewpoint (°F) → **27**
Wind speed

Amount of cloud cover
(approximately 3/4 covered)

196 Barometric Pressure
(1019.6 mb)

+19/ Barometric Trend
(a steady 1.9 mb rise
the past 3 hours)

.25 Precipitation
(inches past 6 hours)

Wind direction
(from the southwest)

whole feather = 10 knots
half feather = 5 knots
total = 15 knots

(1 knot = 1.85 km/hr)

PRESENT WEATHER SYMBOLS

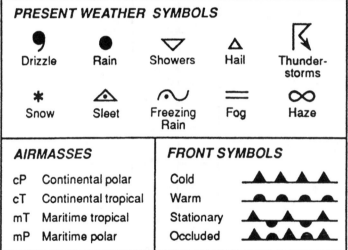

Drizzle   Rain   Showers   Hail   Thunderstorms

Snow   Sleet   Freezing   Fog   Haze
Rain

AIRMASSES

cP   Continental polar
cT   Continental tropical
mT   Maritime tropical
mP   Maritime polar

FRONT SYMBOLS

Cold
Warm
Stationary
Occluded

figure 13c

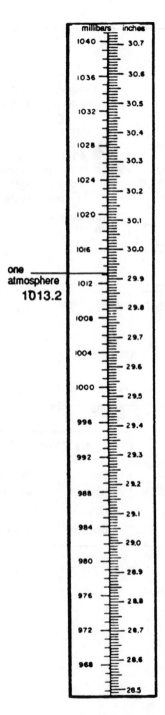

figure 14a

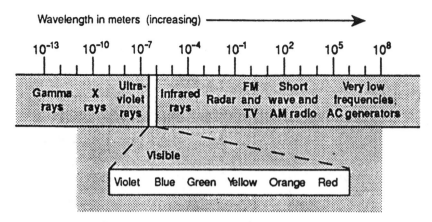

Wavelength in meters (increasing) ⟶

10⁻¹³ 10⁻¹⁰ 10⁻⁷ 10⁻⁴ 10⁻¹ 10² 10⁵ 10⁸

| Gamma rays | X rays | Ultra-violet rays | Infrared rays | Radar | FM and TV | Short wave and AM radio | Very low frequencies; AC generators |

Visible

Violet Blue Green Yellow Orange Red

figure 14b

Planet	Mean Distance from Sun (millions of km)	Period of Revolution	Period of Rotation	Eccentricity of Orbit	Equatorial Diameter (km)	Density (g/cm³)
MERCURY	57.9	88 days	59 days	0.206	4,880	5.4
VENUS	108.2	224.7 days	243 days	0.007	12,104	5.2
EARTH	149.6	365.26 days	23 hours 56 minutes 4 seconds	0.017	12,756	5.5
MARS	227.9	687 days	24 hours 37 minutes 23 seconds	0.093	6,787	3.9
JUPITER	778.3	11.86 years	9 hours 50 minutes 30 seconds	0.048	142,800	1.3
SATURN	1,427	29.46 years	10 hours 14 minutes	0.056	120,000	0.7
URANUS	2,869	84.0 years	11 hours	0.047	51,800	1.2
NEPTUNE	4,496	164.8 years	16 hours	0.009	49,500	1.7
PLUTO	5,900	247.7 years	6 days 9 hours	0.250	2,300	2.0

figure 14c

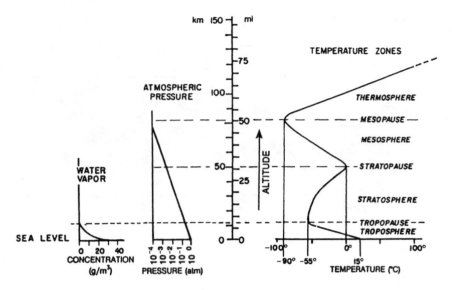

figure 15a

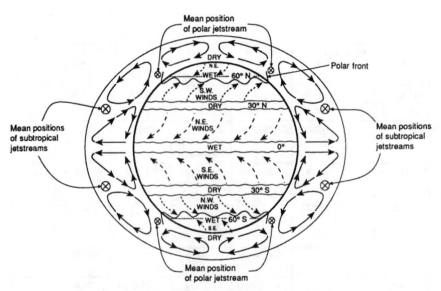

The drawing shows the locations of the belts near the time of an equinox. The locations shift somewhat with the changing latitude of the Sun's vertical ray. In the Northern Hemisphere the belts shift northward in summer and southward in winter.

figure 15b

Equations

Percent deviation from accepted value	deviation (%) = $\dfrac{\text{difference from accepted value}}{\text{accepted value}} \times 100$	
Eccentricity of an ellipse	eccentricity = $\dfrac{\text{distance between foci}}{\text{length of major axis}}$	
Gradient	gradient = $\dfrac{\text{change in field value}}{\text{change in distance}}$	
Rate of change	rate of change = $\dfrac{\text{change in field value}}{\text{change in time}}$	
Circumference of a circle	$C = 2\pi r$	
Eratosthenes' method to determine Earth's circumference	$\dfrac{\angle a}{360°} = \dfrac{s}{C}$	
Volume of a rectangular solid	$V = \ell wh$	
Density of a substance	$D = \dfrac{m}{V}$	
Latent heat	$\begin{cases} \text{solid} \longleftrightarrow \text{liquid} & Q = mH_f \\ \text{liquid} \longleftrightarrow \text{gas} & Q = mH_v \end{cases}$	
Heat energy lost or gained	$Q = m\,\Delta TC_p$	

C_p = specific heat
C = circumference
d = distance
D = density
F = force
h = height
H_f = heat of fusion
H_v = heat of vaporization
$\angle a$ = shadow angle
ℓ = length
s = distance on surface
m = mass
Q = amount of heat
r = radius
ΔT = change in temperature
V = volume
w = width
Note: $\pi \approx 3.14$

Proportions

Kepler's harmonic law of planetary motion	(period of revolution)$^2 \propto$ (mean radius of orbit)^3
Universal law of gravitation	force $\propto \dfrac{\text{mass}_1 \times \text{mass}_2}{(\text{distance between their centers})^2}$ $\left(F \propto \dfrac{m_1\,m_2}{d^2}\right)$

EURYPTERID
New York State Fossil

figure 16a

Properties of Water

Latent heat of fusion (H_f)	80 cal/g
Latent heat of vaporization (H_v)	540 cal/g
Density (D) at 3.98°C	1.00 g/mL

Specific Heats of Common Materials

MATERIAL		SPECIFIC HEAT (C_p) (cal/g·C°)
Water	solid	0.5
	liquid	1.0
	gas	0.5
Dry air		0.24
Basalt		0.20
Granite		0.19
Iron		0.11
Copper		0.09
Lead		0.03

Radioactive Decay Data

RADIOACTIVE ISOTOPE	DISINTEGRATION	HALF-LIFE (years)
Carbon-14	$C^{14} \longrightarrow N^{14}$	5.7×10^3
Potassium-40	$K^{40} \begin{smallmatrix} \nearrow Ar^{40} \\ \searrow Ca^{40} \end{smallmatrix}$	1.3×10^9
Uranium-238	$U^{238} \longrightarrow Pb^{206}$	4.5×10^9
Rubidium-87	$Rb^{87} \longrightarrow Sr^{87}$	4.9×10^{10}

Astronomy Measurements

MEASUREMENT	EARTH	SUN	MOON
Mass (m)	5.98×10^{24} kg	1.99×10^{30} kg	7.35×10^{22} kg
Radius (r)	6.37×10^3 km	6.96×10^5 km	1.74×10^3 km
Average density (D)	5.52 g/cm^3	1.42 g/cm^3	3.34 g/cm^3

figure 16b

Index

cleavage   55, 74
climate   185
compound   48, 74
condensation   167, 185
conduction   159, 185
constellation   201, 216
continental shelf   107, 122
continental slope   107, 122
controlled experiment   6, 10
convection   159, 185
Coriolis effect   100, 123, 164, 185
corona   221, 241
creep   131, 146
current   100, 123
cycle   3
cyclone   165, 185

D
delta   95, 123
density   14, 44
dew point   167, 185
downcutting   138, 146
drumlin   80, 88

E
economic geologists   5
element   47, 74
engineering geologists   5
environmental geologists   5
epicenter   19, 44
erosion   130, 146
escape velocity   216
esker   80, 88
estuary   95, 123
evaporation   185
exfoliation   126, 146
exosphere   2, 10

F
fault   44
fjord   96, 123
flares   223, 241
floodplain   139, 146
fracture   55, 75
framework silicates   57, 75
fronts   172, 185

G
geochemists   5
geochronologists   5

geochronology   245, 276
geological time   246, 277
geology   3, 10
geomorphologists   5
geomorphology   245, 277
geophysicists   5
geosphere   3, 10
glacial till   79, 88
glaciers   77, 88
glaciologists   5
globular cluster   207, 216
Gondwanaland   84, 89
gravity   208, 216
greenhouse effect   117, 123
guyot   108, 123

H
heliopause   223, 241
heliosphere   223, 241
heterosphere   155, 185
homosphere   155, 185
humidity   167, 185
humus   142, 146
hydrogeologists   6
hydrologic cycle   3, 10, 169, 185
hydrologists   5
hydrolysis   127, 146
hydrosphere   3, 10

I
igneous   63, 75
insolation   150, 185
invertebrates   260, 277
ion   75
ionosphere   157, 186
isolated tetrahedra   56, 75
isotope   49, 75

J
jet streams   166, 186
joint   44

K
kaons   216
kettle   80, 89
Kuiper Belt   191, 217

soil profile   142, 147
solar eclipse   233, 242
solar wind   221, 242
solubility   56, 76
space-time   208, 217
specific gravity   56, 76
speleology   129, 147
spicule   221, 242
statistical forecasting   178, 186
stratigraphers   6
stratigraphy   245, 277
stratosphere   155, 186
stream   135, 147
structural geologists   6
subduction zone   15, 27, 45
submersible   109, 123
sunspots   222, 242
supernova   199, 202, 217
surface wave   19, 45
syncline   32, 45
synoptic forecasting   178, 186

T
talus slope   126, 147
terminal moraine   79
terrane   24, 45
thermonuclear forces   242
thermonuclear fusion   220, 242
thermosphere   155, 186
tidal forces   232, 242
trench   108, 123
tropics   151, 186
troposphere   155, 186
tsunami   105, 123

U
uniformitarianism   125, 147
unit cell   52, 76

V
valley   130, 147
variable star   222, 242
varve   248, 277
vertebrates   262, 277
volcanologists   6

W
water cycle   1, 11
watershed   93, 123

weather   149, 187
weathering   65, 76, 126, 147
wind   151, 187

Z
zooplankton   111, 124

ABOUT THE AUTHOR

Michael L. Bentley taught high school earth science in Virginia and Pennsylvania. He has also been the director of a special state magnet high school for science and technology. Dr. Bentley received his masters from the University of Pennsylvania and his doctorate in science education from the University of Virginia. Dr. Bentley lives in Salem, Virginia, with his wife, Susan, a daughter, Sarah, two sons; Alexander and Matthew, and his Golden Retriever, Maggie. He is now an associate professor at Virginia Tech, where he writes, conducts research in science teaching and learning, and helps prepare new science teachers.

NOTES

NOTES

NOTES

NOTES

NOTES

NOTES

NOTES

NOTES

NOTES

NOTES

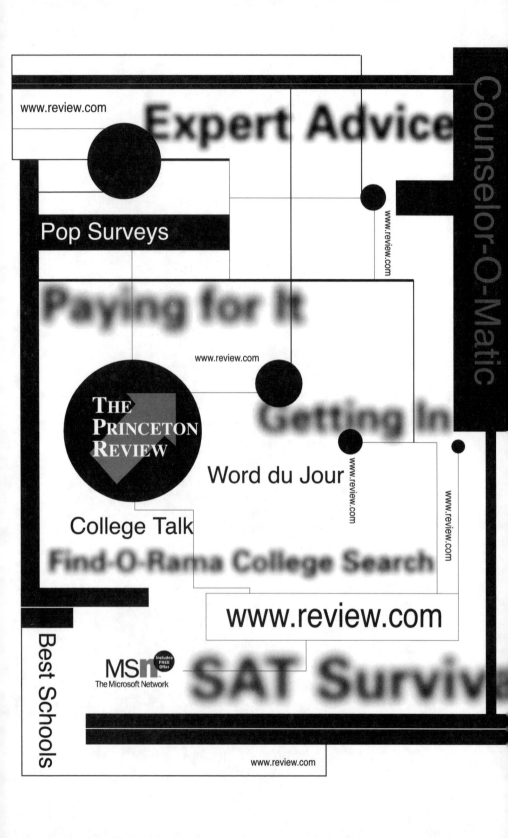

Free!

Did you know that The Microsoft Network gives you one free month?

Call us at 1-800-FREE MSN. We'll send you a free CD to get you going.

Then, you can explore the World Wide Web for one month, free. Exchange e-mail with your family and friends. Play games, book airline tickets, handle finances, go car shopping, explore old hobbies and discover new ones. There's one big, useful online world out there. And for one month, it's a free world.

Call **1-800-FREE MSN,** Dept. 3197, for offer details or visit us at **www.msn.com**. Some restrictions apply.

Microsoft Where do you want to go today?®   MSn.
                                                    The Microsoft Network

FIND US...

International

Hong Kong
4/F Sun Hung Kai Centre
30 Harbour Road, Wan Chai,
Hong Kong
Tel: (011)85-2-517-3016

Japan
Fuji Building 40, 15-14
Sakuragaokacho, Shibuya Ku,
Tokyo 150, Japan
Tel: (011)81-3-3463-1343

Korea
Tae Young Bldg, 944-24,
Daechi- Dong, Kangnam-Ku
The Princeton Review- ANC
Seoul, Korea 135-280,
South Korea
Tel: (011)82-2-554-7763

Mexico City
PR Mex S De RL De Cv
Guanajuato 228 Col. Roma
06700 Mexico D.F., Mexico
Tel: 525-564-9468

Montreal
666 Sherbrooke St.
West, Suite 202
Montreal, QC H3A 1E7 Canada
Tel: (514) 499-0870

Pakistan
1 Bawa Park - 90 Upper Mall
Lahore, Pakistan
Tel: (011)92-42-571-2315

Spain
Pza. Castilla, 3 - 5° A, 28046
Madrid, Spain
Tel: (011)341-323-4212

Taiwan
155 Chung Hsiao East Road
Section 4 - 4th Floor,
Taipei R.O.C., Taiwan
Tel: (011)886-2-751-1243

Thailand
Building One, 99 Wireless Road
Bangkok, Thailand 10330
Tel: (662) 256-7080

Toronto
1240 Bay Street, Suite 300
Toronto M5R 2A7 Canada
Tel: (800) 495-7737
Tel: (716) 839-4391

Vancouver
4212 University Way NE,
Suite 204
Seattle, WA 98105
Tel: (206) 548-1100

National (U.S.)

We have over 60 offices around the U.S. and run courses in over 400 sites. For courses and locations within the U.S. call 1 (800) 2/Review and you will be routed to the nearest office.